John 17
and the
Power of Prayer

A Study of the Prayer of Jesus in the Fourth Gospel

JUDITH A. DIEHL

ISBN 979-8-88685-621-7 (paperback)
ISBN 979-8-88685-622-4 (digital)

Christian Faith Publishing
832 Park Avenue
Meadville, PA 16335
www.christianfaithpublishing.com

Printed in the United States of America

Preface

I am blessed to be able to live west of Denver in the Rocky Mountains. We are nestled in a natural valley, about 8,700 feet above sea level, surrounded by tree-covered peaks. We ski in the winter months and hike in the hills all summer. I am not the only one who enjoys the freedom of living on the edge of the wilderness. One of the first things we learn is the importance of communication. No one ever wants to be alone in a remote area with no means of contact with other people.

A couple of summers ago, I was hiking with a group of ladies. We descended down a rocky, craggy trail, and one woman slipped and fell. She was seriously injured. Quickly, everyone with a cell phone attempted to call for help. We realized that in our position on the mountain, no one had any cell phone service. Our fearless leader had a rescue *Garmin* device and was able to get a message out. Unfortunately, the operator at the central station called her back to confirm our location, but she could not reach us because she had one number wrong in the callback number.

It was a critical lesson for all of us. What a helpless feeling to desperately need rescuing, but there was no communication available! We knew where we were, and we were fairly close to the end of the trail and to safety. So close and yet so far; trauma stopped us in our tracks. The minutes ticked by; still no answer. No one hears us; no one knows where we are.

This is a picture of prayer. It is easy not to even think about prayer until trauma happens. Everything seems to be going very well, until we slip and fall. Life is filled with beauty and joy, until it isn't. Then, where is God? When we do cry out to God in prayer, it is frustrating to wait for an answer—any answer. Is he listening? Silence is deafening and the lack of communication is frightening.

Even after more than thirty years of serving in Christian ministry, for me, there is still an element of the mystic about prayer. Most of my adult life has been serving in the church and teaching students on the seminary level. I have learned a great deal about prayer and people's perception of prayer. Everyone knows the familiar "Lord's Prayer" found in Matthew 6:9–13, and for good reason. Many of us memorized it in our childhood.

But what *is* prayer really, and how does one *do* it correctly? How can I help other people to pray "better"? I noticed that many Christ followers knew little about prayer or tried to avoid it altogether. I have taught a wonderful collection of people from numerous "religious" backgrounds: various Protestant denominations, Roman Catholics, no religious background at all, and even non-Christian traditions. Within these varied customs, people had rituals and practices about prayer that were deeply ingrained and imprinted in cement in their brains. Some were very helpful and valuable, but some did not raise prayer above a mysterious obligation and a duty. Backgrounds and practices can divide us as believers, but prayer should be the one uniting force in which all of us can participate together (John 17:20–23). Sadly, I think we lose our "prayer innocence" with time, traditions, and the painful experiences of life.

In graduate school, I decided to write a doctoral dissertation on the prayer of Jesus in the Gospel of John 17. I had not paid much attention to this long prayer, and it never occurred to me that it could actually affect my own relationship with God. At the time, putting John 17 "under the microscope" was an academic exercise. After three years of research, I was still left with gnawing, unanswered questions about this prayer. To change metaphors, there were a number of pieces missing from my jigsaw puzzle of this is prayer.

Specifically, I needed to find out why the author of the prayer put two unusual epithets (titles) for God on the lips of Jesus—the "Holy Father" (John 17:11) and the "Righteous Father" (John 17:25). Aren't these just descriptions of God? But why are they included in a *prayer*? Each of these titles appear nowhere else in the entire canonical Bible. Furthermore, why would Jesus refer to himself in the third person—as "Jesus Christ" in a prayer to his Father (who knew him well) (John 17:3)? And finally, why did John use the title of *Paraclete* for the Holy Spirit in the Farewell Discourses (John 14:16, 16:7)? I needed to understand about God's holiness and his righteousness. I needed to comprehend exactly who the *Paraclete* is. What do such titles have to do with prayer? I did not anticipate that a better understanding of who God is can have a profound effect on one's own prayer life.

Knowing God does move us toward a more effective prayer life out of love, not obligation. Yet there are tons of books on "effective" or "successful" prayer in the "religious" section of the local bookstore or on the internet. This is not one of those books. It is not about methodology—*how* to pray—but it is a book about the One to whom we pray.

My intent is not to suggest more methods of "doing" prayer, but it is to create more love for the awesome God who wants very much to be in a relationship with us. Life is a rocky, craggy trail; and we all need totally dependable, reliable, and available help when we slip and fall. In addition, we need to lift our hearts and thank Someone who is bigger than we are when we experience the incredible beauty of this world. That is what prayer is all about. Please read on.

Introduction

"I believe in prayer," my friend said, "because I know who I am talking to." As Christians, do we really know who we are talking to when we pray?

Over the centuries, scholars, pastors, and laypersons have dissected and taught what we commonly call the "Lord's Prayer" of Matthew 6:9–13. It has been sung, preached, and recited in churches for no doubt hundreds of years; it is familiar and comfortable, repeated in even the most harrowing of circumstances. Yet for some people, it has lost its deep meaning and its significance because it is just another obligatory thing to do, words to repeat, and an address to God in odd language that is not common in our vernacular today.

On the other hand, relatively few people have spent much time and consideration on Jesus' prayer of John 17, the longest prayer on the lips of Jesus in the New Testament. In the past, it has been regarded as "The High Priestly Prayer," which somehow removes it from the common person, the ordinary *pray-er*. The prayer of John 17 is not reserved for the church hierarchy today, and it is a very rich passage that informs and assures everyone.

Indeed, Dr. Craig Blomberg states that a "better designation for the Lord's Prayer" is John 17, as it really is a prayer of Jesus spoken on behalf of his followers. The familiar prayer in Matthew might be better labeled the "Disciples' Prayer," spoken to teach his followers, then and now (see also Luke 11:1).[1] John 17 is less "preachable," less "teachable," and less memorable than Matthew's prayer. It is not an example of human requests brought before God that is easy to follow. Actually, John 17 is the Son communicating with his Father for the benefit of his human listeners. The Johannine prayer is not so much about getting God to do something for believers; it is more about what believers should be doing with God and why. If the familiar "Lord's Prayer" is Jesus' instructions on "*how*" to pray (Matt. 6:9), then John 17 helps believers to understand "to *whom*" they should pray.

David Clark recently explored the historical and functional background of the "Lord's Prayer" as presented in early literature. He investigated the familiar prayer in the Gospels of Matthew and Luke. Clark also explored the comments by the writer (or compiler) of the *Didache* (an early noncanonical Christian text), as well as comments made by the early Christian theologian Tertullian. What Clark suggested about Christian prayers in the New Testament is worth noting because he enlightens modern readers to the origins and intentions of the ancient authors as they interpreted and preserved early Christian prayers. Clark determines that to fully understand the "Lord's Prayer," we must consider how the prayer was received and used historically. For example, historically the Matthean prayer may have "close parallels in the standard Jewish Kaddish prayer."[2] With Clark, the same can be said about the importance of how John 17 was received and used by the original readers of John's Gospel. Even more than the Matthean "Lord's Prayer," John 17 is rich in depth, purpose, and meaning. Hopefully, an exploration of the history and literary features of the Fourth Gospel can help present-day Christians to grasp the fullness and the beauty of the Johannine prayer, as well as understand the identities of the divine Persons who actually hear our prayers.

John 17 and unique titles

This study will investigate some very unusual names for God found in Jesus' Farewell Discourses (John 14–17). Why did John choose to use very unique epithets (titles) for God in Jesus' final instructions to his followers and in his final prayer? The distinctive titles used by John are an expression in human words (language) of the divine nature of God. To be sure, it is difficult to fully define the character and role of the God of the Old Testament and of the Messiah of the New Testament.

The historical milieu of John's Gospel can give us insight into the culture, the setting, and the original readers of the Gospel, which can help us to understand the names and titles for God. In the culture of the first-century AD Roman Empire, titles given to human beings would have been perceived as claims about the nature and character of that person. So the names used for God and for Jesus Christ by Christ-followers could be seen as direct challenges to the entitlements given to the Roman emperors, gods, and goddesses. Furthermore, the identities, roles, and positions of the Father and the Son introduced in the Johannine Prologue (John 1:1–18) can be mystifying to readers; and it may have been the intention of the Johannine author to "unpack" these titles in the rest of his Gospel.

In the Fourth Gospel, the author freely and explicitly used epithets to highlight his characterization of three main characters: God, Jesus, and the Holy Spirit. In fact, Prof. Larry Hurtado wrote that,

> One of the distinctive features of the Gospel of John is the emphasis on the divine name, and (a related topic) divine glory. The Gospel of John associates Jesus with the manifestation of God's name and glory. The author of the Gospel of John was inspired by the prophetic themes of a future manifestation of God's name and glory in Isaiah. Jesus is the fulfillment of the promise that God will bring eschatological salvation by manifesting his name and glory.[3]

In particular, the Farewell Discourses and the prayer of John 17 reveal additional information about the triune God through the use of epithets. In the opening verse of the prayer (John 17:1), Jesus refers to God as "Father" and to himself as the "Son." These are not unfamiliar designations for God and Jesus, as the author of John has referred to them as such in previous verses (i.e., John 6:37, 40). John 17:3 describes God as "the only true God." The Greek grammar in

17:3 implies that these adjectives are descriptors of God, showing his authentic nature. In the text, there are no commas around *"ton monon alethinon theon."* This indicates that the adjectives are not used as a title for God; they are an explanation of his uniqueness, especially in contrast to the polytheistic religious beliefs of the Romans familiar to John's audience.

The unique and distinctive epithets which are used for God in John 17—"Holy Father" (17:11) and "Righteous Father" (17:25)—beg for further research and attention from readers today. Both titles appear *only* in the Fourth Gospel and nowhere else in the entire Bible. We will also consider the theological truths which the titles reveal to the readers, especially concerning the theology of prayer, since that is where they occur. Our first consideration, then, will be the Old Testament background of the epithet "Holy Father" (chapter 2). What is the literary backdrop for such a title? Did Jesus create this title for God, or did the Gospel author borrow a title that was well-known to his congregation? What was Jesus' aim in using such a name before his central group of followers *in a prayer*?

Second, we will study the historical and cultural background of the exclusive epithet "Righteous Father" (John 17:25). If the original readers of the Gospel were indeed a congregation of both converted Jews and Gentiles who lived in the powerful Roman Empire, this would affect why the author subversively employed the title of "Righteous Father" (chapter 3). Again, why did Jesus use this particular attribute of God as a title *in a prayer*?

In addition, Jesus entitles himself "Jesus Christ" in John 17:3. It would be very odd for Jesus to refer to himself with the third-person title of "Jesus Christ" in a prayer to his Father and in the presence of his earliest followers. This odd phrasing implies that the titles in this prayer were created by the author of the Gospel, John. In fact, the first three verses of the prayer appear literarily to be the innovation of the Gospel author and not the actual words of Jesus. The words are lofty and are not indicative of an intimate relationship between the Father and the Son.

These verses serve as the closing "bookends" to the true identity of Jesus, which began in John's prologue, where Jesus is identified as the "Word" of God participating in creation (John 1:3). Although he is God and exists "with God" (John 1:1), he is apart from God and is "at the Father's side" (John 1:18). The title "Son of God" is used of Jesus in John's Gospel as a key to his Christology (chapter 4). This is revealed in the author's explicit purpose statement in John 20:30–31. John employs the title "Son" or "Son of God" twenty-nine times in the Gospel and refers to God as "Father" over a hundred times. The author's emphasis on Jesus as the divine "Son of God" is stronger than what we find in the other Gospels.[4] There is a sense of mystery about the identity of Jesus as the "Son," but in both the ancient Jewish and the Roman cultures, the idea of a "son" was critical to a man's lineage and character.

Fourth, John is the only Gospel writer to make reference to the "*Paraclete*" (the Holy Spirit), as found in the Farewell Discourses (chapter 5). The gift of and the functions of the Paraclete to the followers of Jesus are distinctively Johannine. In the Farewell Discourses, John also called him the "Spirit of truth" (John 14:17, 15:26, 16:13), which is a rare title. While there are numerous biblical names given to the third Person of the Trinity throughout Scripture, the author of John's Gospel stands alone in his use of the title "*Paraclete*" (John 14:16–17, 15:26, 16:7).

The passages about the Holy Spirit, placed on the lips of Jesus in his farewell address, tell the readers that the presence of the Spirit in their lives is a gift from the Father through the Son (John 14:16, 15:26). By using this title, Jesus was telling his earliest disciples about the new nature of the Holy Spirit in their lives. While the work of the Spirit is apparent from the beginning of time (see Gen. 1:1), he takes on a new role in the lives of believers after the departure of the incarnate Son from the earth. Thus, Gospel readers today may notice quickly that the Johannine author emphasizes all the three persons of the Trinity—Father, Son, and Holy Spirit—in the final discourses of Jesus, especially in his climactic prayer (chapter 6).

As we explore the deeper artistic significance of John 17, we will consider what the author is *doing* for his readers by employing specific theological titles. We need to understand what Jesus is *saying* in the Farewell Discourses, specifically about the intertwined Trinity.

Then, we can better determine what John is *doing* with the words of Jesus for the readers then and for Christian readers today. The prayer of John 17 was both redemptive and transformative for the original readers, just as it is for present-day Christians.

Biblical interpretation

How can we interpret the Johannine prayer in such a way that it is meaningful to every Christian who tries to communicate with God in prayer? Current biblical scholarship notes that biblical interpretation is "both a science and an art." That is, the meaning of a communication is implied by the recognition of established "codes": spelling, grammar, paragraphs, even tones of voice, which indicate the meaning of the communication (oral or written).[5] We use these tools to help comprehend what we read (or hear). For example, we can perceive rules, principles, humor, irony, or other patterns of expression. As a result, we can evaluate the texts strictly as literary compositions, such as a poem or a story, with a happy ending. It is a good idea to ask what rules of communication is the author following to express his or her ideas? Indeed, we must also consider discrepancy or familiar commonality with other texts or passages.

In addition to the "rules" of communication, we must also investigate the historical and cultural backgrounds of the texts because there may be large "gaps" of time between our known culture and the culture known to the ancient authors and readers. There are time "gaps" as well as differences in language, acceptable behavior, political, and social systems as well. Even so, ancient texts can be descriptive of common human nature; and they can give us knowledge, evidence, and insight. Yet critical evaluation and "decoding" of a text may not ultimately reveal the human emotions expressed in the words. This approach to a text may not be totally adequate to determine what a text "means."

Thus, there is also an "artistic" approach to the texts that goes beyond scientific expressions of information and empirical data. There is an analysis of the text on a different level, which brings to light expressions of emotions, beliefs, perspectives, attitudes, and wisdom. What does the text arouse or evoke in the reader? Ordinarily, an author intentionally expresses his or her thoughts and ideas in such a way as to create a response from the readers. That is, texts can give us "feelings" of despair, or grief, inadequacy, confidence, hope, and power. These are expressions of human sentiments, passions, and emotions. As we read biblical texts, *both* of these approaches— the "scientific" and the "artistic"—are necessary and deliberate. The meaning of the text is not one or the other; it is both. Meaning can be distorted or completely missed if we neglect either approach.[6]

To determine the full "meaning" of the biblical texts is, of course, a bit more complicated than these two brief approaches; but it is important to realize that understanding Scripture is both a "decoding" of the perfunctory text and a discerning of the implied artistic features. The latter are matters that are not expressed through the mechanics of communication and must be perceived through other types of expressions, such as imagery, symbols, and literary nuances. It has been suggested that as readers, to help us decipher this "artistic" approach, we can ask these types of questions: What does the text *do* to us? How does the text make us *feel*? What *experience* do we have in reading a passage? What is the author of the text *doing* or *showing* to his or her readers? What is the "emotion, power, and pathos" of a given passage?[7]

As we study the Bible, we are taking the approach that we are studying the very words of God given to his people through human authors to reveal himself for their transformation and edification. To teach and preach God's Word correctly becomes an awesome task. This book is an investigation that takes into account all three of these aspects of interpretation with respect to John's Gospel: the historical and cultural background to the Gospel; the language, vocabulary, imagery, significance, rhetoric, and emotional power of the given literature; and what is ultimately disclosed about who God is.

While it is important to "decode" the text as it is, it is also vital that we understand the texts in their fullness, as the chosen words of the human author (and the divine Author) who is attempting to *do* something that *affects* the readers. Briefly, then, the more scientific aspect of the study of a text discloses the *what* about the text (what is the grammar and the structure; what is the historical background of the text?), while the more artistic approach helps to answer the question *why* the author presented things as they are (why did he choose *these* words and why did he choose to use *this* image?).

Specifically, then, what was the author of John's Gospel *doing* to/for his readers in chapters 14 through 17? Perhaps it was quite intentional that the author chose to close the Farewell Discourses with a *prayer* to give his readers a sense of intimacy, unity, confidence, and hope. We can assume that the ancient author carefully chose specific words and phrases to intentionally offer care and support for his readers in their Christian walk. In the same way, it is not unusual for Christians today to close a worship service with a benediction or a prayer, sending the worshipers out of the service with hope and assurance.

Names and titles

As an educator, I thought it was very important to remember the names of my students, and I made an effort to know them by their names. After years of practice, I realized that I could easily remember the outstanding students (the A students), as well as the struggling students (the "failing" students who liked to skip class). But I had a hard time remembering the names of the average, C students. They disappeared into the ocean of average papers, average scores, and average participation.

Then, when I worked as a pastor in a fairly large church, the same thing happened. I remembered the names of the faithful attenders and volunteers and the struggling families who came to us for help. But the names of the typical attenders or the occasional participants escaped me. A wise pastor once told me that it was his goal to know all the people in his congregation by name—a worthy goal, and he was successful at attaining it. It was not an easy goal for me. What I realized is that we can recall the names and faces of those people that we *know* the best. Names are critical to our own identities and to our human connections; when our names are forgotten, it can disappoint or even hurt us. Everyone wants to be a "somebody," and our names are central to who we are and to our construction of relationships.

Most often, titles are given to a person in addition to his or her "proper" name. Titles are a vehicle to reveal what needs to be known about a person. They reveal who a person is and what role they play in an organization or a family or in a society. Names preserve the nature and character of someone passed along through descendants. Who is president of the United States, for example, and what does he/she do in that position? Presidents are remembered for who they were (or are) in that position. In addition, a title also reveals how other people react to that titled person. What is expected from a speaker when one comes face-to-face with "king" or "the emperor"? What does it mean in my life personally when someone with a title enters into my space? What emotions are present when a student encounters the "principal" or a soldier meets a "general?" By extension, the son of a titled person often demands the same respect as his father, such as a crown prince, or the son of a Mafia "don." An excellent example of this was the speech of George W. Bush (forty-third president of the U.S.) at the funeral of his father, George H. W. Bush, the forty-first president of the U.S. In his speech, the younger Bush told the audience what they needed to know about this great man, what he did in his position, and how he served and earned the respect of people for his accomplishments and his character. The son revealed to us the nature and character of his father.

Old Testament names

In the same way, names and titles in the Old Testament are used to reveal the character of the person so named. Names reveal the very nature and character of God. They illustrate who he is, what he is like, and how he interacts with his people. The writers tried to describe One God who is entirely "Other" from human beings and from any other so-called "gods." There are three major categories of names for God in the Old Testament; each category includes various compounds and forms of the basic title.

The first group is 'ĕlōhîm (i.e., Gen. 1:1 and 811 times in the Pentateuch), a common noun for "God" or "gods." The second word group is *yhwh* (YHWH), which is the personal, proper name of "LORD" (Gen. 2:4 and 1,827 times in the Pentateuch). Third is the title, or epithet, of 'ădōnay, which is the equivalent of the English words "lord(s)" or "master," or "sir" (Gen. 15:2 only seventeen times in the Pentateuch and 439 times in the Old Testament).[8]

Each title reveals a perception of an invisible God, while each title also implies the position of the people in relation to God. God is "in" his name; that is, God's "tabernacling presence is in his name," just as his presence and glory were in "the cloud" at Mt. Sinai.[9] Isaiah the prophet must have intentionally used the title of "Sovereign Lord" (Isa. 25:8; 40:10; 50:4; 61:1, 11) as a direct reference to who God was to him. The prophet Zechariah identified a God who would eventually reign over all the nations totally and completely: "The Lord will be king over the whole earth. On that day, there will be one Lord, and his name the only name" (Zec. 14:9).

The name YHWH implied a very personal relationship between God and his people (Exod. 20:2). For the Hebrews, God's name was his very presence; in fact, for fear of misusing his sacred name, they used substitutionary titles and did not say or write "proper" his name.[10] The writers of the Old Testament adapted numerous names for the promised "Messiah," which means "the Anointed One" (see Psalms 2:2, 28:8, 84:9, 89:38, 105:15). A hundred years before Jesus' birth, the members of the enclave at Qumran attributed the nature and characteristics of God to a Messiah, one chosen by God, consecrated to his service and endowed with his name and his power (1QIsaª. 51.5; Isa. 42:8, 56:5, 57:15).

New Testament names

Likewise, Christians down through the ages have attempted to define and title the One called "Jesus Christ" (John 1:17, 17:3).

With this realization, the early Christians gave great significance to his "*name*":

> The Name of the Father is the Son...He gave
> Him His Name which belong to him...One does
> not pronounce the Name of the Father; but He
> reveals Himself through A Son. Thus, then, the
> name is great (From the Valentinian Gospel of
> Truth).[11]

Only after Jesus' life, death, and resurrection did the early Christians understand the references to Jesus in the OT:

> Just as 'the name' was a pious Jewish surrogate for
> God, so for the early Jewish Christians it became
> a designation for Jesus, the Lord's Christ. As in its
> earlier usage, so with the Christians it connotated
> the divine presence and power.[12]

Thus, in the New Testament, we find numerous titles for Jesus that also reveal his character: the "Christ" (*Christos*: Matt. 16:13–16; Mark 8:27–29; Luke 9:18–20); the "Son of God" (1 John 4:15, 5:12); the "Son of David"; and his favorite name for himself, the "Son of Man." During his baptism, the very voice of God introduced Jesus as God's "Son" (Luke 3:21–22; Heb. 1:5). John the Baptist identified Jesus as the "Son of God," sent and loved by God (John 3:31–36). Even a frightened Roman centurion, a Gentile, at the foot of Jesus' cross, declared, "Surely he was the Son of God!" (Matt. 27:54).

In his opening prologue, the author of the Fourth Gospel referred to God as "the Father" (John 1:14), and to Jesus as "the Word," (John 1:1–2) and understood Jesus to be the "One and Only" (John 1:14, 18). Also in John's Gospel, people were converted to Christianity "in his name" (John 1:12, 2:23, 3:18); believers have life "in his name" (John 20:31); and the readers were instructed to "ask in my [Jesus'] name" (John 14:13, 15:16,16:23–26). Likewise, Jesus calls believers ("his own sheep") by their names, and "shepherds" them (John 10:3).

The Synoptic Gospels also reflect the importance of Jesus' name (i.e., Matt. 6:9, 18:20, 24:5; Mark 9:41, 10:29; Luke 11:2) as recognition of who he is as the divine Agent and Son of God, his position to the Father, and his authority on earth.

Names and labels

To be sure, the *name* of a person is different from a *label*. Labels are something we place on things to describe them as we see them. Unfortunately, they are not necessarily a correct interpretation of the nature and character of another person. Labels can carry a lot of baggage and misinformation, both good and bad: "he is an aristocrat," or "she is a gossip," or "he is a conservative," or "she is a liberal."

It is interesting to note that in the Fourth Gospel, God names believers as his "children" (John 1:12) because they are "born of God." This is not a label, as it is as ontological as it is positional. By nature, believers are born of God in his image as their "Father." It is societal culture that labels believers as anything different than people who are loved and accepted by God. It is also interesting that the author of the Fourth Gospel apparently intentionally left some of his characters "nameless." This anonymity draws the readers' attention to the distinction between the named characters, such as Jesus, the Christ, and the unnamed characters (such as "the Beloved Disciple").

The author? The "Beloved Disciple"?

Indeed, it is strange that nowhere in the Fourth Gospel does the author reveal to the readers the true identity of the "disciple whom Jesus loved" (John 13:23, 21:20). Strictly speaking, references to this person appear linguistically as descriptions, not titles (see also the "other disciple" in John 20:3). The author is very careful to use proper names and titles for many other key characters, but it appears that he intentionally sought anonymity about himself. Yet ironically, down through the centuries of the Christian church, it has become a title for one particular disciple who may have composed this "beloved" Gospel. If so, the author chose to humble himself and remain unnamed, in contrast to such honorific titles such as "my Lord and my God" (John 20:28), the "Lamb of God" (John 1:29, 36), "Rabbi, the Son of God and King of Israel" (John 1:49), and "*Rabboni*" (John 20:16).

The use of numerous thoughtful, meaningful titles in this Gospel lends credence to the idea that the author highlights his narrative characters, while keeping his own identity in the shadows. It appears that the author of the Fourth Gospel, perhaps the "Beloved Disciple" himself, worked very hard to preserve and record the revelations of and encounters with Jesus the Messiah, and to personally testify to his "seeing" Jesus. It also appears that the author was very intentional about the names of the trinitarian God in his Gospel to help his readers to "see" the extraordinary vision of the divine.

In our society today where names, titles, and authorship are so important, it is almost inconceivable to us that the author of the Fourth Gospel would seemingly go out of his way to hide his identity through the lack of a name. Perhaps "the Beloved Disciple" name is a metaphor for an entire community of believers in the second century AD. Perhaps the "beloved disciple" was a literary role model, a perfect example, for the reader to emulate. More likely, the Gospel author (at least chapters 1 through 20) did not want to separate himself, or distinguish himself, from all the other nameless people in a very early Christian congregation (the original readers).

If they are one and the same, the Gospel author was given the title of "Beloved Disciple" by later readers over the course of history. The writer of the Fourth Gospel was *not* perfect but was certainly taught and transformed and loved by Jesus, like all the other early believers, and he wanted to humbly remember and record his story of all that Christ accomplished (John 21:24). In addition, we see the use of titles for the Trinity in the *epistles* of John: we can compare 1 John 1:1 to the Gospel of John 1:1–2 and see 1 John 2:22 and 4:2 as prime examples. If the author of the Gospel and the pastoral Johannine epistles was the same person, who experienced the humility of Jesus firsthand (i.e., John 13), it is understandable as to why he considered his own identity as secondary, especially in relationship to the risen Christ (John 20:8). The first readers of the Gospel would have known exactly who authored the text, and they believed his message (John 21:24). More important than the author's name or his own descriptive title is the names and identities that he gave to the trinitarian God.[13]

Suffice it to say that while we fully recognize the anonymity of the author of John's Gospel, we can still think about what the author was *doing*. Outside of the discussion concerning his true identity is the most important discussion of the content and the motivation of the author to record and share what he considered to be "*truth*" with his readers (John 1:14, 17; 4:23–24; 14:6, 17; 15:26; 16:13; 17:17; 18:37; 21:18). We can discern this authorial intention from the literature itself, and this leads to the basic theology embraced by the author. He was granting assurance that faith in Jesus as the Messiah Christ is valid, effective, authoritative, and compelling. The trinitarian God loves all those who believe (John 17:23) and those who believe will "have life in his name" (John 14:18; 17:26; 20:26–29, 31).

Farewell Discourses

The prayer of John 17 is the climax to the Johannine Farewell Discourses. Not everyone agrees on the length of this section of the Fourth Gospel, but it is often regarded as chapters 14 through 17 because in these four chapters, the main focus is on the words of Jesus. Literarily, these "speeches" of Jesus are unlike any discourses that we find in the three Synoptic Gospels. They are a collection of monologues and dialogues between Jesus and his disciples at the final Passover meal they would share together (John 13:1–2).

As his time on earth was drawing to a close, Jesus still had many things to say and to teach his followers (John 16:12). They needed some preparation for the strange and awful events that would culminate Jesus' time on earth. Jesus offered comfort to his disciples and presented them with a number of paradoxes and amazing statements that must have been very confusing to them at that time. Because Jesus often spoke in hyperboles, parables, images, and metaphors, his followers were left questioning his teachings.

How much greater would be their confusion as they witnessed his crucifixion and resurrection? He predicted his own exit from their lives but promised them he would never leave them. He said that if they "knew" him, they "knew the Father" (John 14:9–11), and his little band of followers would do "greater things" than what Jesus did on the earth (John 14:12). He told his disciples that they were his "friends" (not students); but their final assignment was to "abide" in him, obey his words, and "love one another." If they did so, they will "bear" amazing "fruit." Most importantly, Jesus pledged to send "another Advocate," the Holy Spirit, to live *within* them (John 14:16–18).

His teachings and revelations alternated between the disciples' present, the near future, and the distant future; so it was difficult for them to discern his clear meaning and time frame. In fact, it is still difficult for readers today. Yet Jesus promised "peace" to his own in the midst of all the turmoil that was about to take place (John 16:33). How astonishing, amazing, fearful, and mystifying! It is no wonder the disciples asked Jesus to "speak clearly, without figures of speech," so that they could "see" everything more clearly (John 16:29–30).

So why did the author of John include these unique speeches in his Gospel? Matt Searles perceives a number of purposes articulated by Jesus in the Johannine discourses. Searles points out that Jesus repeated the phrase "I have said these things to you…" or "I have told you…" (*taũta lelálēka 'umĩn*). This phrase appears only six times in the entire canonical Bible, and they are all in John chapters 14 through 16. Each brief discourse ends with a statement that tells the readers *why* Jesus said what he did. The phrase, then, is key to our understanding of what Jesus was saying and a fitting conclusion to a section of the text. As Jesus prepared his disciples for his departure, his discourses were a reassuring glimpse into what would happen after he is gone, and what they should do after his departure.[14]

Thus, the literary setting, structure, and determined purposes of the Farewell Discourses are the background to the prayer. But why a *prayer*? In fact, the content (themes) and position of the prayer at the end of the discourses appear to be quite intentional. Jesus promised that his *"going"* would mean union with God and not separation; a prayer is only fitting because it is the final visible public connection Jesus had with his Father in the presence of his followers. At the end of the Farewell Discourses, perhaps a "pep talk" would have been more appropriate. Like a coach, preparing his team for the big game, perhaps Jesus should have been more positive and encouraging ("high fives" all around) because the disciples had no idea what was in the near future. But for his central group of followers, the closing prayer after his discourses was a preparation for the unexpected experiences of Jesus' looming betrayal, passion, crucifixion, and resurrection.

Nearing the end of his assignment on earth, Jesus was pleased to share with the Father that there were those people who did believe and were ready to follow him (John 13:37, 14:11), even if they did not fully understand what was coming. It was even more import-ant, therefore, that his followers stay closely connected to the Father as they faced fear, opposition, doubt, and disappointment during Jesus' final days on earth. John 17 is Jesus' last "will and testament" spoken to his followers, as well as a "commissioning" of *those first disciples* for their ministries that would develop after Jesus' death, resurrection, and ascension. Knowing what was ahead of him and wanting to equip his followers for what was to come, Jesus prayed for himself, for his immediate group of followers, and for the future believers that were to come after them, like the Johannine readers. In spite of all his preparations, of course, events did not go exactly smoothly for the first disciples at Jesus' crucifixion and for quite a time afterward. Nevertheless, his "going" would inaugurate a time of new belief, love, obedience, joy, and peace that would arise from the ashes of his crucifixion.

Jesus' prayer and practices

Intimately connected to God, Jesus sought private and personal space to connect with his Father (i.e., Mark 1:35; Matt. 26:39; Luke

6:12). While we recognize that the Fourth Gospel, including the prayer of John 17, was written decades after the actual events of the narrative, it is clear that during his time on earth, Jesus practiced personal and public prayer. The first listeners of Jesus' prayer, his earliest followers, who were likely confused and fearful with regard to his words of departure, were years into their ministries or were not even alive at the time of John's writing. The readers of John's Gospel were already familiar with the events surrounding Jesus' life, death, and resurrection; so preparation for such events was unnecessary. The next generation of believers—"those who will believe in me through their message" (John 17:20)—were actually the people to whom John was writing. Thus, the author used a prayer as a strategic literary technique to affect his intended audience. This is *not* to say that Jesus did *not* say a prayer with his disciples at their last supper together; it is merely a consideration of John's intention as he chose to include a prayer at the end of his Farewell Discourses.

Consequently, John 17 was Jesus' *prayer of preparation* for his earliest followers during his lifetime on earth, and it was John's *prayer of assurance* composed for his audience many years later. The Johannine author collected all of Jesus' final intentional words of grace and instructions for his *first followers* and culminated them with the prayer for his *first-century audience*. Köstenberger suggests that the Gospel was written after AD 70 and before AD 100; and, "if Thomas's confession of Jesus as 'my Lord and my God' [John 20:28] is intended to evoke associations of emperor worship under Domitian (AD 81–96), a date after AD 81 would appear most likely."[15] What did the early Christians to whom John wrote think about this final prayer? How did the death and resurrection of Jesus affect the way that people prayed to God?

After the destruction of the Jerusalem Temple (in AD 70), the Jews and early Christians were scattered abroad within the Roman Empire. By the end of the first century, the power of Rome was felt across the province of Asia Minor, especially in a city like Ephesus, plausibly the location of the Johannine community. With this in mind, the overall purpose of the Gospel was to show that "Jesus is the Christ, the Son of God, and that by believing, you may have life in his name" (John 20:31). This "purpose statement" indicates that John had an evangelistic purpose in writing; he wanted to reach unbelieving people through his believing congregation. Of course, there were no recording devises to capture Jesus' exact words of the spoken prayer. In fact, our studies of the New Testament Gospels are all based on the memories and interpretations of the ancient authors concerning the life of Jesus, his words, and his teachings. The authors' testimonies are not untouched by their own experiences and settings. However, we can be sure that the Holy Spirit brought to John's mind the voice and intentions of Jesus, just as Jesus said he would.

So we can ask, what is the purpose of John 17 for the original readers first and then for readers today? What is the author *doing* by placing this final prayer at the end of Jesus' Farewell Discourses? Is he evoking or creating particular comparisons, emotions, desires, images, or experiences for and in his audience? What is the author *saying* to his readers, and rhetorically speaking, what is he trying to persuade his audience to *do*? The meaning and implications of the prayer are very profound for people of any age who "hear" it. The goal of this study is to answer those questions, to glean the purpose and the significance of the prayer for the earliest Christ followers and then for Christian believers today. The discoveries will aid in our confidence in our own prayers and will help clarify the Trinity to whom we pray.

Who are the "believers"?

The Fourth Gospel records various types of people who began to follow Jesus during his earthly ministry. They were characters in a full dramatic production: first, we note the "Twelve" (John 6:67, 70–71), a narrow group of men chosen by Jesus, one of whom betrayed him (John 6:70, 20:24, also, my "brothers" in 20:17). Second, it is plausible to think that "the Twelve" were a part of a broader group of people, perhaps including women, who were following Jesus during his ministry, listening to him, seeing his miracles, perhaps supporting him and the "Twelve" financially, and believing in his message

(John 4:28, 39–42; 8:31; but see 6:66). This broader group of "disciples" know God through Jesus (i.e., John 16:29–31). The "crowd" to whom Jesus spoke appears to be ambivalent toward him, seeking physical "signs" and "works" (John 6:1–2, 5, 14, 22–31, 64). "The world" can be seen as a Johannine shorthand for those people who reject Jesus and stand in opposition to his message. "The Jews" refers specifically to those Jewish leaders who rebuked and confronted him (John 8:23, 14:27, 15:18–18, 17:14, 18:36).

By the time the original readers heard John's Gospel, we can assume that John was writing to a small community of committed believers—people who had chosen to follow Jesus in spite of their cultural circumstances. Perhaps John's congregation was in or near the Roman city of Ephesus in Asia Minor. While the identity of the first-century author of this Gospel continues to be debated in scholarship, the exact nature of the original audience is debated too.

No doubt the author presented his personal recollections of the mission of Jesus the Christ and reported to his readers as an eyewitness to many events and discourses. The community to which he "testified" about Jesus accepted his words and knew his words "to be true" (John 21:24). Assuming this Christian community was composed of both Jewish and Gentile believers, and if Ephesus was the location of the church, they were taking quite a risk to gather together in a time and place ruled by the strong hand of the Roman emperor. The mixed audience was apparently under political persecution and was ostracized by the surrounding culture. They were "hated by the world," but were "chosen" out of it and separate from it (John 15:18–21). The author notes that the formerly Jewish Christian believers were "put out of the synagogue" for their faith in Jesus as Messiah (John 16:1–4).[16]

Believers, in any day and age, are those people who were/are committed to knowing and following Father God through the Son Jesus in the power of the Holy Spirit. As an assurance to believers across the centuries, even in difficult circumstances, Jesus promised that if they stay committed to their faith, he has "overcome the world" and that they will have his "peace" (John 16:33).

Knowing God

Indeed, the Bible is a revelation of God; our knowledge of God is possible only because he has chosen to reveal himself to people. God's self-revelation was through the Hebrew covenants and laws, and then though his Son, Jesus Christ (John 1:17, 5:45–47, 6:14, 7:16–19). God revealed himself in divine acts and promises and commands in the Old Testament. In the New Testament, God's revelation was completed in the life, death, and resurrection of a person—his Son. A key theme of John's Gospel is the "testimony" of those who "saw" and "heard" and knew Jesus. That is, accurate firsthand authentication of words and events leads to true knowledge of who Jesus is (John 1:15, 21:24).

Thus, humanity cannot truly know God without knowing Christ (John 5:19–25, 30, 36–40; 15:25; 1 John 5:5:11–12). In fact, prayer is an important part of a person's *knowing* God, and knowing God is an important aspect of prayer. Prayer is a tool that connects the pieces and builds a sturdy foundation of a relationship with God. Even so, not everything has been disclosed to us yet, and there are always new things we can learn about our Mighty God and about his divine plans and purposes for each person and for the community of believers (John 21:25).

On the one hand, human beings tend to talk more with the people that they already know: we talk to our spouses, our parents, our children, and our close friends. It can be much easier to talk to people that we know and trust, that accept us as we are and still care about us. On the other hand, people pay a lot of money to talk to psychologists, counselors, and doctors (who they may know little about), hoping that they will know themselves better! So this is one of the first things that the author of John's Gospel is *doing*. In writing his Gospel, the author wanted his readers to *know* what they *know*: to know the Father, the Son, and the Spirit more fully; to "abide" in them more closely; to cultivate an intimate relationship with the divine Trinity; and to "have life, and have it to the full" (John 10:10). There is a difference, of course, between knowing God and knowing *about* God. A person can study the Bible and memorize the Scriptures in his/her head without having a real "heart" knowledge of God.

John 17 and knowing God

In the Hebrew language, the most common root word for the verb "to know" is *yada*. It means "to know, to recognize, to understand, to be respected, to have sexual relations." This word does *not* describe intellectual, academic information; it implies something much more: an intimate, bonded, relational *knowing*, as deeply as a couple married for fifty years *knows* one another. Knowing God helps people to trust him and to understand who we are in relation to him. In fact, God knows everything there is to know about each one of us, and he wants us to know him in the same way:

> Those who *know your name* will trust in you,
> For you, Lord, have never forsaken those who
> seek you (Ps. 9:10; emphasis mine).

> Be still, and *know* (*yada*) that I am God;
> I will be exalted among the nations,
> I will be exalted in the earth (Ps. 46:10).

The Old Testament prophets clearly indicate that it was a lack of knowing God that was the underpinning of the Israelites' sins and idolatry against God:

> There is no faithfulness, no love,
> No acknowledgement of God in the land…
> My people are destroyed from lack of knowledge
> (*yada*). (Hosea 4:1, 5).

> Let us acknowledge (*yada*) the Lord;
> Let us press on to acknowledge him. (Hosea 6:3).

In the Greek New Testament, common words for "to know" are *oida* (to see, to know, to understand) and *ginōskō* (to come to know, comprehend, to distinguish between, recognize). In English, the two verbs appear to be the same, but they each have a nuanced meaning in Greek. Both are used frequently in the Fourth Gospel, indicating that the "knowledge of, and self-revelation of God" is a key theme of the Gospel.[17] God revealed himself to his people so they would know him as the "only true God" (John 17:3). Jesus noted that the Samaritans "worship what you do *not* know," while the Jews "worship what we *do* know" (John 4:22). He also reminded the Jewish leader Nicodemus that,

> You are Israel's teacher and do you not understand (*ginōskō*) these things? I tell you the truth, we speak of what we know (*oida*) and we testify to what we have seen, but still you people do not accept our testimony? (John 3:10–11).

While there are many other times in John's Gospel when people come to "know" God through knowing and believing in Jesus (i.e., John 4:42, 8:32), it is also apparent that unbelievers—the "world" or "the crowd"—did *not* know God because they did not know Jesus as the Christ (John 1:26; 7:28; 8:19, 55; 12:35; 15:21). The Jewish leadership was condemned because they did *not* know (*oida*) Jesus or his Father. That is, to know the Son is to know God; *not* knowing the Son is *not* to know God (John 1:26; 7:28; 8:19, 55; 15:21). On the other hand, Jesus knew his followers, and they knew his voice (John 10:4, 14, 27). He wanted his followers to know his teachings as truth (John 13:17) so that they could witness to other people about the truth (John 21:15, 24). Ultimately, knowing Jesus is key to knowing the Father (14:7).[18] Since we are *fully known* by God, and it is God's earnest desire *to be known* by his people, we can know the One who hears and answers our prayers because of our faith in Christ.

Knowledge, it seems, is more than just an intellectual pursuit of factual information. The human mind, heart, and spirit are all involved in true "knowing." That is, experience, awareness, participation, judgment, and discernment are not inferior to a revelation of facts but supplement our intellectual reason and "knowing." In particular, we need an informed "knowledge" of God, as revealed in his Word, which are the Scriptures given to us so that we can learn about him. But God cannot be fully explained by intellectual study; we know God more deeply by participating in his work, experiencing his presence, and by returning the love he has for us.

It is true that we may love another person—a spouse, a parent, or a child, for example—and we know that person in such an intimate way that it is difficult to reasonably explain why we do so. There are obvious reasons why we love a person, but there are also less obvious reasons felt in the heart. It is on this deeper level of love that we *know* God. John says that "eternal life" is *knowing* God: that is, knowing the one true God and his Son Jesus Christ, who was sent by God to live among human beings (John 17:3).

Jesus' first followers *knew* that everything that was given to Jesus—all his devoted human followers and his glory—came from God (John 17:7). The earliest believers who trusted the words of Jesus while he was still on the earth were, in fact, a gift from God to his Son (John 17:9). The first followers of Jesus *knew* "with certainty" that Jesus was sent by God, and thus they believed that he was who he said he was—God's Son (17:8). These first believers were the "eyewitnesses" to Jesus and to his life and ministry, providing testimony of that knowledge to the readers of the Gospel who perhaps did not see Jesus, nor did they hear his words (see John 20:29). In contrast, the "world" does not *know* God as Jesus *knows* God (John 17:25). But believers *know* God, as Jesus does—truthfully, intimately, and without reservation—because they believe that God did send Jesus to them (John 17:25). Jesus made God *known* to them and continues to make God *fully known* (John 17:26) to those who receive his word in obedience (John 17:6) and believe (John 17:20). Thus, the *knowledge* that humans have of God is rooted and revealed in the love that God has for his Son. Jesus "made God known" to those who believe and will continue to "make God known" because the love God has for the Son will be "in them," and the Son himself will be "in them" (John 17:26).

John chose to use the Greek verb *ginōskō* in John 17:1, as well as in the last few verses of his final prayer (John 17:23, 25, 26). *This is key to understanding the gospel message.* Believers can know God experientially because, in his love, God sent his Son to redeem humanity. He made himself known to people in the Old Testament in various ways, but there were people who still did not know God (John 7:28–29). Then, it is the Son who "made God known" and who revealed his divine purposes (John 12:45; 14:7, 9–10).

Knowing God nourishes human life, like the simple but essential "bread" (John 6:48–59) and the "living water" pictured by Jesus (John 4:10, 13–14). Through his life, death, and exaltation, Jesus made the Father "known" to people in an entirely new way: to know God is to know his Son, and to know the Son is to know the Father. From the earliest followers of Jesus to the original readers of John's Gospel and to believers today, "all those" who believe in the Father and the Son are united into "one" (John 17:20–22). From the past to the present to the future, all believers can know the love of God because Jesus is "in" them (John 17:26).

"Knowledge" in Johannine Epistle

While scholars still debate the authorship of the epistles of John, it is worth noting that the author of 1 John, perhaps the Gospel author as well, used almost the exact the same language about "knowing God" that we find in the Gospel of John: "We know (*ginōskō*) that we live in him and he in us because he has given us of his Spirit" (1 John 4:13, compare to John 14:16–17, 20).

As he concludes his letter, the author reassured his readers that they can rest assured *("know," oida)* that their belief in "the *name* of the Son of God" does lead to eternal life and confidence in the one true God (1 John 5:13–14). Then the author gives three specific affirmations in verses 14–20, using the phrase *"we know."* He affirmed the fact that God hears the prayers of the faithful (*oida*, 1 John 5:14–15), which is comparable to John 14:13–14 and 16:23. He confirmed the fact that God considers the believers as his "children" and protects them from an evil world (*oida*, 1 John 5:18–19; John 17:15). And the author *knew* that the Son of God was sent to give people an "understanding" so that they might *know* the one true God (*oida*, 1 John 5:20; John 8:19). In summary, the author removes any doubt about the truths expressed in this letter concerning the distinctiveness of the "Son Jesus Christ" who is fully God, and the provider of "eternal life" (1 John 5:13, 20).[19] The themes and words in the epistle very closely match the assurances given in the Fourth Gospel.

Therefore, names describe who God is, what he does, and how he interacts with his creatures. God is "otherness" and not like human beings. While he is necessarily "far away" from us by his "otherness," he has a strong desire to be present with us. What we know about a person affects the way we deal with that person. The same is true of God. If we believe that he is remote and far away, connecting with him in prayer seems feeble and useless. But if we truly *know* God, prayer is a vehicle to being in an intimate relationship with him. Prayer makes God accessible and close at hand; God makes prayer relational and a privilege.

The question is, how?

This leads to the expected question: *how* does one know God? The author of the book of Revelation in the New Testament, perhaps even the same John, gave his readers in Ephesus three steps to a better understanding of how to stay connected to God. The Ephesians had "forsaken your first love," and had forgotten about their initial loving, intimate relationship with the Lord (Rev. 2:4). The "angel" told them three things: "remember" (or "consider"), "repent," and "do the things you did at first" (Rev. 2:5). The struggling believers in Ephesus were to "remember" the "height," the joy, the "mountain-top experience" of a young, "just-born-again" believer. In our daily struggles and "perseverance," we too can forget the pure joy of remembering what Jesus has done for us and the tremendous love and mercy and grace God has given us.

In light of his grace, the readers were to "repent" or "change their minds" about the way they viewed God. Did they blame God for their hardships? (Rev. 2:3). Did they think God had deserted them? If they truly knew God and understood his character and his promises, they would not maintain such thoughts. Finally, the believers were to "do the things you did at first," which was to see life with a new, fresh, joyful outlook and with an excited testimony to share with others.

This is good advice for all of us. It is not the "doing *for* God" or the activities that we do in our own power that are important. What is important is what we do *with* God to improve, restore, and invigorate our relationship with him. We will find that he is, remarkably, more faithful, more loving, and more trustworthy than we ever expected.

Further, exactly *how* do we pray to this God with enthusiasm and devotion? We live in an age of advancing technology where communication is primarily through devices like the internet, cell phones, and tablets. Such devices can limit the amount of face-to-face contact that we have with one another: parents and children, teachers and students, employers and employees. As good as technology is, it cannot replace a *real* handshake, smile, tears, or a hug. It has been said that in this high-tech world that we need to make an intentional effort to bring high touch to our relationships. The same is true with God; if we really want to know God, we need to make a concerted effort to "reach out and touch" him through every means possible, including prayer.

Indeed, it is a personal challenge for Christian believers today to evaluate their own prayer life and how it affects both their relationships with God (the "vertical relationship") and with other people ("horizontal relationships"). It is my contention that the writer of the Fourth Gospel wanted his readers to respond to his deliberate use of the divine titles, which taught his readers about *who God is*. This leads to a deeper understanding of the nature of human prayer. The author John used titles which can teach Christians about prayer—about who it is that we are praying *to*. What are we to *do* having discovered the true identities of the Father, Son, and Holy Spirit? The

Farewell Discourses and John 17 give us clear indications as to how we should respond to *knowing* God.

We must recognize that God is shaping his people into those who reflect his own nature and character. One cannot live a godly life if he or she does not know God; and that means we still struggle under our own weaknesses, arguing, rebelling, and giving up hope. Prayer is not an attempt to manipulate God; it is a molding of our wills to his, not the other way around. We need to know that God does listen, does speak to his people, does care, and is extraordinarily gracious in his responses to us. In fact, it is only by his grace that he chooses to listen and to care deeply about his creatures at all.

Thus, knowing God more deeply and cultivating a meaningful relationship with Father God—in Christ, by the Spirit—are crucial to the writer of the Fourth Gospel. Notably, the Johannine author uses a prayer to demonstrate this for his readers. Prayer, in fact, has an indisputable place in the rapport between the Trinity and the followers of Jesus. The Farewell Discourses and the final prayer of Jesus in John 17 can bind believers to God and move readers toward a healthy theology of Christian prayer. Our prayers are the bond between us, not unlike an internet worldwide link that is invisible and unbreakable. An ineffective prayer life can be the result of an inaccurate knowledge about God.

Toward a theology of prayer today

We can get caught up in methodology; that is, every author, every speaker may have a different view of how to *do* prayer. This comes with our own guilt trips. Do we really believe the promises of God in the Bible? How much should we pray? Are my motives pure? I forgot to pray before my meeting yesterday—was God there anyway? Are God's only answers *yes, no,* or *just wait*?

Scot McKnight observes that today, Christians may be more concerned about their own lack of a prayer life than about God's intentions in answered prayer. It is a vicious circle: we feel guilty for not praying, and then we tend to pray less often.

> But, instead of using guilt to motivate, we need
> to cast a compelling vision of the goodness of
> the Father. Knowing God's love, knowing God's
> goodness, and learning to embrace those attri-
> butes of God prompt us to pray.[20]

Humanity seems so small and insignificant in relation to a God who is so "immense, omnipotent and omniscient"; and we get so bogged down in our own little worlds. On the other hand, we imagine that we can figure things out on our own, and we need not bother God with all our trivial circumstances.[21] No doubt, we can tell God how to solve a problem, but then we are frustrated because he does not do as we have told him to do. So how does a sincere pray-er find a clear picture of who God is and how to talk to him?

Our "theology of prayer," then, is based on a clear understanding of who God is *really*! What we believe about prayer reveals our honest, personal knowledge of the three Persons of the Trinity. How can we obey someone we do not know? If, indeed, we know a God who is holy, just, and righteous, who loves us so much he died for us and who actually lives within us, how can we *not* build a prayerful relationship with him and allow him to transform us into the persons he wants us to be? Our faith and trust in God are demonstrated in our ordinary everyday life—a life of obedience and humble gratitude.

"What I believe about God is the most important thing about me," said A. W. Tozer.

Human responses

This book is written for all of us who have found the practice of prayer to be a difficult task. Most Christian leaders are extraordinarily busy, and it is hard to find a spare moment to converse with God in true personal prayer. Yet it is critical to fully know this God so that we can help other people to fully know him. Unanswered prayers can be painful for anyone, and they can lead to an incorrect and distorted "theology of prayer." We all know people who have "given up on God" because they have had hollow experiences with prayer.

Helping people to have a more intimate and exciting prayer life is truly a blessing for students and teachers! What the author of John's Gospel is *doing* is putting followers of Christ into a brand-new living prayer relationship with God through Christ and by the Holy Spirit. Indeed, this is one goal of Christian relationship and leadership: to help people deepen their connection with Christ through an intimate prayer life.

With this in mind, in the following chapters, we will unpack the titles or names that the author of John used for the Holy Trinity. Hopefully, this will indeed help us to *know* God in a deeper, more heartfelt way, and affect the ways we communicate with him through prayer. That is, the concept of prayer, from the Old Testament Jewish Temple worship to the advent of the New Testament "*Paraclete*," was modified over the centuries as people learned to know God. The "new covenant" accomplished by the blood of Jesus and the presence of the Holy Spirit in Christian believers initiated a new way of communicating with the Almighty God. *Prayer moved from ritual to a relationship.*

It seemed important to John that his readers fully understand who God is, both individually and collectively, which impacts how believers relate to God in prayer and to each other as a community of believers. It was important to "decode" the identities of the triune God so that an authentic, cherished relationship can be relished by all of God's people.

C. S. Lewis summarized the intentions of this book rather succinctly:

> Prayer is either a sheer illusion or a personal contact between embryonic, incomplete persons (ourselves) and the utterly concrete Person. Prayer in the sense of petition, asking for things, is a small part of it; confession and penitence are its threshold, adoration its sanctuary, the presence and vision and enjoyment of God its bread

and wine. In it God shows Himself to us. That He answers prayers is a corollary—not necessarily the most important one—from that revelation. What He does is learned from what He is.[22]

Notes

1   Craig L. Blomberg, *The New American Commentary; Matthew*, ed. gen. ed. Dockery, David, vol. 22. (Nashville, TN: Broadman Press, 1992).

2   David Clark, *On Earth as in Heaven: The Lord's Prayer from Jewish Prayer to Christian Ritual* (Minneapolis: Fortress Press, 2017).

3   Larry Hurtado, "A New Book on Christology in the Gospel of John," Word Press, https://wp.me/pYZXr-297) Accessed 12/13/17.

4   David R. Bauer, "Son of God," in *Dictionary of Jesus and the Gospels*, eds. Joel Green, Scot McKnight, and I. Howard Marshall (Downers Grove: InterVarsity Press, 1992), 769–75.

5   William W. Klein, Craig L. Blomberg, and Robert L. Hubbard Jr., *Introduction to Biblical Hermeneutics*, 2nd ed. (Nashville, TN: Thomas Nelson, 2004), 5.

6   Klein, et al., *Introduction*, 6.

7   Abraham Kuruvilla, "Time to Kill the Big Idea? A Fresh Look at Preaching," *JETS* 61.4 (2018), 825–46, 840–841.

8   D. W. Baker, "God, Names Of," in *Dictionary of the Old Testament Pentateuch*, ed. T. Desmond Alexander and David W. Baker (Downers Grove: InterVarsity Press, 2003), 359–68.

9   M. F. Rooker, "Theophany," in *Dictionary of the Old Testament Pentateuch*, ed. T. Desmond Alexander and David W. Baker (Downers Grove: InterVarsity Press, 2003), 859–64, 861.

10 Baker, "God, Names of," *DOTP*, 364.

11 Richard N. Longenecker, *The Christology of Early Jewish Christianity* (Naperville, Illinois: Alec R. Allenson Inc., 1970), 41–42.

12 Longenecker, *The Christology of Early Jewish Christianity*, 45–46.

13 Michael J. Kok, *The Beloved Apostle? The Transformation of the Apostle John into the Fourth Evangelist* (Eugene, Oregon: Wipf & Stock, 2017).

14 Matt Searles, "'These Things I Have Said to You': An Investigation of How Purpose Clauses Govern the Interpretation of John 14–16," JETS 60.3 (2017), 511–32, 511–512.

15 Andreas J. Köstenberger, John; Baker Exegetical Commentary on the New Testament, ed. Robert; Yarbrough and Robert H. Stein (Grand Rapids: Baker Academic, 2004), 8.

16 Köstenberger, *John,* 8.

17 E. Schütz, "Knowledge," in *NIDNTT*, vol. 2, ed. Colin Brown (Grand Rapids: Zondervan Publishing, 1986), 390–409.

18 Schütz, "Knowledge," 390–409.

19 Judith M. Lieu, *I, II, III John; A Commentary* (Louisville, Kentucky: Westminster John Knox Press, 2008), 229–233.

20 Scot McKnight, *The Sermon on the Mount*, ed. Tremper Longman III and Scot McKnight (Grand Rapids: Zondervan, 2013), 245.

21 McKnight, *Sermon*, 245–246.
22 C. S. Lewis, "The Efficacy of Prayer," in *The World's Last Night and Other Essays* (New York: Harcourt Brace Jovanovich, 1960), 8.

Chapter 1

The Passage of Prayer,
Past and Present

> Theologians would like to think that their tomes trickle
> down to the masses and shape Christian discourse and
> prayer. However, it is often the case that theological trends
> emerge more in response to the actual life of the church
> and the insights and experiences of the faithful.[23]

Over the centuries, how have faithful, God-loving people learned to
pray to an invisible, transcendent, yet intimate God? In the past, how
have devoted Christian leaders experienced, practiced, and taught
other people how to pray? No doubt, prayer is one of the most complicated and wonderful aspects of the Christian faith that leaders
today can teach, model, and foster.

Prayer in the Hebrew and Jewish traditions

If we assume that the practice of prayer was common in antiq-
uity, how was prayer a unique practice in ancient Israel, among the
people of God? What did the Israelites believe about prayer that was
different from the prayers of the neighboring pagan cultures? Such

questions help us to understand what role prayer played at the time of the biblical writings.

We can observe how prayer changed and developed from the ancient Old Testament Israelite nation to the presence of the permanent Holy Spirit as revealed in the New Testament. If prayer moved from ritual to relationship in the Hebrew nation, it has moved that direction even more so in the New Testament. Furthermore, early prayer traditions are the seeds that were planted to teach humanity about who God is—past, present and future—and how we can be in a communicative relationship with him today in the shadow of early prayer conventions.

Historically, prayer is a common element of human worship, practiced for as long as anyone can remember. People prayed to stone idols, to ancient gods and goddesses, as well as parts of nature, such as the sun, moon, and the stars. Prayer was often associated with sacrifices and other rituals performed to or for a deity. Certainly, the most common prayers were requests placed before a deity for his/her help in a wide variety of situations ranging from agriculture to wars.

Ancient practices included types of oracles, dreams, magic, amulets, folk medicine (healings), astrology, and fate, as well as personal curses and blessings. In the ancient prayers, we often see the use of divine titles, epithets, and descriptions of the deity, pointing out divine attributes and perhaps the god's previous benevolence toward humanity. The person praying often reminded the deity of his/her great human deeds and gave significant reasons for the god/goddess to comply with the human requests. Prayers then were sometimes formal, sometimes informal. They could be primitive and self-serving; but they could also be hopeful, reverent, and contemplative.[24]

Thus, the early Israelites were unique in their practice of prayer to an unseen God, both within a structured religious system and in very personal, informal addresses to their deity. The heart-wrenching emotions, passions, and pleas of the Hebrews who prayed exclusively to one God is apparent throughout the book of Psalms (i.e., Ps. 4:1). We have recorded prayers of the prophets (Jer. 29:7, 12; 42:3), and later, the appeals of the apostles (i.e., Rom. 15:30; Eph. 6:18; 1 Pet. 3:7). The major difference between the Hebrew God and the "pagan" deities is the evidence that YHWH God is intimately concerned about his people and closely involved with all of his creation (Deut. 4:7). As a personal God, who is both transcendent and near to his creation, human prayer is an expression of the desire on both parts to be connected to one another.

In the early Hebrew tradition, psalms, hymns, liturgy, and prayers to God were very much a part of the worship and devotion to YHWH God. Prayers were generally conducted by the nation's leaders, especially in connection with the Tabernacle or the Temple. In the presence of God in his Temple, prayers and sacrifices were conducted by the Israelite leaders who prayed to the Lord for the people. Less often, individuals prayed for themselves, like the beautiful prayer of Hannah (1 Sam. 1:12). "Blessings and curses" were part of the Israelite faith, rooted in the idea that the spoken word had great power over actions and behavior. Thus, if a curse was spoken *in the name of YHWH*, it was he who carried it out; and it was YHWH that finally carried out all of his promises and blessings.[25]

It is interesting to note that the revelation of God to Moses was through *God's name*, which was a disclosure of his distinctive, divine nature and character as both Judge and Lord (Exod. 3:13–15). As leader of God's people, Moses went before the Lord and prayed for the people. Because God had put his Spirit on Moses, he had a direct line of communication with the Lord. Moses was assigned to do a difficult task—to lead the nation based solely on the *words* that he received from God (i.e., Num. 11:2, 16–17, 21:4–7).

In the Old Testament, *petitionary* prayers are common. The Israelites never hesitated to ask God for something specific, either for the nation or for an individual or both, and sought his help in times of need. The Hebrew verb "to pray" is related to the idea of "to call or cry out," and we find various Hebrew words in the Old Testament which reveal subtle nuances in meaning that are not immediately perceived in English. For example:

"To entreat, make supplication" (Heb. *bea, beah*):
In times of great trouble, Daniel prayed (Dan. 6:10–11).

"To make supplication" (*athar*):
Job was an intercessor and prayed for his "friends" (Job 33:26; 42:8, 10), believing that his righteous prayers would be answered.

"To entreat grace" (*chanan*):
Second Chronicles 6:37–39 is a prayer of repentance by the people and a plea for forgiveness from the Lord.

To judge the self, pray habitually (*palal*):
Gather together and come; assemble, you fugitives from the nations. Ignorant are those who carry about idols of wood, Who prays to gods that cannot save?" (Isa. 45:20).
(see also Deut. 9:20, 26; Isa. 37:15, 21; 38:2; 44:17)[26]

We see other examples in Abraham who prayed for healing and God answered his prayer (Gen. 20:17). In her distress and bitterness, Hannah prayed "continually" for a son (1 Sam. 1:5, 10, 12, 20). The priests and the prophets prayed to the Lord for the people (Exod. 32:31–32; Jer. 27:18; 1 Sam. 12:22–23). Jeremiah instructed the people to pray (Jer. 29:7, 12; 42:3), but God even asked Jeremiah *not* to pray for the rebellious nation (Jer. 7:16, 11:14, 14:11). The prophet Elijah displayed his great faith and prayed to defend the superiority of his God before the worshippers of Baal (1 Kings 18:36). Yet soon after, at a weak and dreadful moment, Elijah prayed for himself that he "might die" before the Lord (1 Kings 19:4). In a familiar and summary verse, God asked for his people to "humble themselves, pray and seek my face" (2 Chron. 7:14).

King David poured out his emotions to God in prayers, psalms, and praises. The "songs and praises" (*tephillah*) in the Book of Psalms are often cited in the New Testament, indicating that the Jews and the early Christians highly valued the prayers and the poetry of this book. This word ("songs and praises") is used thirty-one times in the

Psalms, five times as a title. Certainly, the most familiar and loved prayers in the Old Testament are prayers of joy and praise for who God is. In Psalm 23, for example, the poet (probably David) realizes that God does provide, meeting the needs of his people even in ways that he could not imagine. The poet reacts with confidence and trust in the Lord who provides, protects, and supplies. The Lord answers with goodness and mercy, and his people lacked only what they did not need.

We see that prayer was used by Israel's leaders in times of emotional highs, such as a military victory, and in times of tragic lows, doubt, and defeat (1 Chron. 5:20, 30:27).). Certainly, "Israel was a praying nation."[27] Prayer was as much a part of the nation as her sacrifices, her marvelous victories, and dreadful defeats. Israel's prayers were not incantations, mystical or formal; "rather, its marks are a childlike simplicity, sincerity and confidence." Prayer reflected a genuine and humble strength that the people found in communication with their personal and present God. "Real adoration and lively religious feeling lend force even to public worship."[28]

Second Temple Judaism

The Pentateuch and other ancient Hebrew texts, including worship, prayers, and praises, were the foundation of Second Temple (or Intertestamental) Judaism. This time frame begins post-exile after the Israelite people returned to their homeland from exile in Babylon. The prayer life of the Israelites changed dramatically. Having been in Babylon for decades, the nation was redeemed, and they began restoration. The pattern of the worship of God became more rigid and prescribed in an effort to strictly follow in obedience the commands and instructions of God. "Prayer became an obligatory and meritorious work of the pious, with prescribed times, forms, and apparel for prayer." The pious Israelite became a "warrior" who fought, even in prayer, for a strong leader, a national king, for possession of the land, and for peace.[29]

This period gave birth to many noncanonical Jewish writings, such as what we now call the Apocrypha books. These writings were nationalistic in nature and record a number of prayers that are indicative of the religious feelings of the people. Worth noting is the "Prayer of Azariah and the Song of the Three Jews," which dates to the late second-century BC and accompanies our canonical book of Daniel.

It is a compilation of three literary compositions: a prayer, a prose narrative, and a hymn. The prayer is a communal confession of the sins of Israel against God but with the hope of forgiveness and heartfelt repentance.[30] Another example is the similar "Prayer of Manasseh" (150–50 BC), which recognized the great sins of the nation, the true power and eminence of God, and the sincere desire for repentance and forgiveness. It includes a phrase (verse 11) that is as beautiful as it is descriptive: "And now behold, I am bending the knees of my heart before you; And I am beseeching your kindness."[31]

In later Judaism, the Jewish synagogue developed primarily as a result of the loss of the temple and accompanying traditions (AD 70). The people were steeped in rabbinic traditions: the synagogue became the center of Jewish life, featuring the study of scriptures, prayer, and worship. Prayer was regarded not as a substitute but as a "supplement to Temple worship and services."[32] At that time, there were "three pillars of Judaism: prayer, fasting and almsgiving."[33] The *Shemoneh 'Esreh* ("Eighteen Benedictions") was recited in communal worship and as the prayer of individuals on a daily basis. These prayers were based on Deuteronomy 6:4–9; 11:13–21 and Numbers 15:37–41. At some point in the first-century AD, the wording of the twelfth benediction was modified to include the condemnation of the Jewish Christians as "insolents," "apostates," and "Nazarenes" (or "heretics") (see John 9:22, 12:42, 16:2).[34]

Even so, *petitionary* prayers for the entire nation became problematic. What if God does not answer the prayer of the prophet or the king or the common farmer? Is God really a good God that is concerned about his people? Remembering the bonds of exile, the nation sought to know if and when God really would save and redeem his people from droughts, tyranny, and political oppression. It was to this issue that Jesus spoke to his followers.[35]

Prayer in the New Testament

At the time of writing of the New Testament, the ruling Roman Empire was basically polytheistic in nature. The people recognized that gods and goddesses were very powerful and omnipotent, far beyond human understanding and abilities. At the time of Jesus, we know that many of the Jewish leaders had misconceptions concerning prayer; they forgot that the Temple was a "house of prayer" for *all* people and they became very exclusive (see 1 Kings 8:41–43; Isa. 56:7; Matt. 21:13). They vied for attention, praying specific prayers (usually impressively out loud) three times a day as prescribed by their laws. Jesus implied that the leaders' prayers were hypocritical in nature because the leaders were "clean" on the outside, but inside, they were "full of greed and self-indulgence" (Matt. 23:5–32). In Jewish tradition, the "ask and receive" prayer structure was very common (Prov. 8:17; Jer. 29:13–14); but in reality, of course, everyone knew that God did not answer all prayers as prescribed by the person praying.

Because of this doubtful environment, it was necessary for Jesus to address the topic of prayer with his disciples. His teaching in Matthew 7:7–8, for example, is a call to pray and promises that, indeed, God does answer prayers. They could be assured that God is trustworthy and that he loves his people. The reason why his followers could depend on answered prayer is rooted in the true *character* of God. That is, if a person truly knows God and knows of his goodness and trusts his words, he or she can be assured of answered prayer even if it is not the way one might expect or desire. "God is good, and he gives nothing but good things" (Ps. 37:4, 84:11; Isa. 49:15; and Jas. 1:16–17).[36]

The early Christian believers recognized that worshiping Jesus as "Lord" was the most distinguishing feature about their faith. They held the conviction that both Father God and the Son Jesus were worthy of their devotion, worship, and prayers. It is worth noting that very early in the history of Christianity, Jesus was worshiped as God and as the central figure in the Christian faith. Although he was separate from the Father God, love and devotion for *both* were expressed in prayers, hymns, and liturgical words. The Christians sang and prayed the Old Testament Psalms, aware that some were messianic and were prophetic of Jesus as the promised Messiah. They also created new Christian hymns of praise and worship that were about Jesus and honored him as divine. Perhaps an example of this is the confessional prayer in Paul's letter to the Philippians (Phil. 2:6–11).

In the Synoptic Gospels, Jesus taught his followers "how" to pray (Matt. 6:9), which is set in the context of Jesus' discussion of three "acts of righteousness" in Matthew's Gospel: giving (alms), prayer, and fasting (Matt. 6:1–18). Jesus also taught them how *not* to pray; that is, his followers were not to pray "like the hypocrites" who were more concerned about how they appeared to other people than to God (Matt. 6:5, 23:5). In Jesus' words, God becomes "*your* Father" illustrating an intimate, personal connection to God. Self-gratifying, forced, rote prayers performed for show were not acceptable to God (Matt. 6:6–8). By way of example, Jesus often went to a "solitary place," "up on a mountainside" to pray to *his* Father, away from the crowds (Mark 1:35; Matt. 14:23). Furthermore, and against all known reasons for prayer, Jesus challenged his followers to pray for the ones who "persecuted" them (Matt. 5:44, 46; Luke 6:28).

It is interesting to note some key similarities between the "Lord's Prayer" of Matthew 6:9–13, and Jesus' prayer of preparation with his disciples in John 17. First, we see in Matthew 6:9, Jesus refers to God as his "Father" and recognizes that the name of God is "holy" ("hallowed by your name"). This description of God is repeated in John's title of "Holy Father." Second, Matthew 6:10 says, "your kingdom come, your will be done," which matches nicely with John's title of "Righteous Father." Because God is holy, just, and righteous, his people want his kingdom and his will to be accomplished on this earth in contrast to the corrupt Roman Empire "kingdom" that so controlled the culture in the first-century AD. We can safely assume that the Fourth Gospel was written sometime after Matthew's Gospel so the people to whom John wrote may have already been aware of Matthew's instructional prayer. Thus, John remolded the descriptions of God found in the earlier prayer into two distinctive epithets for God. But what was John's intent to create titles for God that echo the descriptions of God in Matthew's prayer?

As we consider this question, we must also recognize two other brief prayers in the Fourth Gospel which prepare the readers for the

Farewell Discourses in chapters 14–17. In John 11, Jesus performed the miracle of raising his friend Lazarus from the dead (John 11:17–44). He used the event to further disclose his true identity to those people who placed their faith in him: "I am the resurrection and the life" (John 11:25); and "if you believed, you would see the glory of God" (John 11:40). As the tomb of Lazarus was opened, Jesus prayed to his Father with gratitude, affection, and confidence (John 11:41–42). The miracle and the prayer were done for the benefit of the people "that they may believe that you [the Father] sent me" (John 11:41–42).

In John 12, Jesus was uncharacteristically "troubled" as he spoke to some people who were "God-fearers" (they were non-Jews who were attracted to the monotheistic faith). They were curious about this Jesus person and wanted to meet with him (John 12:20–22). He took the opportunity to prepare his followers (and the seekers) of what was to come; that is, he spoke of his impending death, resurrection, and exaltation.

But in the shadow of these unexpected events, decisions would be made by his listeners as to whether they would "serve" him or desert him (John 12:23–26). At the thought of his impending "hour," Jesus still refused to pray for a reprieve from his death. Instead, he prayed that the Father's "name" would be "glorified" because his redemptive events were the "very reason I came to this hour" (John 12:27–28). In fact, his atoning work was completed for all of humanity, the Jews and the non-Jews alike. Following both of these short prayers, there was an immediate positive answer from the Father to support and defend the Son (John 11:44, 12:28).

John's unique "asking"

In the New Testament, where the forms of the English words "pray" or "prayer" appear, the corresponding Greek words are much more numerous and varied. It is interesting to see how the distinctive Greek words are used and what words John chose to use in his Gospel. Like the Hebrew usage in the Old Testament, the verbs translated "to pray" in the New Testament reveal several nuances and implications that are not so obvious in the English versions. For example:

"To want, pray, beseech" (*Greek: deomai*):
(Matt. 9:38; Luke 10:2, 21:36, 22:32; Acts 4:31;
    8:22, 24, 34; 10:2; 2 Cor. 5:20, 8:4)
This word does not appear in the Gospel of John.

"To pray, wish" (*euchomai*):
(2 Cor. 13:7; Jas. 5:16)
This word does not appear in John.

"To call for, or alongside of" (*parakaleo*):
(Matt. 26:53; Mark 5:17–18; Acts 16:9, 24:4,
    27:34)
This word does not appear in John, except in the
    noun form of the title of the Holy Spirit,
    Paraclete.

The most common Greek word for "to pray or wish for" is *proseuchomai*. It appears thirteen times in Matthew (26:42, 44), nine times in Mark (14:32, 35, 38, 39), eighteen times in Luke (22:40, 41, 44, 46), and sixteen times in the book of Acts (20:36; 31:5; 22:17; 28:8). But the word is not used in the Fourth Gospel at all! Instead, John chose to use the word *erōtaō* in his lengthy prayer of John 17:

"To ask *of*, to interrogate" (*erōtaō*).
(Luke 5:3, 14:18–19, 16:27; John 4:31 (not in
    the NIV); 14:16; 16:26; 17:9, 15, 20; 1
    John 5:16).[37]

Moreover, the act of requesting or "asking of" (*erōtaō*) is found primarily in the Farewell Discourses (John 14:16, 16:26) and in the prayer of John 17 (vv. 9 [twice], 15, 20). Why did John select *this* particular word to put on the lips of Jesus in these chapters? Perhaps he was implying that Jesus was specifically "asking of" his Father from a position of equivalence. As "one" with the Father (John 10:30, 38), Jesus was making "requests" that he knew would be granted; it was not just wishful thinking on his part.

Jesus was *interceding* for his immediate followers and for those who would believe in him because of their ministry (the readers of the Gospel). The One who came from God returned to God, leaving his people united as "one" (17:21). There was never any doubt that the requests would be granted because of the relationship ("the one-ness") between the Father and the Son (see John 11:41b–42).[38]

Jesus' departure prayer

We can imagine a what-if narrative: what if you worked for a company for about three years, and one day the boss came into your office and closed the door? Your boss told you that he was leaving—soon (but he really didn't say when). Not only that, but he was also placing you in charge of the company. He looked you straight in the eye and told you it was your duty to take the reins of the organization and lead it into the next century. If that was not enough to paralyze you with fear, he also said that the whole company, all the other employees were depending upon you for their future and their jobs.

That is a very loose analogy to what happened to the very first followers of Jesus. The disciples, his "friends" and closest followers, sat down to a Passover dinner together with Jesus. Excitement was high, for they were in Jerusalem! Then, one of them is accused of being disloyal to Jesus, and he makes a hasty exit. Suddenly, Jesus starts talking about his departure. He is going away, but he really can't explain to them where he is going.

They might see him again, but who knows when? They had no idea what was going on or what was going to transpire in the next few days. This scenario is critical for us to understand the Johannine Farewell Discourses in general and the prayer of John 17 in particu-lar. Chapter 14 opens with an explanation of Jesus' imminent depar-ture from this earth in the presence of his closest followers. Jesus' disciples have been with him for about three years, but suddenly, he is about to leave them. What a shock! His departure was unexpected and terrifying to his first followers.

Even in his words of preparation, Jesus is positive. In fact, he is "preparing a place" for all those who believe (John 14:1–4). His disciples, of course, did not understand any of this (John 14:5–6). They could not grasp the fact that he was just going to leave them, yet he would not "leave them as orphans" (John 14:18). He proceeded to assure them about his unity with the Father and his unity with them as his *followers* (John 14:7–11) and his *friends* (John 15:14). He promised them that in the future, they would receive from him the "baton" of Christian ministry. They would have much work to do; they would have a future purpose and a mission (John 14:12–14). The next chapter of their lives would be very important; and oh, by the way, he would not be with them to help. How could they "remain" in him (John 15:4) if he was going away?

Then, Jesus *interceded* for his immediate followers and for those believers who came after them. He made a startling claim: They would do "even greater things" than what Jesus did (John 14:12). The disciples' ministry would be post-Easter after the work of the cross, which is a more advanced stage in God's plans and purposes of salvation for believers. In their missionary, evangelistic, church-planting efforts, God was with them through Jesus by the Spirit. So the "greater things" would be performed by his followers through the Holy Spirit.

Jesus went on to explain to his disciples about the "other helping presence," the "*Paraclete*," or the "Advocate" (John 14:16–18). That is, the way the "branches" (believers) remain attached to the "true vine" (Jesus) is by the Holy Spirit. In fact, the only way the "branches" can "bear fruit" (in their case, the creation and sustaining of the church) is by "abiding" in Jesus through the Holy Spirit (John 15:1–4). Even after he is gone, believers will not be left alone as "orphans" (John 14:18).

Asking "in Jesus' name"

The words of Jesus in chapters 14 and 16 of John's Gospel reveal both promises and warnings. It is good to remember that these words were first directed to Jesus' first followers, who were his "friends." Their lives were about to change dramatically, and Jesus' preparation for imminent events continued. Jesus instructed his followers to ask or pray to the Father "in *his* name." Never before had the Jews asked for anything in the *name* of someone other than Yhwh himself. We must remember that Jesus' first followers were faithful Jews, born and raised in a culture that did not allow the "proper" name of God to pass on their lips. They would not say it, nor would they write it.

But Jesus told them to pray "in *my* name," with the assurance that the Father would answer them. That is, through the *name* of Jesus, humanity can draw near to the Almighty God and speak directly to the Father. That is revelatory and remarkable! This is not a magical charm or spell, but to pray in Jesus' name is an expression of faith in the person and character of Christ. When his disciples faced their short-term grief and fear at the cross and then faced their long-term ministry tasks to come, it would have been a great assurance that they could come before God in prayer because of their faith in the One he sent. To help support his earliest followers in their assignments to come, Jesus guaranteed that he himself would answer their prayers "so that the Son may bring glory to the Father" (John 14:13).

Even so, we must reconsider Jesus' pledge that "I will do *whatever* you ask in my name" (John 14:13). Whatever? Is this a miraculous formula that *guarantees* that the one praying will get "whatever" he/she asks for? This promise must be put into context because it is no more a self-centered guarantee in today's world than it was in the first-century AD. Praying "in Jesus' name" states the fact that people *know* the Son as the Savior and place their faith in him as an agent of God's purposes and desires.

To pray "in Jesus' name" means that we believe in his whole person, his divinity, his integrity, his nature and character, his messages, his words, and his actions (see John 2:23–24; 17:6, 8). Therefore, Jesus told his disciples that they could ask for "whatever" "in my name, *as long as it brought glory the Father and the Son*," and it was not intended for selfish gain (John 14:13–14, 5:19–20). As his earliest disciples entered into a time of despair, followed by a dangerous time of carrying forward the work that Jesus did on earth, this is a promise from Jesus to hear any and all prayers in reference to the continuation of his ministry and mission.

"Asking" in John 16

Again, within his Farewell Discourses, Jesus taught his disciples to "ask for *anything* in my name, and I will do it" (John 16:22–28). Why did he repeat this promise, and did he mean something different than the promises of chapter 14? One key to our understanding of these verses is the phrase "*In that day*" in verses 16:23 and 26. Jesus predicted his own death and resurrection, as well as the grief and despair of those people he left behind. One day, however, their temporary grief would be turned into joy at his resurrection (see Jer. 31:31; Isa. 61:2–3). In their near future, their pain and confusion would cease, like a woman in labor, whose pain and agony is turned into great joy with the birth of a baby (John 16:20–22; Isa. 27:17–19).

After Jesus' physical departure, the disciples would be unable to ask Jesus questions about "anything": about trust and betrayal, death and resurrection, crucifixion and exaltation, and about their future as those people who followed in his footsteps. Jesus warned them that it was not going to be easy (John 16:1–4, 32–33). But "*in that day*," on the other side of the cross, postresurrection, they would see Jesus again (John 16:16, 19, 22). Then, he would put an end to all their confusion and questions; there would be "peace" and "joy." Jesus would not be a physical "intermediary" between God and his people in prayer because both the Father and the Son sent the Spirit to intervene and "guide [them] into all truth" (John 16:13).

Thus, Jesus opened the door of prayer to the Father "in *his* [Jesus'] name" so that their "joy would be made complete" (John 16:24). On the other side of the cross, after Jesus' return to the Father, his followers would have a "direct pipeline" to the Father through the Son (John 16:26–27). Thereafter, since they could not ask questions of Jesus in the *physical* realm, they could ask the Father directly "in Jesus' name," and the Father would answer because "the Father himself loves you, because you have loved me" (John 16:27).

This was a brand-new avenue of prayer for those who believe—through the Son to the Father by the Spirit. In this sense, this explanation of prayer by Jesus matches his prayer promises in chapter 14. Jesus' promise is that when believers truly seek God in advancing Jesus' kingdom and ministry, their prayers will not go unanswered.

Of course, the words of Jesus created all kinds of questions in the disciples' minds. In Jewish tradition, it was important for the students to ask questions of their teacher; that was a well-established didactic method. An experienced teacher could anticipate the students' questions and answer them before they were even asked. So Jesus knew the disciples would have many fears, thoughts, doubts, and disappointments; and knowing their lack of understanding, Jesus attempted to reassure his followers even before the passion events would change their lives forever. The disciples finally began to grasp the answers to their own questions and acknowledged Jesus' divinity (John 16:18, 29–31), yet in fact, they still did not have a clue. They were just beginning to learn about Jesus' true identity and purposes.

Because of the birth, death, and resurrection of Jesus on behalf of believers, we can ask God anything, *through* the Son and *by* the Holy Spirit, and he will hear our prayers. If we place our trust in Jesus and pray in his name, our prayers are heard because we are "loved by the Father" (16:27). Our prayers should be rooted in "whatever" brings glory to the Father and the Son, grounded in obedience to Jesus' word and in love for one another, which is the path to "fruitful discipleship."[39] The outcome of prayer "in Jesus' name," is fourfold: believers "*remain* in Jesus and in his love," they "*bear* much fruit" in this world (John 15:8), they have *joy* (John 15:11), and they have the "*peace* of Jesus, because he has overcome the world" (John 16:33; 14:1, 27).

Johannine Epistle and prayer

It is also helpful to reflect on the conclusion of a Johannine epistle as it relates to the answered prayer. First John is written in the style of the Johannine Gospel, and there are distinctive similarities between the two. The author of the letter presents a positive conclusion to his explanation of "eternal life" for those who choose to follow Christ (1 John 5:13). "*We know*" is the author's formula for true "testimony" about the Father and the Son (1 John 2:3–4, 5:11–20). Knowing God, believers can "approach God" in prayer with the confidence that God will "hear" their prayers: "And if we know that he hears us—whatever we ask—we know that we have what we ask of him" (1 John 5:14–15).

However, the author of the letter also reiterates *conditions* that must be met by the one praying before he/she can expect answered prayer:

> Dear friends, if our hearts do not condemn us, we have confidence before God and receive from him anything we ask, because we obey his commands and do what pleases him. And this is his command: to believe in the name of his Son, Jesus Christ, and to love one another as he commanded us. Those who obey his commands live in him, and he in them. And this is how we know that he lives in us: We know it by the Spirit he gave us (1 John 3:21–24).

In agreement with the Gospel, this letter assures believers that whatever we ask of God, with all our humility, and with his grace, it is preceded by belief in Christ (see John 6:29), by obedience to his commands (John 14:23), by love for God and for other people (John 13:34–35, 15:9–12), and by the power of the Holy Spirit within us (John 14:16, 16:7).[40] This is, in fact, a rather humbling recognition; God acts on behalf of his "children" for their benefit and maturity. What the Johannine author is *doing* is giving the followers of Christ a new confidence and putting them into a brand-new living prayer relationship with God through Christ and by the Holy Spirit so that they can be a joyful, active part of spreading the gospel message in the world.

Summation and John 17

Furthermore, what was the Johannine author *doing* to and for his readers by including the prayer of John 17 after the promises and warnings of chapters 14 and 16? None of the other Gospels have recorded this prayer; and no other New Testament writer summarizes the Father, the Son, and the Holy Spirit in quite the same way as John. Jesus, and the author John, were both teaching, exhorting, warning, and assuring all of Jesus' followers throughout all time with a summarizing prayer:

> *John 17:1–3.* These verses are an explanation of the true identities of the Father and the Son so that the one praying knows who he/she is talking to.
>
> *John 17:4–5.* Jesus prayed for himself.
> It is not incorrect to pray for ourselves—not like a selfie, with the camera turned on ourselves for our own glory, but for clarity of his will, his purposes, and how we can be a part of that.
>
> *John 17:6–19.* Jesus prayed for his immediate followers, "those whom you gave me out of the world."
> His first disciples were about to experience the worst time of their lives—the arrest and crucifixion of their Lord and their leader. But they belonged to God and would be covered by his divine protection.
>
> *John 17:20–26.* Jesus prayed for all believers who would come after his first disciples, a wider circle of humanity and "those who believe in me through their message." This includes the original readers of the Fourth Gospel as well as readers today!

First, Jesus interceded for his earliest, closest followers and asked the Father to set them apart for their ministries, with the "full measure of my joy within them" (John 17:13, 17; 15:11). He prayed that the disciples would be protected from the "evil one," "in the power of your [the Father's] name" (John 17:11, 15). The disciples were commissioned and "sent" into the world, just as Jesus was "sent," to spread the gospel truth from God, and they would be blessed for doing so (John 15:27; 17:18).

Second, Jesus interceded not only for John's readers in the first century but also for Christ followers of today. The small circle of disciples did indeed take the gospel message out into the world, and "their message" was received across the Ancient Near East and all the way to Rome (John 17:20). Through their mission and message, empowered by the Holy Spirit, the Christian church blossomed and grew rapidly across the globe. Jesus' prayer redeems and unifies all Christ-followers from the first disciples until today, all across the world, united in the one Father, one Son and one Spirit. This unity has already been given though the sacrifice of Christ, and it is not achieved by human effort (John 17:21–23).

By his example, Jesus taught us that we can pray for our own guidance and direction. We can intercede for other people, especially those close to us; and we can broaden our prayers to include our church, our nation, and our world. What we are to *do* is to pray for ourselves, pray for other people, and pray for the whole world around us *that all may see the glory of God* (John 17:24).

Prayer in the church

The confession of faith in Jesus as the Messiah is the turning point in a person's life (Matt. 16:16), and the gathering of confessing persons is called the "church" in Matthew's Gospel (Matt. 16:18, 18:17). The task assigned to the earliest Christ followers was to establish and grow local congregations of believers—that is, the church of Christ. In Matthew's Gospel, we see that the authority and duties of the church are to proclaim the gospel truths by witnessing, preaching, and doing ministry ("loose on earth"—Matt. 16:19, 18:18). Being a part of the "kingdom" on earth may also include confrontation, forgiveness, and fellowship (Matt. 18:15–20). Like the passage in John 14 about asking in prayer, Matthew 18:19–20 can be misunderstood and misused as a pledge that the Father will grant "anything you ask for" (Matt. 18:19). Again, this is not a guarantee that God will fulfill every prayer we ask of him as we so desire. But God assures the church that he will be present in all acts of reconciliation among believers (as in Matt. 18:15–18).

Note the connection between the "two or three witnesses" in Matthew 18:16 and the "two or three gathered together in my name" in Matthew 18:20. In addition, immediately following these verses is a parable about the kingdom and forgiveness (Matt. 18:21–35). Thus, Jesus (with the Father) will remain present in the church (in the form of the Spirit) to guide and help the process of forgiveness and restoration.[41]

Moreover, in Matthew's Gospel (Matt. 7:7–12), Jesus recalls the pattern of *petitionary* prayers of the Israelites before him: "Ask, seek, knock." Many Christians are familiar with the pattern of "asking and receiving" as seen in these verses; the instructions to "ask, seek, knock" becomes the paradigm of prayer: "*ask.*" Again, is this a guarantee that if we are persistent that God is obligated to answer our prayers as requested? If we "knock" hard enough, will the "door" finally open? Experience teaches us otherwise. From these verses in Matthew's Gospel, however, we can learn that persistence and patience are important. If a congregation of believers prays together in agreement, and if we truly seek God and his will for his people, he will surely answer.[42] Furthermore, the church is "*in*" Christ to be witnesses to the world (John 17:21) and all the prayers of all believers are "unified" in the power of the Spirit and in the love of God (John 17:23, 26).

The unified church that prays in faith appears much simpler on the surface than it is in reality. Human faith falters; it stumbles and falls. It crashes and burns; it goes up and down like an elevator. The faith of Christ-followers is never higher than a person's view of God; our faith will never exceed the character of the Person we are talking to. More often than not, what appears to be a *fear* issue for people is really a *faith* issue.

We have faith in God because we *know* who he really is. This is apparent in the stories of Jesus calming the Sea of Galilee found in the Synoptic Gospels. In a boat during a dreadful storm and fearing for their lives, the disciples awaken Jesus, telling him *to do something about their circumstances*. After his miraculous calming of the winds, Jesus does not address his disciples' *fears* but their *faith* (Matt. 8:26; Mark 4:40; Luke 8:25). So if fear is a lack of faith, then a lack of faith is a lack of knowledge of God ("What kind of man is this?" Matt. 8:27). Surely, believers can pray in faith, as the prophet told the whole nation: "do not be afraid," because we have a *very big* God (Isa. 40:9–20).

Conclusions and responses

In summary, we can observe that faithful, God-loving people learned to pray by experiencing the Almighty. The Old Testament nation experienced God in his miraculous acts and his commanding words. They learned to pray with awe and devotion, and he answered their prayers in familiar and in unexpected ways. Inspiring leaders guided the ancient people to pray sincere prayers to a God they could not see. In the New Testament, believers experienced God in the Word, in Jesus Christ, who was God from eternity past and who was God incarnate to be among his people in the flesh.

If prayer moved from ritual to relationship in the Hebrew nation, it moved in that direction even more so in the New Testament. As the divine Son, Jesus reflected the essence of prayer by being so intimately connected to God his Father. Finally, the Holy Spirit is given to all faithful believers to complete the task of recreation, redemption, and to tighten the incredible bond between God and his people. We can see how prayer has changed and developed from the ancient Old Testament Israelite nation to the gift of the permanent Holy Spirit revealed in the New Testament in lives of Christian believers.

Over the past countless years, devoted, God-fearing leaders have experienced, practiced, and taught other people how to pray because they can't do otherwise. Once a person experiences a rich connection with God through prayer, it drives one to share those experiences with others. Those Christian/church leaders who have had visions of a kingdom of God on earth know how important prayer is to that vision. Prayer was the foundation of a chosen nation; it is now a foundation for churches, schools, hospitals, sermons, small groups, songs, writers, and every mission imaginable. Through prayer, we know God. Through God, we know prayer.

Notes

23 Michael Horton, *Rediscovering the Holy Spirit* (Grand Rapids: Zondervan, 2017), 17.

24 N. C. Croy, "Religion, Personal," in *Dictionary of NT Background*, ed. Craig Evans and Stanley Porter (Downers Grove: InterVarsity Press, 2000), 926–31.

25 Walther Eichrodt, *Theology of the Old Testament*, volume 1, sixth (Philadelphia: Westminster Press, 1961), 172–175.

26 Robert Young, *Young's Analytical Concordance to the Bible* (Nashville, Tennessee: Thomas Nelson, 1982), 767–68.

27 Scot McKnight, *The Sermon on the Mount*, ed. Tremper Longman III and Scot McKnight (Grand Rapids: Zondervan, 2013), 242.

28 Walther Eichrodt, *Theology of the Old Testament*, volume 1, sixth (Philadelphia: Westminster Press, 1961), 175.

29 Eichrodt, *Theology*, 176.

30 Larry R. Helyer, *Exploring Jewish Literature of the Second Temple Period* (Downers Grove: InterVarsity Press, 2002), 51.

31 James H. Charlesworth, ed., *The Old Testament Pseudepigrapha*, volume 2 (New York: Doubleday, 1985), 634–637.

32 J. Julius Scott, *Jewish Backgrounds of the New Testament* (Grand Rapids: Baker Books, 1995), 130.

33 Larry R. Helyer, *Exploring Jewish Literature of the Second Temple Period* (Downers Grove: InterVarsity Press, 2002), 67.

34 Scott, *Jewish Backgrounds of the New Testament.*, 141–42; 366–67.

35 McKnight, *The Sermon on the Mount*, 242.

36 McKnight, *The Sermon on the Mount*, 244.

37 Edward W. Goodrick and John R. Kohlenberger, eds., *The NIV Exhaustive Concordance* (Grand Rapids: Zondervan Publishing, 1990), 899–900.

38 Young, *Young's Analytical Concordance to the Bible*, 767.

39 Andreas J. Köstenberger, *John; Baker Exegetical Commentary on the New Testament*, eds. Robert Yarbrough and Robert H. Stein (Grand Rapids: Baker Academic, 2004), 474–479.

40 Judith M. Lieu, *I, II, III John; A Commentary* (Louisville, Kentucky: Westminster John Knox Press, 2008), 222–234.

41 Craig L. Blomberg, *The New American Commentary; Matthew*, ed. gen. ed. Dockery, David, vol 22. (Nashville, Tennessee: Broadman Press, 1992), 254, 280–81.

42 Köstenberger, *John; Baker Exegetical Commentary on the New Testament.*, 474–479.

Chapter 2

"Holy Father" and Holiness

Critical to the background of the Reformation was Martin Luther's unique terror and trepidation because he did not know how to please the Holy One. He tried everything—doing every conceivable sort of penance, beating his own body mercilessly, confessing the smallest of sins, and even some he had not committed—and yet he was utterly aware that he could never please a holy God.[43]

Truly, how can ordinary, everyday people, who sin and error and make mistakes, *ever* live in the presence of a holy God? How do we reconcile the biblical demand for holiness and the reality of human nature? Can we say that we ever *feel* "holy" in our hearts? We may strive to "become" holy, but how do we know if we have achieved holiness or not? It is so difficult to let go of familiar "former things" that stand in our way on the journey to holiness—selfish behavior, addictions, ambition, the drive for wealth and position—and truly follow the holy, omnipotent God of the universe.

We desperately need to understand the holiness of God in our Scriptures and the biblical command for holiness among God's people. Of course, the meaning and significance of a passage of Scripture (or of any writing) should not interpreted apart from its historical background. This chapter is primarily concerned with the background of one of the unique titles for God in John's Gospel; of particular interest is the title of "Holy Father" in John 17:11. This distinctive name for God appears nowhere else in the canonical Bible (Old Testament or New Testament).

Previously, biblical scholars have noted that "Holy Father" is a formal address, a name used to describe an attribute of God. God is holy, so John refers to the "Holy Father." To see God as "holy" is not unusual in Jewish thought. "Holiness" is an expression of something that is, by nature and character, separated from a sinful world. Since God is holy, then he is, by definition, distinct and detached from that which is "unclean" or "impure," including a rebellious, sinful world.

It follows that God would desire "holiness" in his chosen people so that he could communicate and interact with them. In his final prayer in John's Gospel, Jesus asks God to "sanctify" his followers; that is, he asks that they be "made holy," apart from an "unholy world" (John 17:17). Jesus "sanctifies himself," or separates himself for his assigned purpose for the benefit of those who place their faith in him (John 17:19).

Because the followers of Jesus "are still in the world" and are sent out into the world to be witnesses to the truth, they need the separation and protection of a "Holy God." By attributing such holiness to God, John is indicating to his readers that he is a God who can and does separate the believing ones from the unbelieving world by his truth. This was valuable assurance for the readers of the prayer of John 17 in the first-century AD, just as it is for believers today.

God is holy

And yet we may ask, why holiness? Why does John make reference to *this* attribute of God and not another divine attribute in the final prayer of Jesus? Blending the diverse cultures in the first-century society, the author of the Fourth Gospel had the insight to show his readers the true nature of God as revealed in the Old Testament, as well as the true natures of the human rulers in the Roman Empire. Long before the rulers in Rome, the Old Testament prophets spoke of the self-serving practices of human empires as contrary to God's justice and holiness, as well as God's redemptive plans for human beings of all nations (Isa. 41:1–4). "Holiness" is the umbrella description of God under which we find all the other divine attributes. He is all-powerful and all-knowing because he is holy. We would not want it otherwise!

Throughout the Old Testament, the holiness (and the uniqueness) of Yhwh God is clear. God is "set apart" from all other false gods, goddesses, and deities; only he is worthy of human devotion and worship. His distinction and his holiness are evident from the time of Moses and the "burning bush" experience when God instructs Moses to "take off your scandals, for the place where you are standing is holy ground" (Exod. 3:1–6). Thus, any place God directly interacts with human beings is holy because *God made it holy.*

Holiness was the worship and devotion *only* to Yhwh God and none other. Furthermore, God powerfully guards his name, his reputation, and holy character: "Do not swear falsely by my name and so profane the name of your God. I am the Lord" (Lev. 19:12).

> The Lord, who redeemed Abraham, spoke to the people of Jacob: When they see among them their children, the work of my hands, *they will keep my name holy;* they will acknowledge the holiness of the Holy One of Jacob, and will stand in awe of the God of Israel (Isa. 29:22–23; emphasis mine).

Like the prophet Isaiah, Marva Dawn perceives that, "YHWH is unparalleled, unrivaled, unequaled. What or who could be set up as similar in value to the LORD?"[44]

Indeed, *holiness is the presence of God.* The ground was holy when Moses encountered God in a burning bush; God was present there. The innermost chamber of the Jerusalem Temple was called the "Holiest of Holies" because God was present there. Thus, God is *separate* from his creation and his creatures; he was not with them visibly and physically like the stone and wooden false idols. He revealed that his presence, power, and authority in his creation, in his covenants, and in his words to and actions with the nation. Even as an invisible God, Yhwh proved to be far superior to any human ruler or emperor, any human-created image or idol. This revelation was a

completely novel experience for a nation of people who had lived for
so long under the thumb of an Egyptian pharaoh and his gods.

> God dwells in his creation and is everywhere
> invisibly present in all His works. He is transcen-
> dent above all His works even while he is imma-
> nent within them (A. W. Tozer).[45]

The idea of God's holiness was beyond the understanding of
Israel's "pagan" neighbors. Other gods may have been terrifying,
capricious, and cruel; but Israel's God thoroughly changed humanity's concept of the divine. While he is holy, YHWH is not remote and
withdrawn. It was his constant desire to communicate and interact
with his people and to mold them into a nation that reflected his
holiness and his glory. Ultimately, YHWH God is the "*only* being in
existence of whom that term [holiness] may be justly used."[46]

> I am the Lord and there is no other… I form the
> light and create darkness, I bring prosperity and
> create disaster; I, the Lord, do these things (Isa.
> 45:5a, 7).

Knowledge of God through the laws and the prophets

It was the covenantal laws given to the people by God that
divulged the true nature and character of this exclusive God. His
holiness is paramount in the covenant agreements from the beginning of the exodus occurrence in Exodus 3 all the way to the climax
in Joshua 5. The covenants were contracted to bring about the holiness in the individual person and in the collective community. His
laws, commands, and ordinances were given to teach the people how
to live, to work, and to worship together as a community within the
sacred holiness of a God who was unlike any of the other gods in
their neighboring cultures. A brief example is found in Leviticus 19,
where the people are commanded to adhere to laws of ceremonial

and moral "holiness," culminating in the most important command to "love your neighbor as yourself" because "I am the Lord" (Lev. 19:18).

The "Holiness Code" of Leviticus 18–27 is a collection of groundbreaking instructions on how people should live, built on God's holiness and on love for one another. That is, the people were to follow God's rules to be a reflection of his holiness: "*Be holy, because I, the Lord your God, am holy*" (Lev. 19:1–2). Therefore, the Old Testament laws, covenants, and promises established between God and his chosen nation were vehicles by which human beings could be in relationship with a holy God.

They were also the standards set by God for his people as individuals and together as a congregation. From the very beginning, the holiness of God's people was intended to mirror his holiness and bring glory to their personal God (Lev. 20:7–8). Unfortunately, the Old Testament demonstrates that it was difficult (if not impossible) for the nation to perfectly obey his laws and commands; therefore, the relationship between God and his covenant people was a struggle with fear and failure and disappointments.

Because God is unique in his holiness, he is therefore the only suitable judge of human behavior. As a result, a common response by people to a holy God is *fear* (Ps. 34:7–9, 111:10, 118:4, 128:1). In fact, the Lord "delights" in those who "fear" him (Ps. 147:11), and "fear" of the Lord is the "beginning of knowledge" (Prov. 1:7). What does it mean to "fear" the Lord, and is this the proper human response to the holiness of God? The most common Hebrew word we find is *yārē*, which can mean "fear" or "reverence, respect."[47] It is a positive concept; perhaps the modern English equivalent of this word is "*awesome!*" He is an awesome God! It was very common in the ancient world for people to feel real terror and dread with respect to their gods and goddesses; the deities could be quite unpredictable and uncaring toward humanity. In this sense, however, "fear" is the adoring reverence for a holy God which yields correct submission to his sovereignty and authority. Those who "fear" the Lord and who bow before him (physically and/or metaphorically) begin to truly know him and humbly listen to his "wisdom and discipline" (Prov. 1:7).

As the nation learned to follow God, the people gained knowledge of who he is. As witnesses and examples to all other peoples and cultures, the Israelites were to follow only the one true God. Over and over again, the primary purpose of the established covenants and the laws is repeated in God's words: "I am the Lord…then you will *know* that I am the Lord your God" (Exod. 6:6–7; emphasis mine). God chose to disclose himself to his own in his *name*; therefore, in many ways, their knowledge of God was expressed in various epithets (or titles) for God. For example, he is called the "Most High God" (*elyon*) in Psalm 78:17 and 78:35; in the latter verse, the psalmist also called God his "Rock" and his "Redeemer." After he was given rest from his enemies, in an earnest prayer to God, King David addressed his God as the "Sovereign Lord" (*Adonai YHWH*) seven times: 2 Samuel 7:18–19 (twice), 20, 22, 28, 29. In addition, David "found the courage" (2 Sam. 7:27) to address God as the "Lord Almighty" (*YHWH Saba* in 2 Sam. 7:26–27). The Lord kept his promises to David so that the "name of God" would be "great forever" (2 Sam. 7:25).

Furthermore, the Israelites' understanding of who God is and how he interacts with his people increased through the Old Testament prophets (Jer. 31:33–34). Certainly, the prophets spoke with God's voice in "foreknowledge," concerning future events and warnings with respect to the nation's disobedience and their struggling relationship with God. But there was also "forth-knowledge" given from God to the prophets about himself and his purposes and plans for the people.

For the Israelites then, knowing God was being in relationship with him, being obedient to his commands, having faith in his promises, and recognizing their unique calling to reflect his holiness among all the other nations. They came to know a God who was both imminent and transcendent—far above but close at hand. What they were told about God, what they knew, and how they experienced him was to be taught to and shared with each subsequent generation by remembrance and with great accuracy (Ps. 78:2). By way of example, being in the presence of the Holy One is pictured vividly in Isaiah 6. The prophet draws away from God with genuine terror as he has a vision of the Holy God "high and exalted" (Isa. 6:1). The prophet is racked with grief and guilt with the recognition of his own sin and the lack of holiness in his life (Isa. 6:5). Before an awesome and holy God, it is not uncommon for human beings to feel of little value to him or to anyone else.[48]

The covenantal God pledged to love his own, and he remained faithful to his portion of the covenants. But the nation gave in to disobedience and sin and could not uphold their end of the deal. The prophets warned the people that holiness cannot tolerate sin and evil cannot look upon holiness. Therefore, the answer is found in the commands of the sacrificial system (see Lev. 1–17). This system did not put sinful people into a relationship with a holy God; in fact, those who offered sacrifices to YHWH were *already* in a covenantal relationship with him. The followers of YHWH, who should have already been enjoying the presence of their God, fell out of favor with him because of human sin and disobedience and they had to pay for it with a sacrifice. There is no forgiveness without the shedding of blood. Thus, an authentic relationship with a holy God was made possible only through constant "blood" atonement:

> Unless God makes continual provision for our sin, known and unknown, we will be destroyed by his perfect holiness. Fellowship with God rests forever upon God's provision of atonement.[49]

It is the atoning sacrifices which reestablished the covenantal relationship between a forgiving God and his erring people. In the end, of course, it was the sacrifice of Jesus which was God's provision of atonement forever. Jesus created a "new covenant," an "eternal covenant" that provided the grace, atonement, and forgiveness for believers in the present and in the future (Matt. 26:28; Luke 22:20; 1 Cor. 11:25; John 17:4).

In summation, then, the Old Testament covenants and his appointed prophets revealed the holiness of God and his moral compass for his chosen people. His covenantal names emphasize his sovereignty, power, glory, and his holiness. In view of such names as "King" and "Lord," the view of God could be harsh and judgmental. But other names disclosed his grace, mercy, "undeserved and unexpected faithfulness" toward his own. Martin Luther (like all of us) was finally set free by receiving God's grace and love and by acknowledging the sacrifice of his Son for the sake of sinful humanity.[50] Ultimately, it is the will of a holy God that he should live in a loving fellowship with his people who share his righteous, glory, moral and ethical character.[51]

Isaiah and the Fourth Gospel

The discussion of how the author of the Gospel of John used the ancient book of Isaiah in his Gospel is gaining recognition in the field of New Testament studies. There are, in fact, perceivable connections, especially between "Deutero-Isaiah" (chaps. 40–55) and the Farewell Discourses (chapters 14–17) in the Fourth Gospel. Careful study reveals the fact that the prophecies of Isaiah serve as a background and a source for the theology, the themes, and even the language used by the Gospel writer. Perhaps more than any other prophet in the Old Testament, Isaiah's words about redemption and holiness come alive in John's Gospel.

First, the Johannine chapters resemble the distinctive character of Deutero-Isaiah in themes, motifs, and theology. Second, the Johannine author used direct quotations from the book of Isaiah in his Gospel on more than one occasion: John 1:23 (Isa. 40:3), 6:45 (Isa. 54:13), 12:37–41 (Isa. 53:1 and 6:10). Scholars have noted that the book of Isaiah is quoted or alluded to in the New Testament more than any other Old Testament book except the Psalms. Third, and one of the most interesting connections between Isaiah and the Fourth Gospel is the use of names and titles. To the ancient Israelites, divine and human names were very important. In Isaiah, the readers may wonder, exactly who is this God (YHWH), and is he able to save his people from certain annihilation? The prophet answers these questions, particularly noting the *name* of God:

> For this is what the high and lofty One says—He
> who lives forever, *whose name is holy*: "I live in a

high and lofty place, but also with him who is
contrite and lowly in spirit, to revive the spirit of
the lowly and to revive the heart of the contrite"
(Isa 57:15; emphasis mine).

The ancient prophecies in Isaiah struck a chord for the author
of the Fourth Gospel, and they were carried into his remembrances
as he tried to capture the words of Jesus in his final discourses with
his disciples. Perhaps as John's audience heard his Gospel, they too
remembered the promises of God to Israel and saw how they were
fulfilled in the Redeemer—Jesus. In Isaiah, *it is his name* that reveals
God's character and intentions (see Isa. 49:26, 52:6). God is their
only "Savior" (Isa. 45:15, 21–22), and their promised "Redeemer"
(Isa. 46:4, 48:17), not unlike the same titles attributed to Jesus much
later in time.

Certainly, God is characterized by his holiness, but he is not so
remote and separate that he cannot connect to the contrite, humble
spirit of his people. He even reveals his own desire to be in a relationship with his people by calling them "by name" so that they will
know that he is the Lord (Isa. 45:3–4).

"The Holy One of Israel"

The prophet Isaiah frequently used a distinctive name and title
for God—"*The Holy One of Israel.*" This exceptional title is used for
a holy, transcendent God who is significantly different from the idol
deities worshiped by human cultures outside of Israel. Isaiah insists
that this mighty God is not only *the* Creator but also as *the* Redeemer
of his people:

> I, even I, am the Lord, And apart from me there is
> no savior. I have revealed and saved and proclaimed,
> I, and not some foreign god among you. You are
> my witnesses, declares the Lord, that *I am he* (Isa.
> 43:11–12; see John 6:35, 8:12, 10:11, 15:1).

> This is what the Lord says, Your Redeemer, the
> Holy One of Israel…I am the Lord, your Holy
> One Israel's Creator, your King (Isa. 43:14–15).

> Do not be afraid, O worm Jacob, O little Israel,
> for I myself will help you, declares the Lord, your
> Redeemer, the Holy One of Israel (Isa. 41:14).

The "Holy One of Israel" title for God appears thirty-one times in the Old Testament, and twenty-six of those occurrences are in Isaiah, making it distinctive in this prophetic book (the only occurrence in the Bible of "The Holy One of Jacob" is in Isaiah 29:23). The epithet occurs thirteen times before chapter 40 and thirteen times after chapter 40. Such an observation could lend authenticity to the idea that the book was written by one author. References to the "Holy One of Israel" are particularly apparent in Deutero-Isaiah (that is, 43:15, 47:4, 48:17, 49:7). Outside of Isaiah, the epithet "The Holy One of Israel" is not at all common but is found in 2 Kings 19:22, which is a duplicate of Isaiah 37:23; Jeremiah 50:29, 51:5; and Psalms 71:22, 78:41, 89:18.[52]

In addition, Isaiah chapters 40–55 are addressed to a dejected nation—the people felt hopeless. "The Holy One of Israel," then, is the God, Redeemer, and Protector of Israel in need of redemption and hope. Isaiah encouraged the Israelites by showing them that YHWH alone is God and that he will use the nation to witness to that fact.[53] They were to be a "light" to the other "pagan" nations; God made it clear that "still others" outside of the nation of Israel would be part of God's redemption plan (Isa. 49:26b). This promise is clear, even to the Gentile readers in John's congregation.

The climactic purpose of the prophetic "Suffering Servant" songs is found in Isaiah 52:13–53:12. The individual pictured in these songs "poured out his life unto death," bearing on the cross the "sin of many" (note the singular use of "sin"), and he suffered to "make intercession for the transgressors." The singular "Servant"— that is, Jesus Christ—who carried the "substitutionary suffering" in these songs of Isaiah is called to cleanse and restore *all* the people of

God, Jew and Gentile.[54] Thus, the Suffering One, the Resurrected Redeemer makes atonement for people once and for all. Perhaps this was a great encouragement to the earliest Christians, living in a difficult Roman culture to renew their faith and give them hope.

"Holy One of Israel" is the "Holy Father"

Still, why did the author of the Fourth Gospel intentionally connect the Isaianic "Holy One of Israel" and "Father" as a name for God in a distinctive *prayer*? If the title "The Holy One of Israel" casts light on precisely who God is, his nature, and character, as well as his plans and purposes, then "Father" implies a close, intimate relationship with the same God. The unique holy God is also a gracious Father God, bringing compassion, redemption, peace, and love to the ones who are faithful to him. He is holy and imminent yet close enough to his rebellious people to hear their cries and prayers and to save them (see Isa. 45:20–22, 47:12–15).

The use of the title "Father" for YHWH God is customary in the Old Testament (Deut. 32:6; Ps. 2:7, 89:26; Isa. 9:6, 63:16; Jer. 31:9; Mal. 2:10). Of course, the use of "father" (with a lowercase *F*) in many Old Testament verses is likely a reference to the human patriarchs of the Israelites, especially to Abraham who was considered the "father" of the nation (see Mal. 2:10). As a revelation of God, there is a much deeper connotation with this epithet (with a capital *F*). No other Old Testament culture was so audacious as to call their gods by such an intimate, relational name. The mere fact that the people of Israel could address their God as "Father" is remarkable; it illustrates that they did trust him to save and redeem the nation.

Isaiah 63:7–64:12 is a *prayer* of the prophet, who asked the Lord to finally bring about the redemption of his people as he promised (just like John 17). Within the prayer, Isaiah addressed the Lord as "Father" three times—Isaiah 63:16 (twice) and 64:8. Because he is their Father, Isaiah prayed that the Lord would not abandon the nation, even if human leaders had done so.

Isaiah also recognized that only God is their "Father," and that redemption is only in *his* "name"—his nature, his identity (Isa. 63:16). To illustrate his words, Isaiah created a vivid picture of God as a "potter" and his people as "clay":

> Yet, O Lord, you are our Father. We are the clay,
> you are the potter; we are all the work of your
> hand (Isa. 64:8).

He then prayed that the Lord would not "remember our sins forever" (Isa. 64:9). The prophet used the same metaphor in Isaiah 29:16 and 45:9. The image shows that he knew that God was sovereign over the people, and *they had no right* to question God's motives and actions. The "potter" metaphor is extended and duplicated by the Apostle Paul in the New Testament (see Rom. 9:21), where Paul used the metaphor to emphasize the sovereign freedom of God in dealing with human beings. Thus, God is not a doting grandfather but a *Holy Father* who has every right and claim to demand covenant obedience from his "children" for their own benefit.

Fatherhood

Fatherhood was critical in the Jewish culture; the father was the leader and patriarch of the family. It is well-known that the sons carried their fathers' names (also implying his characteristics), inherited the fathers' wealth, and were loyal and obedient first and foremost to their fathers. Wives were scorned and rejected if they did not give birth to sons to follow in their fathers' footsteps. In the tribal sense, Hebrew families were everything, and they were headed by strong fathers.

Certainly, God is most holy and sovereign, but he is also a God who is concerned enough about his people that he has a plan to redeem them and love them as their "Father." This stands in direct contrast to the wicked leaders in the nation in the days of Isaiah (see Isa. 30:1–14) and to the corrupt human authorities that controlled the Roman Empire in the first-century AD. In the New Testament, "fatherhood" is a new and extraordinary glimpse into the plan and work of God through the lens of his agent, his Son. Within the context of the final prayer of Jesus, John's use of "Holy Father" is a promise to the readers. The "Holy Father" cares enough to "protect" his children and "keep them safe" because there is "power *in his name*"— the same name, and thus the same power, that the Father gave to his Son (Isa. 17:11).

Perhaps there are people today who dislike the title of "Father," as it may raise images of a painful childhood or reflect an image of a male-dominated, controlling regime. However, this is attributing fallen human character to a perfect divine Being who is completely different from sinful, immoral, "unredeemed" humanity. That is, God is pictured as a divine Father who never fails to love his own: tenderly redeeming, caring, keeping, saving, comforting, and discipling his people, even if they sin and reject him.

God desires the intimacy and immediacy of the devoted title of "Father" who loves his "children." If it were not so, Jesus would not have called his Father by this familial name in the presence of his disciples. As a combination of the title "Holy One of Israel" from Isaiah and the Johannine title "Father," it bears all the meaning and significance of both titles (Deut. 1:31; Isa. 63:15–16, 66:13). To all the Johannine readers, a combination of these two names is the assurance that God is far more than able to protect, to love, and to save them in a time of corruption.

Trial theme

It is true that if God is genuinely holy, he cannot, by nature, ignore evil, corruption, and disobedience. On the one hand, he is perfectly forgiving and compassionate; on the other hand, he is perfectly holy, pure, right, and just. His laws have been set, the boundaries and limits are established, and his people swore obedience to him. When they swerved off the path of righteousness and obedience, God could not stand by and just let it happen any more than human parents should allow their children to consistently indulge in that which is wicked, wrong, and not for their own good. As holy and righteous Judge, God is forced to discipline his children.

This leads to an important "trial" theme in Deutero-Isaiah (41:21–24, 43:26). We can see a parallel in the Fourth Gospel, as the Johannine author "brings to bear another legal model from Scripture, the covenant lawsuit; and it is Isaiah 40–55 that provides the resources" for the author of the Fourth Gospel.[55] The Isaiah chapters "take the form of a lawsuit between Yahweh and Israel," where the "Holy One of Israel" defends his power, authority, his uniqueness, and his exclusivity, especially in relation to other gods or idols. "He is the Creator, and he is the instigator and controller of all of history":[56]

> "Present your case," says the Lord.
> "Set forth your argument," says Jacob's King (Isa.
>   41:21).

> "Review the past for me, let us argue the matter together; state your case for your innocence" (Isa. 43:26).

The nation is challenged to provide evidence of its innocence in spite of its past history of disobedience and idolatry before God. In "court," the "King" (God) asked the nation to reveal their "former things"—plural in nature! (Isa. 41:21–22—which appear to be human achievements: military victories, idol worship, human power and prestige, or any other "god" which detracted from their faith in and their loyalty to their God. Of course, the nation could not uphold its case against God. They were guilty of rejecting God, and they could not produce anything conceived by human beings, "good or bad" (Isa. 41:23) that was superior to the plans and works of the "Holy One of Israel" (Isa. 41:20).

It is also interesting to see the section known as Deutero-Isaiah (Isa. 40–55) as a literary "pause." The shift in tone at the end of chapter 39 causes a break in the prophetic narrative. Court was out for the day. After warnings of destruction and departure, chapter 40 opens with a tone of reassurance: "'Comfort, comfort my people,' says your God." Despite their circumstances, God is the Holy Father who comes in power to redeem his faithful people. Chapters 14–17 of the Gospel of John also interrupts the Jesus narrative and provides a "long pause" before the passion narrative. The discourse material in these chapters is used to inform and assure the readers concerning their faith in the Redeemer Jesus and in a Holy God. The discourses ensure John's people of God's ultimate judgment on a corrupt, distorted, and unbelieving world, as well as the vindication of his faithful people.

"Redeemer"

Moreover, in Isaiah, the title of "Redeemer" appears thirteen times in conjunction with the title "The Holy One of Israel." Doubtless then, "The Holy One of Israel"—Yhwh—is the only "Redeemer" of Israel and it is *he alone* that must redeem them:

> But now, this is what the Lord says—he who created you, O Jacob, he who formed you, O Israel: "Fear not, for I have redeemed you; I have summoned you by name; you are mine" (Isa. 43:1).

In Deutero-Isaiah, "The Holy One of Israel" appears together with the title "Redeemer" at least seven times (41:14, 43:14, 47:4, 48:17, 49:7 [twice], 54:5), showing that "The Holy One of Israel" is both the "Redeemer" (Isa. 54:5) and the "Savior" of the nation (Isa. 43:3): "Then all mankind will know that I, the Lord, am your Savior, your Redeemer, the Mighty One of Jacob" (Isa. 49:26).

But exactly *how* does the "Holy One of Israel" redeem and restore his people? That is, if Isaiah 41 is the legal challenge by Yhwh against the false idols that had infiltrated Israel, then Isaiah 42 is "how" God intended to resolve the situation. False idols, corrupt leaders, and military conquests would not save the nation from certain destruction. Is it done through more offerings and sacrifice? In fact, it is accomplished by the actions of "my [S]servant," introduced in Isaiah 42:1, that will save God's people. Isaiah's prophesies were fulfilled in God's Son. God revealed himself in the Suffering One, the obedient Jesus who made atonement for human sin. The prophet Isaiah warned the people that they would not be redeemed through human effort but through faith in the promised Savior and Messiah, sent by God, who is God.

Then we can ask, *why*? Why would God choose to redeem his wandering people? The nation was rescued and redeemed so that they would be a "light for the Gentiles, that you may bring my salvation to the ends of the earth" (Isa. 49:6). This plan and purpose of God is foundational to the survival of the nation of Israel; they were saved in order to make known the name of the "*only* true God" (John 17:3; see Acts 13:47 and Rom. 1:16). Just as the prophet Isaiah said, God's redemptive plan was completed by his divine Servant— Jesus—whose mission and purpose was to redeem *all* of the Lord's people (Isa. 61:1–9; John 17:8). Together, the Father and the Son accomplished the promises of Isaiah (Isa. 44:6; 52:13; 53:1–12). It is the continuing mission of Christian believers, then, to spread the "good news" of the holy Father God and his redemption across the world to all people (John 17:18).

The intent of God was and still is to bring his covenant people to "wholeness" and to "holiness." "Wholeness" is the same idea as "*shalom*," that of "peace, tranquility" (see Ps. 29:11; Isa. 26:3, 12). It is being made "whole, complete, to be made sound" (see John 7:23, 13:10). In fact, for people who hear and follow God, "holiness" is "wholeness." God's perfect will has always been to redeem his people completely, create "wholeness," and not to leave them in "the darkness" of the world (John 1:5, 3:19).

This is divine salvation; it is accomplished through divine love, which was epitomized by the cross of Jesus. The prophetic poetry of Isaiah 40–55 urged the redeemed people to have faith, just as Jesus' prayer stimulates faith in John's readers. John drew parallels from Deutero-Isaiah as a distinctive form of redemptive literature presented for the benefit of those reading or hearing the Gospel. Not unlike the ancient Israelites, John's readers were struggling to live within a perverse, unbelieving culture that chose to reject the

Jewish/Christian God and cast off the people who did follow him. John was thus speaking to his Christian congregation to assure them that regardless of their cultural situation as a church in the "unholy" Roman Empire, the one and only Holy Father continued to bring about his promise to redeem, sanctify and protect his people, and bring them into "wholeness."

Extrabiblical literature

It is interesting to note that the title "Holy Father" is used very rarely in early Christian literature outside of the canonical biblical books. The epithet appears in *The Didache* (10:2) in the context of a prayer of thanksgiving; it also appears in the *Testaments of the Twelve Patriarchs*, specifically the *Testament of Judah* 24:2. While many scholars date the *Testaments* back as early as the last two centuries BC, it is apparent that many Christian interpolations were added to the text in the first two or three centuries AD. That is, if there was an early original Hebrew text of the *Testaments,* the text was used and adapted by later Christian readers. While there are various sayings that echo the Old Testament "wisdom" literature, other sayings are clearly messianic and are directly applied to Jesus as the promised Messiah.

The *Testament* is written in a type of literary genre that is similar to the Farewell Discourses in John's Gospel, commonly called the "farewell testament." Each of the twelve Old Testament patriarchs gives an ethical and exhortatory speech on his deathbed, complete with warnings and blessings. Of course, the speeches were not actually from the patriarchs, but the later author used their names to lend authenticity to his writings. As such, their farewell speeches urged the following generations to choose to obey the Lord, for only those who live in obedience to God will be protected by him. Within the *Testament of Judah,* there is an obviously Christian passage that is messianic in nature:

> And after these things a star will arise to you from
> Jacob in peace, and a man will arise from my seed

like the sun of righteousness, walking with the sons of men in meekness and righteousness, and no sin whatever will be found in him. And the heavens will be opened to him to pour out the blessing of the spirit of the *holy Father*, and he will pour out the spirit of grace upon you, and you will be sons to him in truth and you will walk in his commandments from first to last.[57]

In this context, the actions of the messianic figure (Jesus Christ) on behalf of believing people are linked with the gracious actions of God (the "Holy Father"). Here, "Holy Father" is used as a title, which speaks to the reader concerning the relational nature of a God who abundantly "pours out" both blessings and grace and whose saving actions toward the believers are fulfilled in the life and actions ("in truth") of the Son. Also, note that in this passage, it is his Spirit that he sends to those who believe and obey his commandments (see John 14:17, 21; 15:10; 16:13).

Even the rare occurrences of this epithet in extracanonical literature supports the fact that it was used in early Christian circles. It may have been a title that developed within the early Jewish Christian church that was based on the prophetic use of "Holy One of Israel" in Isaiah. Consequently, the unusual use of "Holy Father" is symbolic of the salvific aspect of the "Redeemer God" that is accomplished through the redemptive activities of the Messiah Jesus. The use of this title brings to mind the power of God to bring about the promised "salvation" for his people and his grace to even consider doing so through the person and mission of his Son.

Old Testament scholar John Goldingay declared that "the material in Isaiah 40–55 is designed to *do* something to an audience."[58] Similarly, in the context of the whole Gospel, the inclusion of John 17 is designed to "*do* something" or to affect the readers. Isaiah 40–55 both warns the nation and promises ultimate redemption, just like the warnings and promises of John 14–17. Both passages are designed to capture the attention of the readers and to give them some assurance. Both have a positive effect on readers to remind them that God has not forgotten them in their trials. God promised restoration and renewal for those who are obedient to his commands, and he will deliver (John 15:9–10). Thus, the Farewell Discourses were a renewed encouragement to the earliest Christians that God did deliver on his promises by sending his Son and his Spirit (see John 14:1–7, 21).

A *"new thing"*

On their own strength and power, corrupt human beings have never been able to fully redeem themselves. From perpetuity, the world has suffered from the brokenness of self-interest and fractured by human failures, disorder, and deception. The dualism of good vs. evil has always plagued human culture. But the broken parts of humanity are not beyond repair. In Isaiah (especially chapters 40–48), the prophet is declaring that, indeed, God is bringing about a "new thing" into the lives of his people. What is the "new thing" that the prophet Isaiah foretold in 42:9 and 43:19a? And in contrast, what are the "former things" that must go away? God promised to make his plans and declarations clear to the people, and in both passages (42:9 and 43:19a), "former things" must go, before the "new thing" can come.

The nation was instructed by God to "forget the former [human] things, and do not dwell on the past" human accomplishments and failures (43:18) because God is in control and will do something ("a new thing") that is even beyond the imaginations of human beings. It is easy to overlook the fact that in 43:19a, the "new thing" is in the singular form: it is one thing, one divine act, which God declares that he will do. Surely that "new thing" is the sending of his Son, the Messiah, who would "make a way in the desert and streams in the wasteland" (Isa. 43:19).

There is something very Johannine about Isaiah 43—like the prophet Isaiah, the author of John's Gospel emphasized the need for people to turn to God for wholeness and redemption. God and God alone is to be recognized as the one and only Creator, Revealer,

Protector, Savior, Redeemer, and "the only true God" (John 17:3). God's grace was poured out on the nation of Israel, and they were to be his witnesses in the world.

Then, God poured out his grace on *all* the nations in the form of his Messiah, the "Redeemer" Jesus (John 1:1–5, 10–18). Remembering the prophet's words and God's promises, John assured his readers that the "new thing," planned and purposed by God, is the life, death, and resurrection of Jesus. This "new thing," promised in the days of the Old Testament prophets, was finally being fulfilled in Jesus—and in Jesus alone.

Further, the "new thing" accomplished by God is for *all* the people, including the Gentiles, who receive the gift of the Messiah and believe *in his name*. Who would ever have guessed that Isaiah's "Suffering Servant" (Isa. 53) was the vehicle by which God would fulfill his promises to his people? In addition, Jesus' prayer of John 17 reiterates the plan for believers to be "sent" into the world to be witnesses to this "new thing," which is the "sending" of the Son for the redemption of humanity (John 17:3, 8, 18). "Sent out" to be his witnesses on earth, Jesus asked the Holy Father to protect the faithful Christian believers who fulfill this part of God's plans (17:11, 15). This parallels the duty of the nation of Israel who was called to "testify" to all the other nations about the "Holy One of Israel," the "one true God."

Indwelling holiness

The holiness of God entered into the "unclean" world of people with Jesus. God's holiness is maintained in the world even today through the Holy Spirit. Practically speaking, God came into the world in the incarnated Son to "become one of us." When he departed this physical world, the Son left the Spirit to be the presence of God on earth. Now even in his holiness, God desires fellowship with his people. God matures and transforms people, cleansing and purifying human beings so that he can be present and live within us. Holiness is God indwelling us and transforming us into what he intended us to be. Because of the work of Christ, we are God's presence in the world; we live in an unholy world to reflect a holy God and to redeem the world in his name (Heb. 10, Exod. 19, 1 Pet. 2, Isa. 41, Rom. 8). Thus, finite human beings are enabled and empowered to be what God planned for us to be by his own Holy Spirit.

Certainly, believers do not achieve their own holiness; it is a gracious gift. Only a holy God can make people holy. Because he is holy, God can "sanctify" his people through the work of Christ and through the filling of the Holy Spirit (John 17:17). We do not become holy by our own efforts, but we are holy "because the Holy One has already made us so."[59] The living presence of the holy God in the world is demonstrated through his people, who are "set apart for sacred use" to activate his plans and reflect his glory on earth. Not unlike the nation of Israel, believers are to pass on the truth about God to the world, to every generation, and to exhibit the holiness and glory of God (2 Sam. 7:12–16).

Those people who believe in Jesus as the Messiah and Savior are "made holy" by their confessed faith in Christ. This sanctification process ("being made holy") is a radical (but gradual) transformation of the human being to live a life more like Jesus (see 2 Cor. 3:18). Then as a result of the holiness imparted to believers, they are "sent into the world" to continue the message of the knowledge and truth of Christ (John 17:18). God's people are sent into a world of conflict but are "protected...by the power of your [the Holy Father's] name" (John 17:11). Furthermore, this infusion of holiness by God through Jesus is for *all* believers and unites them into one redeemed community. Since the Father is holy and he is "sanctifying" his people through Jesus Christ as he promised, then his believing "children" are united into one reconciled family of witnesses to the unbelieving world of the Father's great power and love.

Conclusions and Responses

Incredibly, we are to be extensions of God's holiness on earth. We carry God's name on us and in us wherever we go. We are "set apart" ("made holy," Ezek. 20:12) by his grace *for him*—to glorify his name in all the world (John 17:22). Holiness is God's name; it is who he is. It is his relationship with us and his presence *in* us. We are to reflect his character and his nature of his holiness in ordinary, everyday occurrences. The holiness of God is revealed through his work in us toward other people: to heal, reconcile, mend, encourage, and build up, not tear down.

In spite of all the challenges, the prophet Isaiah urged people to acknowledge God's holiness, to stand in awe of him, keep his name holy—in our language and verbal speech!—to bow before him with authentic prayer and worship—"our worship teaches us the necessary awe."[60] This is where faith comes in—with joy and wonder we read scriptures and learn more about God. The more we learn, the more we know we can trust. Oswald Chambers wrote, "Faith never knows where it is being led, but it loves and knows the One who is leading."[61]

It is unimaginable to think about what the world would be like if God's holiness was absent (in the form of his Spirit and in his people) to combat the wickedness of the unbelieving world. Remove the Holy Spirit, remove the presence of God entirely from this earth, and the enemy would control and destroy everything. Yet evil will not be victorious (Rev. 20:7–10). On an infinitely smaller scale, all of our actions, words, attitudes, and prayers should reflect to others the nature of the God in whom we believe.

In truth, our "indwelling holiness" is not for ourselves; it is for others. God wants to make us holy so that other people will see his holy character in us.[62] As we put the holiness of God into our worldly context, we ponder: who do we *truly* worship? And to whom are we *really* praying—a "spiritual Santa Claus?" A white-haired man on a heavenly throne, keeping "score" in golden books? Do we treat God as holy and separate and sovereign over us, or as one who can be manipulated and constrained?

Truly, "the fate of the Christian church in America and around the world depends upon what the Church does with the biblical doctrine of holiness."[63] God is, indeed, an awesome God beyond all measure that deserves *all* the reverence and respect that we can give him.

We should be afraid of our own behavior and attitudes instead of his. We must think deeply about our causal language and our informal worship so that neither leads to a reduction of God's magnitude, eminence, and supremacy in our lives.

He is God, and we are not. He is sovereign, and we are not. We must recognize the "idols" in our lives that come before the worship of the holy God. He is the omnipotent Creator and should be feared above all creation (Ps. 96:4–5). When we fully realize the enormity of the Almighty God (if this is truly possible), we should fall to our knees in humility and reverence. John reminded his readers that, on the one hand, they must bow before a *Holy* God. On the other hand, they can rest in the presence of a "Holy *Father*."

> Like the manna in the wilderness, if we try to keep our holiness for ourselves, it will grow sour and rancid in us…holiness is not an end in itself so that we can revel in our own purity, but is for the sake of others…Then we will be free: free to love; free to serve; free to give; free to be self-forgetful. Then we will know that "You must be holy, because I am holy" is not a demand, but a wonderful offer.[64]

The "Holy Father" epithet reminds us today that God's holiness is shown not to destroy us but to empower us to be his agents on earth. Note that in the quotation immediately above, Oswalt does *not* say that we are free to judge other people, to condemn others, or free to be self-righteous in any way. Like the prophet Isaiah, we see that selfish ambition and self-gratification must always give way to submission and humble supplication before a holy God. What a "wonderful offer!" With gratitude and humility, we pray not for more *holiness* but for more of God.

Notes

43 Marva J. Dawn, *To Walk and Not Faint; Meditations on Isaiah 40* (Grand Rapids: Eerdmans Publishing, 1997), 151.

44 Dawn, *To Walk*, 149. See Isaiah 40:25.

45 A. W. Tozer, http://www.Christianquotes.info, access July 23, 2020.

46 John N. Oswalt, *Called to Be Holy; A Biblical Perspective* (Anderson, Indiana: Warner Press, 1999), 17–19.

47 Robert Young, *Young's Analytical Concordance to the Bible* (Nashville, Tennessee: Thomas Nelson, 1982), 338.

48 Dawn, *To Walk and Not Faint; Meditations on Isaiah 40*, 150–51.

49 Oswalt, *Called to Be Holy; A Biblical Perspective*, 29–30.

50 Dawn, *To Walk and Not Faint; Meditations on Isaiah 40*, 151.

51 Oswalt, *Called to Be Holy; A Biblical Perspective*, 38.

52 John N. Oswalt, *Isaiah: The NIV Application Commentary*, ed. Terry Muck et al. (Grand Rapids: Zondervan, 2003), 41.

53 Oswalt, *Isaiah*, 18.

54 Oswalt, *Isaiah*, 19.

55 Andrew Lincoln, "Trials, Plots and the Narrative of the Fourth Gospel," *JSNT*, 56 (1994): 3–30, 20.

56 Lincoln, 20.

57 Howard C. Kee, "Testament of the Twelve Patriarchs," in *The Old Testament Pseudepigrapha*, ed. James H. Charlesworth (New York: Doubleday Dell, 1983), 801.

58 John Goldingay and David Payne, *A Critical and Exegetical Commentary on Isaiah 40–55*, ed. G. I. Davies et al. (London: T&T Clark International [Continuum], 2006), 25.

59 Dawn, *To Walk and Not Faint; Meditations on Isaiah 40*, 153.

60 Dawn, 153.

61 "http:// www.Christianquotes.info," access July 30, 2020.

62 Oswalt, *Called to Be Holy; A Biblical Perspective*.

63 Oswalt, 1.

64 Oswalt, 199.

Chapter 3

Righteousness of God

A pastor once said to me, "Ministry is easy. It is the people who are difficult!" How true. Ministry would be so easy if everyone was honest, faithful, generous, kind, and righteous. So why is it so hard for professing Christians to be "righteous"? Why can we not forgive our own family or our neighbors over petty differences? Why do we disparage and argue with people over political opinions, especially since we can't change much anyway? Why do we cut in line, litter the parks, turn a blind eye to cruelty to people and animals? Perhaps we think too highly of ourselves; we are disrespectful and rude because we do not have the time to care and be sensitive to others. We are above the common "imperatives." In fact, some people are averse to other people who seem to be "so righteous!" In our current society, does it really pay to stand up for what we believe is "right?"

Tied to the idea that God is holy (the "Holy Father" in John 17:11) is the concept that God is also righteous; this attribute of God is found in both the Old Testament and the New Testament. The righteousness of God is revealed in his relationship with the nation of Israel and in their relationships with the pagan nations around them. The background of the epithet *"Righteous Father"* in John 17:25 begins in the Old Testament and is brought to life during the time of the first readers of John's Gospel—those in the Roman Empire. But why did the author of the Fourth Gospel employ this divine attribute as a title for God in the prayer of Jesus? What was the benefit of using such a title for the original readers of the Gospel in the first-century AD, and what is the benefit of understanding the title for Christians today?

Righteousness equals justice

God is righteousness because he always acts according to what is right. His righteousness is another expression of his justice. God is just in all his ways, even in his demands and his assessment of humanity. God does not *have* righteousness; he *is* righteousness. His righteousness is linked to his attribute of omniscience or his "all-knowingness" (Isa. 53:11, 45:21). In view of who he is, and because they agreed to his covenantal rule and reign, the Old Testament people of Israel were to conduct their own lives with faith in their God and in his righteousness and justice (Hab. 2:4).

Those who love and follow God can be assured that because God is righteous, his judgment will always be accurate. In addition, his righteousness is demonstrated in the rescue and deliverance of his people; he promised to secure right and proper circumstances (i.e., land, peace) for those who love him and are faithful to him (Ps. 71:2, 85:10–12). The prophet Isaiah said that God "loves justice, and hates robbery and iniquity" (or unfairness) (Isa. 61:8). In his justice and faithfulness, God promised an "everlasting covenant" of salvation and righteousness with his people, which he would create, cultivate, and sustain (Isa. 45:8, 61:11). This is the promised "new covenant," in Jeremiah 31:31–33 and is completed and made a reality by the blood of Christ for all believers (Luke 22:20; 1 Cor. 11:25; Heb. 8:8, 9:15, 12:24).

God's judgment is not "retributive" justice; it is "restorative" justice. God condemns those human leaders who pervert and distort true justice in the land, especially for their own benefit. The ancient prophets insisted that divine justice was intended to heal the nation (Ps. 23:3, 51:12, 80:3) and redeem the people (Isa. 63:9; Ps. 44:26, 130:8, 34:22). "God 'punishes' Israel by loving them even more, and at even deeper levels, just as God does with every human soul."[65]

Righteousness and justice go hand in hand in the promises of the Old Testament, quite evident in the wisdom literature, as well as in the Old Testament prophetic books:

> You are always righteous, O Lord,
> When I bring a case before you (Jer. 12:1).

> But, O Lord Almighty, you who judge righteously,
> And test the heart and mind (Jer. 11:20).

Furthermore, if God is righteous, then his laws were necessarily also righteous, fair, impartial, and reasonable. He did not demand his people obey bizarre, eccentric, or irrational laws. Psalm 119 is a masterpiece of love for and obedience to God's laws. His righteous laws can be very pleasing to those who know and follow him:

> I hate and abhor falsehood
> But love your law.
> Seven times a day I praise you
> For your righteous laws.
> Great peace have they who love your law (Ps.
> 119:163–164).

Because he loves his people, God acts with justice and righteousness not only toward those he loves, but he also dispenses justice to the wicked nations and those who are condemned for their disobedience and unbelief (Isa. 43:1–6, 45:21–25).

> I will strengthen you and help you;
> I will uphold you with my righteous right hand
> (Isa. 41:10).

> Listen to me, my people; hear me, my nation:
> The law will go out from me; my justice will
> become a light to the nations,

My righteousness draws near speedily; my salvation is on the way,
My arm will bring justice to the nations (Isa.
   51:4–5).

This is what the Lord says: "Maintain justice and
   do what is right,
For my salvation is close at hand,
And my righteousness will soon be revealed" (Isa.
   56:1).

The Song of Moses

In the prophetic and poetic "song" of Deuteronomy 32, Moses spoke specifically about "proclaiming the name of the Lord" (Deut. 32:3). Metaphorically, God is the nation's "Rock" who is "upright and just," in contrast to capricious idols of the neighboring nations (v. 4). In addition, Moses said, "Is he not your Father, your Creator?" (v. 6). So very early in the life of the nation, God was regarded as *the* unique and just Father who "cared for his people" (v. 10), and who deserved their obedience and devotion.

By his choice and by his grace, God bound himself to his rebellious people (by his covenant/promises) and pledged to redeem them and love them. His name reveals who God is, what he is like, and how he interacts with his people. He is both just *and* compassionate. The Israelites, however, acted "corruptly"; they were a "warped and crooked generation" and "to their shame, they are no longer his children" (Deut. 32:5). A "foolish and unwise people" repaid their Father with disobedience and idolatry (v. 6). There were those people in the nation who rejected and "forgot" the God who "fathered" them (Deut. 32:15–18).

The testament of Deuteronomy 33

Immediately after Moses' song praising the nature of God, Deuteronomy 33 is the "last will and testament" of Moses before the Israelite nation, *not unlike* the final prayer of Jesus in John 17. Moses departed from this earth with a benediction for the tribes of Israel, pronouncing blessings and warnings to the people, *not unlike* the preparation of his people by Jesus in his final prayer. Both Moses and Jesus pronounce the justice of God and offer a prayer to the Father to protect and to warn his people:

> There is no one like the God of Jeshurun,
> Who rides on the heavens to help you,
> And on the clouds in his majesty.
> The eternal God is your refuge,
> And underneath are the everlasting arms (Deut.
>   33:26–27a).

In spite of human disobedience and disappointment, God's righteousness and his great compassion were merged together to be a Father to his children.

Faithfulness to Israel

Later, the Jewish Christian readers of John's Gospel worshiped the Messiah Jesus in the shadow of the devastation of the Jerusalem Temple (AD 70). In its entirety, there is a noticeable "Jewish" focus in the Fourth Gospel. John "presents Jesus as the temple's replacement" (John 2:18–22), as well as the "fulfillment of the symbolism" related to the familiar Jewish festivals (see John 5–12).[66]

The "crowds" were mainly Jewish; the argumentative leadership were all Jews. In fact, there are only four "non-Jews" mentioned by John: Pilate, the Roman governor (i.e., John 18:29–38), the Roman soldiers at the crucifixion (John 19:23), the Samaritan woman (John 4:7–26), and the "Greeks" mentioned in John 12:20, who apparently were Gentile "God-seekers." Because of their faith in Jesus, the Jewish Christians were "put out of the synagogue" (John 16:1–4), rejected by their families and fellow Jews. And yet, God's covenant righteousness meant his continued faithfulness to his covenant people, and his demonstration of his redeeming power for their benefit.

Michael Bird succinctly determines that,

> the righteousness of God signifies the fidelity and justice of God's character, the demonstration of his character as the judge of all the earth, and his faithfulness toward Israel in Jesus Christ. The righteousness of God then is the character of God embodied and enacted in his saving actions. It is a saving event that is comprehensive, and it involves vivification, justification and transformation.[67]

The Roman Empire

While the author of the Fourth Gospel was certainly influenced by the Old Testament, and especially by the prophet Isaiah, he was also influenced by the culture in which he ministered and wrote. In the first-century AD, the budding Christian gatherings across the area of Asia Minor were composed of both converted Jews and converted Gentiles (John 17:20). Likely, the author John was writing to primarily (but not exclusively) to Greek and Roman believers in and around the region of Ephesus. At the time of the writing of his Gospel, it was the Roman Empire that wielded heavy power and "justice" over the people.

John reassured both the Gentile believers and the converted Jews that their faith in Jesus was indeed valid. This meant a dramatic change of loyalties for the believers, from the Roman Emperor to a Jewish Messiah as "benefactor" and "savior" of the world.[68] John is quite clear in his "purpose statement" (John 20:30–31) that he was counting on the Christian believers to reach their unbelieving neighbors with the truth about Jesus as the Messiah. The readers were to make it evident that Jesus Christ is the Son of God, and through Christ, all (Jew and Gentile alike) "may have life in his name" (John 20:31). He grants his salvation to all faithful people, not just to the Jews. For people living under the unjust, oppressive thumb of Roman imperialism, this was "good news."[69]

Within the political and social realms of the Empire, the earliest Christians were challenged to maintain their allegiances to an invisible God and to the crucified (by the Romans) and resurrected Christ. Various forms of persecution against the believers were not uncommon. The Gospel writer intentionally wrote to reassure his readers and give them confidence in their Christian beliefs. The epithet "Righteous Father" would have been extremely meaningful to those Gentile believers.

Roman imperialism

At that time, across the vast empire, Romans were expected to venerate, honor, and revere the imperial leader so much that it is said that they worshiped him as a god. Numerous titles were given to the reigning emperor; titles were given to the human leaders as signs of gratitude and devotion. Such reverence began with the reign of Caesar Augustus, who was still in power about the time that Jesus was born.

The goddess *Roma* was an image and symbol of the order, rule of law, peace, and stability of the imperial rule. She was given the epithet of *Aeterna*, which is still attached to the city of Rome today (the "Eternal City").[70] The title *"Sebastos"* (from the Greek *eusebeia*) was an ancient Latin title for Caesar Augustus, which meant "divine favor." Octavius, who became Augustus, was the first and perhaps the most famous of the Roman emperors.[71] *"Pax Romana"* ("Roman Peace") was Augustus' greatest vision and achievement, and it was an acclamation across the empire of visible peace and prosperity.

The "Golden Age of Rome" was pictured as an end to wars and battles, protection from enemy forces, improvements of travel across the land and seas, financial assistance to promote better trade, restoration of (formerly Greek) cities, and better distribution of grain and commodities. After his death, the birthday of Augustus became a national holiday, the first day of the Roman calendar year. Even the language of the imperial cult rivalled that which was known to the early Christians. An inscription near the city of Ephesus reads in part,

> Providence...has set all things in most perfect order by giving us Augustus...that he might benefit humankind, sending him as a *savior* [*sōtēra*] both for us and our descendants...And because he, Caesar, by his appearing, surpassed all previous benefactors...and because the birthday of *the god* Augustus was the *beginning of the good news* [*euangeliōn*] *for the world* that came by reason of him.[72]

The Greek word translated "good news" (*euangeliōn*) in the inscription is the same word that we find in New Testament, often translated "gospel." Obviously for Luke, the "beginning of the good news for the world" was the birth of Jesus, which truly *did* benefit the entire world (see Luke 2:10–11).

The "imperial cult" was widespread in the first-century AD Roman Empire. The presence of Rome was felt every day in every way: Roman soldiers, centurions, proconsuls, palaces, prisons, guards, councils, and decrees. People encountered daily reminders of the emperor: temples, images, inscriptions, festivals, even coinage. Rome was the center of the known universe, and "the Roman emperor was a prominent feature of the 'religious environment.'"[73] There were Roman taxes, tax collectors, customs, tariffs, and authorities. The sitting emperor had to demonstrate that he was, indeed, the recipient of divine favors from the gods. This was evident from his military victories, as well as the display of amazing signs and wonders. To his loyal subjects then, the emperor appeared to be a powerful, caring protector, and a gracious patron of all the people. In total, in language and in power, the Roman culture created an almost "messianic-like ideology" and mindset, so there was an inevitable clash between Roman imperialism and Christians who worshiped an entirely different God.[74]

The empire was rampant with imperial wealth and luxury at the time of the writing of the New Testament. Yet there was an obvious paradox evident in the empire between the ideal and the real. Things were not always the way they seemed. The empire was rife with military strife, persecution, arrests, executions, severe economic conditions, oppression, famine, trials, and executions. Worship of the reigning emperor and his family was not a requirement of all the people, especially outside of the city of Rome. But the people in the outlying provinces vied for the attention of the emperor and from his "elite" upper-crust leaders. Cities displayed their loyalty to the imperial forces through lavish temples and festivals, hoping for the emperor's continued honors and protection.

The exterior or "public" story of Roman imperialism featured the *genius* and the benevolence of the emperor, who appeared to be a just and caring leader and who created schemes to accomplish a perfect, peaceful, prosperous empire. This was the "ideal"; yet the "real" story of the Roman Empire is one of violence, slavery, dominance, self-aggrandizement, deceit, and manipulation. Internally, the empire was incredibly corrupt and unjust. Empires, by their very nature, are created by domineering cultures who conquer weaker peoples and then control the conquered, usually by force.

Ephesus, Asia Minor, and the imperial cult

During these complex times, the early Christians had to learn to navigate their lives, their work, their behavior, their speech, and even their worship around the demands of the imperial cult. Author Schüssler-Fiorenza demonstrated the strong influence of the Roman emperor (especially Domitian) in the seven cities of Asia Minor as found in the book of Revelation 1–3.

Emperor Domitian demanded that the ruled people acclaim him as "Lord and God" and participate in the worship of him as divine.[75] The majority of cities, to which the prophetic messages of the biblical book of Revelation are addressed, were dedicated to the promotion of the emperor cult. Ephesus was the seat of a proconsul, and the city competed with Pergamum for primacy. Like Smyrna, Ephesus was a center of the emperor devotion; it had a great theater and was famous for its gladiatorial games. In 29 BC, the city had received permission to guild a temple to the "divine Augustus and the goddess Roma." Smyrna was just north of Ephesus; and later, that is where Polycarp, the Christian bishop, was executed for his faith in 156 AD. The martyrdom of Polycarp is a paradigm of the Christians who refused to call Caesar "my Lord." In Thyatira, the emperor was worshipped as Apollo incarnate and as the son of Zeus. In AD 26, Sardis competed with ten other Asian cities for the right to build a temple in honor of the emperor, but it lost out to Smyrna. In addition, the Roman city of Laodicea prospered under the Flavian rulers and was one of the wealthiest cities in the Phrygia region.

Under these circumstances, Christian believers in the region of Ephesus were bound to experience growing conflicts with the imperial cult since the believers claimed that Jesus Christ was their "Lord and God" instead of the reigning emperor. The first-century readers would be quite familiar with the aggravation and maltreatment of individual Christians by the Roman officials, "especially in light of Domitian's totalitarianism."[76] The New Testament authors, therefore, were concerned about such idolatrous worship and the "demonic power of Satan," who is the ultimate enemy "clothed" in human rulers.[77]

If we acknowledge this background of the ancient culture in Ephesus and the Gospel of John, we know that worshiping Father God and his Son in the first-century Roman Empire would have been difficult if not very dangerous. "Worship" in the Roman days was, in reality, one big party; "worship" was expressed in parades, feasts, and festivals. The peasants bowed humbly before the returning conquering military hero, the emperor. Under the gauze of imperial concern, many ordinary people in the Roman Empire were bleeding physically, socially, religiously, and economically. The figureheads in Rome and the stone figures in local temples did not really care about human life and the concerns of common people. In fact, true justice and righteousness, though touted as principles of the Roman Empire, were rare in the Roman world.

John's small congregation of believers in the region of Ephesus was a peculiar minority in the empire, with strange (and unacceptable) beliefs and behaviors. The Christians did not participate in the local temple worship rituals, in feasts, and in festivals celebrated to the local deities; nor did they adhere to the common imperial devotion. They were viewed with suspicion by their unbelieving neighbors. Their refusal to worship local gods and revere the sitting emperor led others to name them "atheists." Two of the purposes then, for the writing of the Fourth Gospel, were to give instructions to the growing congregation and to give hope and confidence to the Christians in troubled times:

> The Lord [Jesus], now glorified beyond death,
> is far more powerful, awe-inspiring, and divine
> than even the most impressive alabaster statues
> of the Roman emperor, glowing in the smoky
> light of the oil lamps in the imperial temples, or
> than the most elaborate costumes and accessories
> could ever make the living emperor appear.[78]

"Subversive" writings

In an effort to encourage their readers, it is highly likely that the writers of the New Testament, including John, engaged in what may be called "anti-imperial rhetoric," a mode of writing that included "hidden messages" revealing and opposing the corruption of the reigning human authorities. Such "subversive" writings were necessary because blatant opposition to the imperial powers could have resulted in death for the authors.

It is entirely possible that John used the title of "Righteous Father" (John 17:25) juxtaposed against the controlling, self-centered, unjust Roman emperors who were ruling during the first-century AD. The injustices of Roman imperialism were rebuked by insisting that *only* God is true (John 17:3) and just, and righteous (John 17:25). John responded to the political and greedy secular powers by punctuating the *righteousness* of the One true God (John 17:3); in doing so, he condemned the false "righteousness" of the malevolent Roman authorities.

In contrast to corrupt human emperors, God is recognized as the only truly righteous ruler, and it follows that the Son is also the only righteous Redeemer of the believers (John 10:30). John contended that Jesus, with the Righteous Father God, inaugurated the fully righteous "kingdom of God." Such a kingdom, by its very existence, provoked conflicts and a condemnation of the Roman Empire known to John's readers. In the wake of imperial control, injustice, and unrighteousness, John declared that the Righteous Father God and his Son are superior to any human reigning emperor(s).

Thus, the epithet for God used by John in John 17:25 invited his readers to consider the righteousness of God as far superior to the *unrighteousness* of human rulers. Not only is this a reminder of God's character, but it is also a commentary on how his readers were to respond to the justice and righteousness of God in spite of cultural conditions. It is an encouragement to remain faithful and to follow God with their righteous words and actions toward others.

Why "Father"?

When Jesus used the title of "Father" for God, the implications were numerous. To the Jews, this was a reflection of Israel's use of the title, implying a God who was a supreme Creator, caretaker, protector and guide for the nation of Israel (Deut. 32:6). It also implied Jesus' oneness and unity with God, who sent Jesus as his legitimate Son, and who the Messiah obeyed flawlessly. It also implied Jesus' uniqueness as a special human being (John 5:16–30). Moreover, it is important to note that the title of "Father" was very familiar to the people in the Roman imperial culture. The imperial ruler was the "chief priest" of the Roman world; as such, he was given numerous titles, including *divi filius* or "son of the deified" (also seen as a "son of god").[79] The Roman "acclamations of the emperor were no less than messianic" in the first-century AD.[80] Inscriptions posted throughout the Empire read:

> *To the Emperor Caesar, God, Son of God, Augustus.*[81]

However, the emperors in the first-century AD were far from being just, righteous, and loving fathers. In fact, four of the most notoriously evil emperors lived in the first-century AD:

> Tiberius AD 14–37 (the adopted son of Augustus)
> Gaius (Caligula) AD 37–41
> Nero AD 54–68
> Domitian AD 81–96

Thus, the epithet "Righteous Father" (John 17:25) stood in sharp contrast to the titles bestowed upon the corrupt human emperors. Depending upon the dates that the Fourth Gospel was written and read, there is little doubt that the reigns of the first three emperors were at least remembered by John's readers, and it is plausible that the reign of Domitian was experienced by the readers.

Three Features of the Imperial System

There are three features of the Roman imperial system that highlight the title of "Father." First, "Father" was a common epithet for the Roman emperor because he was head of military power, financial matters, diplomatic functions, and all governmental administration. Caesar was revered as the strong leader of a male-dominated, male-centered, orderly society.[82] This title was more than an honorary title; there was a real shift in administrative belief systems so that it became an actual responsibility and function of the emperor.

Since the time of Augustus, the Roman Emperor was considered to be the "Father of the Fatherland" (*pater patriae*), a name which heightened the emperor's providential care and concern for the citizens. The people considered Caesar Augustus to be the "father of the largest family on earth"—that is, the "father" to fifty million people. Except for Tiberius, every Roman emperor after Augustus accepted this title.[83] Across the provinces, people reacted with great loyalty to their "new father," with the understanding that he was the leader of the entire human race. Thus, ideally, it was firmly accepted that the emperor was the "father" and the empire was the "family."[84]

Adoption

A second feature of the imperial system in Rome was the unusual acceptance of royal adoption. Julius Caesar died in 44 BCE without an heir, but Augustus (born Gaius Octavius) was adopted as the emperor's son and was made his legal heir. Even so, Augustus himself was unable to raise a natural son (see "begotten," John 3:16) to inherit his authority. He therefore had to adopt an heir to follow him. Adoption became a vehicle for the transmission of power and imperial authority. In the Roman culture, the adoption of sons for political reasons was not only accepted, but it was also even encouraged to secure lasting "stability," which actually meant a succession of power, prestige, and position. The title of "Father" not only speaks of the idyllic nature of the benevolent patriarch but also of those he appointed to be his adopted heirs.

Benevolence

The third feature is that of a diplomatic "benefactor." In addition to his role as "Father of the Fatherland," Caesar Augustus was considered to be the ultimate benefactor to his citizens. Like a gracious and generous father, the emperor gave the people what they needed for a prosperous culture: from roads and buildings to grain and bread. However, as the population of the empire increased through a process of military takeovers, the entitlements for ordinary people were severely reduced—or disappeared. The "elites," or ruling class of people, simply indulged themselves and the lower classes provided whatever the "elites" desired. Thus, the ordinary people living in the Roman Empire in the first-century AD were suffering from hardships including poor economic conditions and political unrest. There were military defeats resulting in a disgruntled army. Power achieved in the Julio-Claudian dynasty of emperors disintegrated, and the Flavian dynasty took over. There were four emperors in one year, 68–69 CE, causing great unrest and a lack of confidence in the imperial regime. Emperor Galba was murdered, and Otho was forced to commit suicide. The familiar saying is true in this situation: absolute power corrupts absolutely.

Therefore, in view of these features, the recognition of God as the "Righteous Father" was a strong contrast to the Roman imperial cult. The title used by John implies the deification of the *proper*, just, and righteous God, as well as the *proper* linage of his divine Son. The true divine Father is the universal Creator, Ruler, Savior, and Redeemer—a position that obviously conflicted with the Roman imperial story. The emperor was only human, and a flawed one at that. His immediate family and the other dignitaries (like the Roman senators) fought for and competed for power at the expense of the ordinary population. Only the Righteous Father and his legitimate Son, Jesus Christ, were truly worthy of worship. This epithet is more than a revelation of God's paternal nature to his people; it specifically names God as the *only* righteous and just Ruler who truly loves his own and has beneficial, redemptive plans for his people. The brief epithet is a profound statement over against all "unrighteous" human rulers so familiar to the readers. It is also a guarantee that the justice, the plans, the salvation, and redemption of God's people are fulfilled and completed in the work of "his only begotten" Son (John 3:16).

Declared righteousness

N. T. Wright wrote, "Because he [God] is righteous, he declares in the present time that all who believe in the risen Lord Jesus are in the right, that their sins are forgiven."[85] That is, in the present world, God "declares righteous" those who believe in Jesus as the Christ; in the future, God has also promised a just and righteous kingdom of those people who believe in his Son. Remarkably, God can and does impart his own righteousness into his servants in the present (John 17:22). Of course, human beings are not righteous by nature (Rom. 3:10, 21–24), nor are they filled with the glory of God. It is therefore unimaginable that a deity would impart his righteousness into flawed human beings! In contrast, the present world reflects the same ideology that we saw in the first century—that human beings can achieve a "utopian world" by themselves. It is as much of a failure presently as it has been in the past.

In the Old Testament, human righteousness was following the laws decreed by God as part of the covenant agreements. God assured his righteous people that their prayers would be answered, and he would protect and deliver them from corruption (Ps. 34:15–22). In fact, God promised to bring about his righteousness in his people, in his nation, so that they could shine before the other (corrupt) nations. Nevertheless, knowing that humanity cannot be obedient flawlessly, God sent his Son to redeem the people and fill them with his righteousness. Jesus changed the entire landscape of a relationship with a righteous God. God's people are "declared righteous," not based on their own merit or behavior but on their faith in "the One sent"—Jesus Christ (Rom. 1:17). To receive God's righteousness in place of human sinfulness, people must become the people of God through belief in Christ:

> We implore you on Christ's behalf: Be reconciled to God. God made him who had no sin to be sin for us, so that in him we might become the righteousness of God (2 Cor. 5:20b–21).

Righteousness is not earned by loyalty to a certain human ruler or adherence to a certain set of human beliefs or laws. It is a gift from God to his people because they "accept" the words and work of Jesus Christ (John 17:8) and strive to live in obedience to him (John 15:9–11). "Declared righteousness" is to be "justified" (or receive "justification"), as God declares that believers are "not guilty," and credits righteousness to them. The perfect righteousness of God and of his Son is ascribed to believers apart from the Old Testament law (see Rom. 2:1–16; 3:10, 20–23). That is, believers are in a righteous position by being incorporated into Christ.

Righteousness equals sanctification

But how is this done? How are human beings credited with God's righteousness? How does one attain righteousness if not earned by human merit? Frankly, it all sounds too easy. We can consider the background. The Old Testament promises that "the righteous will live by his faith" in God (see Hab. 2:4; Isa. 26:1–8; Rom. 1:17). The New Testament writers quote this clause to support the teaching that people are made right with God by grace through faith in Christ (Rom. 1:17; Gal. 3:11; Heb. 10:38–39) and not of their own accord. Righteousness is living by faith and trust in God; further, it is a demonstration of that faith in action (Jas. 2:21–24). The first-century believers also recognized Jesus, with Father God, as being "the Righteous One" (1 John 2:1, 29), a title given to Jesus who was the "atoning sacrifice for our sins" (1 John 2:2). Only a Righteous Savior could purify the sins "of the whole world" (1 John 1:7, 2:2).

Then the New Testament reveals that the righteousness of God, in the form of the Holy Spirit, permeates each believer. It is the Spirit who indwells, convicts, and empowers those who have faith in Christ (John 16:7–11; see chapter 5 on the Holy Spirit). In any generation, the disobedient world does not *know* a Righteous Father because it does not truly *know* God (John 15:21–23; 16:3; 17:25). However, the Righteous Father has revealed his nature to his people (Isa. 56:1–

2; John 17:6) and has promised to love them and redeem them from human sin and sorrow.

Those who know God acknowledge his righteousness and humble themselves before him; they are filled with "joy, gladness and thanksgiving" (Isa. 51:1–8, 17:25). Unmerited and undeserved, the Holy Spirit indwells believers, making "right" both the individual person and the family of God collectively (the "church"). The imparting of righteousness by the Holy Spirit is a process, not unlike the process of "sanctification" of the believer. A person is not filled with God's righteousness at one sitting, but as we foster a life of love and obedience, the righteousness of God is revealed in our lives. Jesus said,

> I have made you known to them [his followers],
> and *will continue* to make you known in order
> that the love you have for me might be in them
> and that I myself may be in them (John 17:26;
> emphasis mine).

Like a perpetually running stream, the Spirit of Christ is "in" his followers, flowing through them, revealing the Father and gradually filling the believer with his own righteousness.

N. T. Wright writes that "justification" is both individual and corporate:

> Justification declares that the believer is a mem-
> ber of the covenant community, that community
> itself is called to live as the family who accepts
> one another in love. Justification by faith is indi-
> vidual; the covenant God is restoring his kingly
> rule over the world by creating us "in Christ" as a
> renewed people for his own possession.[86]

So humanity is "made right" before God in terms of a legal position; we are "chosen, adopted, forgiven and redeemed" ("justified") because we accept the atonement of Christ (see Eph. 1:1:4–10; John

17:7–8). But God does not leave us there. The regenerating gift of his righteousness is the gift of the Spirit, who continues to make God's righteousness known in individuals, and then all are united together into one restored collective body (John 17:21–22).

The final question is, why? Why would God promise to make his people righteous? God knows that we cannot redeem ourselves, no matter how hard we try. Human beings cannot and will not ever live up to the demand for perfect righteousness and sinlessness. It is only by the work of the gracious, "Righteous Father" that people can live in harmony with God and with each other. He loves us so much that he was willing to sacrifice his Son in order to assure us of his grace, love, and care (John 12:27). God gives Christians his righteousness so that we can demonstrate his love and care now to other people, and someday experience his divine glory (John 17:22, 24).

Those people who are deemed righteous and made righteous by God are to be models and examples of how to live in this world in accordance with God's righteousness and justice, as a "light to the nations—to all the nations, throughout all time" (Isa. 51:4; John 12:35–36). But we are also examples of his "scandalous" grace, loving and forgiving others just as we have received his love and grace. It is for his own glory that God indwells us with his own righteousness (Isa. 63:14; John 12:28, 13:31–32, 17:24; Rom. 15:9).

It is the larger story of the people of God who replicate his holiness, righteousness, and love in a world that impugns all that he is. With humility, believers can respond by challenging themselves to give fairness, mercy, forgiveness, and grace toward other people. As the righteousness of God was to shine forth from the nation of Israel, so his righteousness is to be a beacon shining forth from his people today.

Prayer and righteousness

Why is it so difficult to pray to this righteous, gracious, trustworthy, all-powerful, all-knowing God? Likely, it is because we do not fully understand who he is. It has been said that people in the modern era often see God as a "spiritual Santa Claus," who exists only to answer our needs and desires. Prayer can be a "grocery list" of what we want and what God can do for us. However, God rejects our primarily selfish concerns. Sometimes, God does know better about how to answer our demands. In the end, God will always do what is right and good for us, even when we do not know it ourselves.

A very beautiful, emotional prayer appears in Daniel 9:3–19. It is a communal prayer of repentance and the confession of sins. Daniel has recognized the righteousness of God and sees, in contrast, the sins of his own and the sins of his people. The rebellious people rejected the warnings of the prophet; they disobeyed the laws of "the Lord our God."

In the prayer, Daniel is pleading for God's forgiveness and mercy in spite of the nation's infidelity and disobedience. He understands that God is "great, awesome, [and] righteous" (Dan. 9:4, 7, 14) and remarkably faithful toward his people. Daniel learned what we need to know—that God answers prayer because of his grace and mercy and not because of our demands and deeds. Daniel's prayer is an expression of humility, praise, and confession (Dan. 9:3–15) *before* his petitions were uttered (Dan. 9:16–19):

> O Lord, in keeping with all your righteous acts, turn away your anger and your wrath from Jerusalem, your city, your holy hill…Hear the prayers and petitions of your servant…We do not make requests of you because we are righteous, but because of your great mercy. O Lord, listen! O Lord forgive! O Lord hear and act! For your sake, O my God, do not delay, because your city and your people *bear your name* (Dan. 9:16–19; emphasis mine).

Christians, in fact, do bear the name of a righteous God; so we should speak and act in ways that glorify his holy, righteous name.

Our prayers then must evolve into a humble connection with a holy and righteous Father. When we recognize who he truly is, it affects our prayer concerns. Our prayers shift from "me" to "thee": what does *he* want from *us*? Prayers become humble requests before a just and caring Father who knows us better than we know ourselves. Our righteousness does not depend on our performance in front of other people. Those believers who humbly and honestly approach God in prayer have hope and confidence in his promises. Believing this, we can have continual praise for a God who is just and righteous, who does not ignore the wickedness around us, but who draws near to those who need him.

Conclusions and responses

It *is* hard for people to be "righteous." Perhaps, in our culture, like the ancient Roman culture, rulers, power, wealth, ambition, and self-importance reign. We can try to achieve a level of "self-righteousness." Social media and other forces urge us to establish for ourselves our own cultural ethics and morality, and we can presume that "rightness" and "wrongness" is all relative ("whatever works for you").

If each individual person sets up his or her own set of ethics, then each one acts as his/her own "god," judge, and final authority. This presents a problem when our opinions conflict with other people who have their relative set of ethical principles. Without recognition of an ultimate authority outside of ourselves—that is, God—our society would be in a greater muddle without any standards, sanctions, or certainty. Without God's righteousness as a baseline, we would live in a constant tension of the boundaries of good and evil.

Righteousness is not a goal to achieve. A young girl practiced the piano for months, learning a piece and preparing for an important recital. The night of the recital came, and she walked out onto the stage. She looked out at what seemed to be a huge audience, and she saw her parents and her teacher. She looked down at the keyboard, but her hands would not move. Terror and panic overwhelmed her. She suddenly ran from the stage and broke into tears. Trying to comfort her, her teacher asked her what happened. She replied, "I was afraid to mess up. I didn't want to let anyone down by making mistakes in my performance." The teacher hugged her and said quietly, "*You are not your performance.* You will make mistakes, but you will also learn to be a wonderful piano player someday. Just keep trying." And she did.

God is like that teacher. He forgives our mistakes and pledges to help us learn not to make them again. It is true that one day, under our own power and intelligence, we realize that we cannot do everything *right*. We do mess things up. It is an admission to God that we need his help. If we could do everything "right" by ourselves, we would not need God. We could be on that piano bench all by ourselves and perform perfectly. Or, we might fail morally or ethically and fall off the bench.

But perfect or not, we are not our performance. When we finally get to know the *real* God who really controls our lives, we are ready to surrender. As we surrender to God's authority, we see that prayer becomes the power to tap into *his* righteousness, *his* grace, and *his* love. "God does not love you because you are good; God loves you because God is good."[87]

Notes

[65] Richard Rohr and Mike Morrell, *The Divine Dance; the Trinity and Your Transformation* (London: SPCK, 2016), 132.

[66] Andreas J. Kostenberger, *John; Baker Exegetical Commentary on the New Testament*, ed. Robert; Yarbrough and Robert H. Stein (Grand Rapids: Baker Academic, 2004), 8.

[67] Michael F. Bird, *The Story of God Bible Commentary: Romans*, ed. Tremper Longman and Scot McKnight (Grand Rapids: Zondervan Publishing, 2016), 43.

[68] David A. DeSilva, *Unholy Allegiances; Heeding Revelation's Warnings* (Peabody: Hendrickson, 2013), 27.

[69] DeSilva, 27.

[70] DeSilva, 23.

[71] Judith A. Diehl, "Anti-Imperial Rhetoric in the New Testament," in *Jesus Is Lord, Caesar Is Not*, ed. Scot McKnight; Joseph B. Modica (Downers Grove: InterVarsity Press, 2013), 38–81, 38.

[72] DeSilva, *Unholy Allegiances; Heeding Revelation's Warnings*, 26.

[73] Michael Peppard, *The Son of God in the Roman World; Divine Sonship in Its Social and Political Context* (New York: Oxford University Press, 2011), 25.

[74] Bruce Winter, *Divine Honours for the Caesars; the First Christians' Responses* (Grand Rapids: Eerdmans Publishing, 2015) 44. DeSilva, *Unholy Allegiances; Heeding Revelation's Warnings*, 27.

[75] Elisabeth Schussler Fiorenza, *The Book of Revelation: Justice and Judgment* (Philadelphia: Fortress Press, 1985), 193.

[76] Fiorenza, 194.

[77] Fiorenza, 196.

[78] DeSilva, *Unholy Allegiances; Heeding Revelation's Warnings.*, 81.

[79] DeSilva, 29–30.

[80] DeSilva, 27.

[81] Peppard, *The Son of God in the Roman World; Divine Sonship in Its Social and Political Context*, 46.

[82] Warren Carter, *The Roman Empire and the New Testament: An Essential Guide* (Nashville, Tennessee: Abingdon Press, 2006), 4.

[83] Peppard, *The Son of God in the Roman World; Divine Sonship in Its Social and Political Context*, 60–63.

[84] Peppard, 60, 66–67.

[85] N. T. Wright, *Pauline Perspectives; Essays on Paul, 1978–2013* (Minneapolis: Fortress Press, 2013), 41.

[86] Wright, 40–41.

[87] Richard Rohr and Mike Morrell, *The Divine Dance; the Trinity and Your Transformation* (London: SPCK, 2016), 110.

Chapter 4

Jesus as Son and Savior

Christ is the lead character in the biblical drama:
the Alpha and Omega, from Genesis to Revelation,
from creation to the consummation.[88]

Who is this "Christ" as presented by John in his Gospel (John 8:25, 17:3)? Who is this Son who becomes a Savior? It is interesting to consider that most Christians would probably assume that the biblical Jesus is unique to Christianity and that Muslims, in particular, do not recognize Jesus. Yet it is true that in the Quran, the scriptures of Islam, Jesus is not only recognized but also revered and honored as a unique prophet of Allah (God). Notably,

> Jesus is mentioned more than Muhammad in the
> Quran. His name appears in fifteen of 114 suras
> [chapters]. While Muhammad is mentioned four
> times explicitly, Jesus is mentioned twenty-nine
> times in twenty-eight verses. He is mentioned by
> his title, the Messiah, the Christ, eleven times.
> Jesus is the central figure in over ninety verses.[89]

Jesus' high position in the Quran begins with his mother, Mary. The only woman mentioned in the Quran, Mary was "dedicated from her mother's womb" and is praised above all other women. The

Quran recognizes that Jesus was "without sin," and he is named "the Word of (or for) God." He was even "strengthened by the Holy Spirit to perform miracles."[90]

Nevertheless, the Islamic Jesus is not the same as the Christian Jesus. The titles given to Jesus in the Quran do not reflect the same meanings as the titles given to Jesus by Christian believers. Most importantly, Jesus is *not* the divine "Son of God." Jesus is only human, and Allah (God) would never have a son. The most critical belief for Muslims is the "absolute oneness" and supremacy of Allah, and he does not need an heir. Therefore, the Muslims totally reject two aspects of the Christian faith as they relate to Jesus: his divinity and his atoning death. The Christian Trinity is misinterpreted as God, Jesus, and Mary; and only "infidels" believe in such. The Islamic Jesus is merely a human messenger, a figure not unlike the Christian Jesus "but with a twist." Ultimately, for Muslims, he is *not* a "savior."[91]

So in dialogues with other people, particularly with non-Christians, can believers really articulate who this second Person of the Trinity really is? Why is it so important to understand the biblical truths about the divinity of Jesus, as well as his death and resurrection? At the heart of John's Gospel, especially in chapters 5–8, the true identity of Jesus is disclosed. As he testified about himself before the Jewish leaders, Jesus clearly set himself "above" the recognized human authorities (John 8:23). If the learned, erudite Jewish leaders did not see Jesus as the promised Messiah to the nation of Israel, how was it possible that the ordinary people can accept him as such (John 8:27–30, 45–51)? In the end, how does knowledge of Jesus as the "Son and Savior" affect a Christian's prayer life?

"Son of God"

The third epithet in the prayer of John 17 that we need to consider—"Holy Father" in verse 11 and "Righteous Father" in verse 25 are the two we have already noted—is "the Son" mentioned twice in

John 17:1. "Jesus Christ" is the title used in John 17:3 for the same Person, the second Person of the Trinity.

"Son of God" is perhaps the most familiar title for Jesus found in the New Testament. It is used in reference to him in various ways among the New Testament writers, but the use of this title in John's Gospel demonstrates the true identity and divinity of Jesus. The Gospel of Matthew uses this title six times (John 4:3, 6; 8:29; 14:33; 26:63; 27:40) with two variations in John 27:42, 54. Matthew also refers simply to "the Son" (Matt. 11:27, 28:19) and to "God's beloved Son" (Matt. 3:17, 17:5). Luke also mentions "the Son of God" six times (Luke 1:35; 3:38; 4:3, 9, 41; 22:70). Mark's Gospel does not use the title at all, while the Apostle Paul used the title only three times (Rom. 1:4; 2 Cor. 1:16; Gal. 2:20). However, in the Gospel of John, "Son of God" appears nine times (John 1:34, 49; 3:18; 5:25; 10:36; 11:4, 27; 19:7; 20:31). The Johannine literature (including the Gospel and the epistles) use the title more than any other New Testament author. Thus, the title, especially by the author of the Fourth Gospel, has an important "confessional significance" given to it, especially by the early Christians.[92]

In Mark's Gospel, the author implied titles for Jesus, more than merely a description, in his introduction to "*the* Messiah, *the* Son of God" (Mark 1:1). Elsewhere in the Synoptic Gospels, God expressed his great love for Jesus by using the title of "Son" at Jesus' baptism, echoing Psalm 2:7 (Matt. 3:17–18; Mark 1:11, 9:7; Luke 3:22). Matthew's record of the baptism quotes Isaiah 42:1, connecting Jesus to the "Suffering Servant" in Isaiah's prophecies. The words of the Father God also authenticated his Son's identity and commission. In John's Gospel, however, there is no baptismal scene; but there is confirmation that his relationship with his Father was a mutual closeness. The Johannine author attempted to explain this unique, eternal, creative, glorious relationship in the prologue (John 1:1–18) and then again in the prayer of John 17:1–5. There is only one divine Son, sent by the Father to do the Father's will on earth. Jesus is thus identified as uniquely God, of God, and by God. The Johannine author calls attention to the exclusive, uniqueness of Jesus as the "*only* Son" of the Father (John 1:14, 18, 34; 3:16). Like Mark,

John gives careful attention to the repeated use of the absolute form of the titles—*the* Father and *the* Son, indicating their uniqueness, their shared purpose, and their strong solidarity with one another. The clear purpose of the Gospel is stated in John 20:31—to validate the readers' belief that "Jesus is *the* Christ, *the* Son of God." Even his mission of coming to the earth was at the Father's bidding (John 8:42). Jesus shared the work of the Father (John 5:19, 9:4, 10:37), including granting life to the dead (Lazarus in John 11:17–27) and executing judgment (John 5:22, 27–29). In fact, the work that Jesus did on earth was actually the work of the Father through him (John 5:17, 30, 36).[93]

As the Son, Jesus called God not by the Hebrew name "YHWH" but by the name "Father." While Jesus' direct references to God as his "Father" are not uncommon in the Synoptic Gospels, John employs the title "Father" ninety times. This compares to five times in Mark, seventeen times in Luke, and forty-five times in Matthew. In the Fourth Gospel, Jesus used the title metaphorically as an implication of a very close "blood" relationship. The tie between the Father and the Son is so close that they are "in" one another (John 10:34–38, 14:10–20). In obedience, Jesus did exactly what the Father told him to do (John 10:17); the Father "set him apart *as his very own* and sent him into the world" (John 10:36; emphasis mine). John is placing Jesus squarely within the Jewish understanding of a son in relationship to his father in a very close union.

In contrast to the Roman emperors, Jesus was not "adopted" by YHWH; he was born of God and is the legitimate, direct descendent of Father God (John 3:16). Only in John does Jesus say that "I and the Father are one" (John 10:30); it is a critical theological (and Christological) claim. Specifically, Jesus opens the prayer of John 17 with a reference to God as his "Father" and to himself as the "Son" (John 17:1). Then, quite oddly, he refers to himself in the third person as "Jesus Christ" (John 17:3). Linguistically, this is so unusual that it is clearly the creation of the author of John in reference to the identities of the two parts of the divine Trinity: the Father and the Son. In the same introduction to the prayer, John contends that the two parts are equal in authority and both share the same "glory"

(John 17:2–5). Jesus made God known to his followers as their "Father," and Jesus will continue to do so because the Father loves his Son and those who follow his Son (John 17:26). The frequency of this title indicates that the Johannine Jesus is portraying a God who is both transcendent and yet intimately involved in the lives of his people. The Johannine epithets (John 17:11, 25) emphasize the Old Testament concepts that God is holy and righteous and that all his ways are perfect. At the same time, God is also a caring "father" to his beloved children. When his unique identity is revealed, it casts light on precisely who his Son is—like Father God, the Son is totally unique and has all the Father's characteristics. God is the Father to all nations and all people who believe in his Son. The epithets used by the Johannine author in John 17 reveal the intimate relationship between the Father and his people who chose to be faithful to him and to his Messiah—Jesus. Knowing God as their "Father" was surely an encouragement and a promise to those readers who received the words of Jesus and are a part of God's plan of redemption.

Perhaps the most important aspect of this entwined relationship is the sharing of love between the Father and the Son. The Son loves the Father (John 14:31) and is loved by the Father (John 3:35, 5:20, 10:17, 17:23). The love of the Father for the Son is demonstrated in the act of giving the Son all things—that is, "placing everything in his hands" (John 3:35, 13:3)—including and specifically those people who have come to love the Son (John 10:29, 17:2).[94] The true love relationship between the Father and the Son is best demonstrated by the Son's obedience to come to the earth, sent by the Father for a strategic mission to redeem the people that the Father loves (John 17:26).

Sonship in the Old Testament

The primary use of the designation of "son" in the Old Testament was given to a human male heir in the family. Sonship was very important to the ancient Israelites; this is apparent from the lists of genealogy in the Old Testament. Each successive generation carried on not only the family name but also its characteristics, joys, sorrows, struggles, and achievements. A person was known by his/her family name, not unlike the way we carry on our family "last" names today from father to son to grandson and so on. In Isaiah, the image of "sons" is used for the "house of Israel," or the people of God; and because they are his "children," God promised to be their "Savior" and to redeem them (Isa. 63:8–9).

In addition, the Old Testament prophets, including Moses, were considered to be "spokesmen" or agents of God; and they spoke on his behalf to the people, communicating the very words of God. Any designated messenger, especially a servant or a family member, was recognized as one who had been sanctioned to deliver messages from one in authority. In the Israelite culture, the messenger was just like the one who did the sending; anyone who failed to recognize the messenger as authoritative actually dishonored the sender. Therefore, the agent or messenger was to be treated with the same respect and honor as the sender. The Son, therefore, is a trustworthy, respected representative and agent of his Father to humanity.

It has been said that if we want to know God, we can read the Old Testament; if we want to know about Jesus, we read the New Testament Gospels. Unfortunately, this is tragically misleading. First, it completely neglects the third person of the Trinity, the Holy Spirit. Second, we cannot divide the Godhead and try to understand the parts of the Trinity as if they stand alone. It is difficult to study the Son apart from the Father and vice versa; it is difficult to know the Holy Spirit without knowing the Father and the Son, both of whom sent the Spirit.

Rejecting the "Son"

Throughout all four Gospels, the authority of Jesus is repeatedly questioned by the Jewish leaders. Who was he, and where did he come from? Why was he challenging *their* authority? Ordinary people, as well as the Jewish leaders, had a difficult time understanding who Jesus is. This is apparent in the first chapter of John's Gospel; the author attempted to introduce Jesus at the beginning of his Gospel through the prologue (John 1:1–18) and through certain characters, such as John the Baptist (John 1:6–36), Andrew and Simon Peter ("Cephas") (John 1:37–42), Philip (John 1:43–44), and Nathanael, who quickly declared that he is the "Son of God" (John 1:45–49).

John the Baptist also testified that Jesus is the "Son of God" (John 1:34), and Jesus said that he was the "light" that revealed the true nature of God (John 1:7–9, 5:35). As the Son, Jesus was both equal with God in nature and in purpose (John 5:18–23). Yet he was subordinate to the Father to carry out the mission on earth for which he was sent. The same was true of emissaries in the Roman Empire who represented the emperor throughout the Empire. Even today, ambassadors from the head of one country are regarded with all due honor and respect given to the ones they represent.[95]

One of the primary reasons the Fourth Gospel was written was to testify to the true identity of the "Son of God" and "that by believing you may have life in his name" (John 20:27–31). This is illustrated by the confrontation with the Jewish leaders in John 5:31–47. That is, a man's testimony about himself is invalid unless the testimony is confirmed by another witness (or better yet, three witnesses in John 5:31). Jesus suggested that only one witness was necessary in his case and that his testimony was greater than the word of John the Baptist (John 5:32–36). God (his "Father") testified concerning the identity of the Son, and the Father's testimony surpassed that of any human being (John 5:34) or any Old Testament Scriptures (John 5:39) or even Moses (John 5:45–47). Yet in John, we see the rejection of Jesus as the "Son of God" because the Jewish leaders did not understand what Jesus taught concerning his Father (John 8:27, 39–41). Those who rejected the Son also rejected the Father (John 8:45, 49, 56) since they refused to believe in the one who God "sent" (see John 5:37–39, 43–44, 47).

Another prominent example of rejection of the Son by the chosen people of God is in a Lukan parable. The "Parable of the Tenants" in Luke 20 is about the rejection of the servants (or the Old Testament prophets) sent by God and the final rejection of the "beloved son" sent to the nation. The owner (God) of the vineyard (the nation of Israel) expected the people to receive the Son as his agent: "Then the owner of the vineyard said, 'What shall I do? I will send my son, whom I love; perhaps they will respect him'" (Luke 20:13). This verse makes it very clear that Jesus' parable was about himself and the lack of acceptance, respect, and honor from the Jewish leadership (Luke 20:14–15). Furthermore, because the nation rejected the Son, they rejected the Father. Therefore, God gave the "inheritance" (the salvation in Jesus) "to others" (Luke 20:16). The promises of God given to the nation of Israel, but who rejected them would be given to other Gentile nations. The redemption of people through the promises of the Messiah is made available to "others," such as the Gentile believers in John's church in Ephesus.

Old Testament Christological texts

The earliest Jewish Christians searched the Hebrew Bible for knowledge of the identity of the promised Messiah. In their efforts to understand and express their beliefs about who Jesus is, a number of texts stand out as "messianic" texts; Psalm 110 and Isaiah 45:22–25 are prime examples. The single most cited and alluded to passage from the Old Testament in the New Testament is Psalm 110. In this poem, the Messiah (position and title fulfilled in Jesus) is pictured as Lord, King ("majestic ruler"), priest, and judge over all the nations. It is a declaration of God's intent to establish the position of a royal priest and ruler king, accomplished by one person who is seated at the "right hand" of God (Ps. 110:5). As the promised Messiah, Jesus fulfilled this multifaceted office as priest, as ruler, and as judge.

The prophet Isaiah spoke of the nation's future redemption in Isaiah 11, which is accomplished by "a shoot [which] shall come out from the stump of Jesse, and a Branch shall grow out his roots" (Isa. 11:1). That is, Jesus is the named Branch who came out of the lineage of David to redeem the nation. In chapter 45, Isaiah records additional declarations of God. The exile of Israel to Babylon is not God's final plan for his people. Certainly, the "Holy One of Israel" is

God alone (Isa. 45:18d); and only his Son, his Messiah, who is also fully God, can complete the task of salvation of God's people:

> Turn to me and be saved,
> All you ends of the earth;
> For I am God,
> and there is no other.
> By myself I have sworn,
> My mouth has uttered in all integrity
> a word that will not revoked:
> Before me, every knee will bow;
> By me every tongue will swear,
> They will say of me, "in the Lord alone
> are righteousness and strength."
> All who have raged against him
> will come to him and be put to shame.
> But in the Lord all the descendants of Israel
> will be found righteous and will exult
> (Isa. 45:22–25; compare to Paul's poem in Phil.
>   2:6–11).

Thus, the Isaiah prophecies reveal the uniqueness and the supremacy of God over all the earth while it confirms the work of Jesus which is completed for all the people in all time, not just for the nation of Israel. Jesus is the one and only God-in-the-flesh sent to save, to rule, and to judge humanity. This righteous ruler is a contrast to any human ruler from King Cyrus (Isa. 45:1) to the emperor in Rome. The Old Testament texts opened up new experiences and new ways to explain why the believing Jews and Gentiles of the first-century AD raised Jesus to the level of the true Son of God.

The prophet Zechariah saw a time when only the "one true God" would reign over the nations; and his words were prophetic of the coming Messiah: "And on that day, living water will flow out from Jerusalem, half to the eastern sea and half to the western sea, in summer and in winter" (Zech. 14:8). The Jewish Feast of the Tabernacles remembered the provision of God in the wilderness for the Jews; Jesus claimed to be the "living water" that is a fulfillment of the Old Testament prophecy (John 7:37–38). Again, Jesus declared to the Samaritan woman that he, indeed, is that "living water" (John 4:10–14; see Rev. 22:1–2); and it is he who grants "eternal life" to those who believe. The words of Zechariah were also accomplished through the "gift" of the Holy Spirit given to all people of all the nations who believe (John 7:39, 16:7).

John 12 and Isaiah 6

Bruce Henning observes that "the Gospel of John frequently points its readers to the Old Testament to make typological correspondences between famous images, and the person of Jesus."[96] In particular, Henning notes that John 12:37–41 is a reference to Isaiah 6, where "Isaiah sees the king in his glory, and is commissioned to be a rejected prophet."[97] In a similar way but in the reverse order, Jesus is the "rejected prophet" and then he is the "king in his glory." Thus, John explained that the "unbelief" of the Jews was a fulfillment of the Old Testament scriptures, specifically Isaiah 53:1 and 6:10.[98]

The writer of the Fourth Gospel names the prophet Isaiah on three occasions just within chapter 12 (John 12:38–39, 41). This overtly connects Jesus with the "rejected prophet" who was told to "callous" the hearts of the people (Isa. 6:9–13; John 12:31, 37–40). First, both Isaiah and Jesus were rejected by the very people they were trying to save (John 12:37–38). Second, God then passed judgment on them with the "blinding" of eyes and the "hardening" of hearts to confuse their understanding (John 12:39). The events of John 9 are an echo of the spiritual "blindness" of the people and the restoration of Jesus. Giving sight to the "blind" by Jesus is contrasted to the searing "judgment" by Jesus of those who refuse to "see" who he is (John 9:39–41). Third, and in contrast to the "blinded" unbelievers, Isaiah "saw" the glory of Jesus. While Isaiah spoke most often about the glory of God, John implies that there was no difference between the glory of God and that of Jesus (John 12:41). Both Isaiah and Jesus were "rejected" by the Jews; both were also "sent" by God. Isaiah responded: "Then I heard the voice of the Lord saying, 'Whom shall I send? And who will go for us?' And I said, 'here I am, send me!'" (Isa. 6:8).[99] At least nine times in John's Gospel, Jesus confirmed that he too was sent from God, his Father:

> Now, this is eternal life: that they may know you, the only true God, and Jesus Christ, whom you have sent (John 17:3).

> As you have sent me into the world, I have sent them into the world (John 17:18).

Thus, there is no doubt that John makes a clear reference back to the "rejected" prophet Isaiah. Then John helps his readers to "see" the connection between the prophet and the Messiah and to understand the mistake made by those who chose not to believe in him as the Messiah.[100] John 12:41 proves to be an editorial comment by the author John to help his readers "see" the connection between Jesus and Isaiah's "glorious king" (Isa. 6:1–4).[101] Even though he is rejected by some people, Jesus is the exalted Lord; perhaps *because* he was rejected, then he was glorified. He obeyed his "sending" all the way to the cross and thus becomes the "glorious King." The glory and power of the Son is exactly the same as that of the Father.

In addition, we read in John 20:10–18 that Mary Magdalene is the first of Jesus' followers to speak to Jesus after the resurrection. Standing near the tomb, weeping, two angels ask Mary why she was crying. Then she turned around and saw a man who asked her the very same question: "Why are you crying?" (John 20:15). She recognized the risen Jesus *only after he called her by name* (John 20:16; 10:3–5, 14). However, Mary was not allowed to touch Jesus, or "hold on" to him, because he had not yet "returned to the Father" (John 20:17). That is, postresurrection and preascension, Jesus had not yet been "glorified" and had not resumed his original position alongside of the Father (John 17:5). Like Mary, we are not allowed to fully "grasp" (or comprehend) Jesus this side of eternity and to fully take hold of him, who now sits in glory with his Father. But also like

Mary, if we are truly looking for Jesus, even in unlikely places, we *will* find him and he *will call us by name*—he knows us! Jesus calls us even today, and then he tells us to "go" and spread the gospel truth about "my Father and your Father…my God and your God" (John 20:17, 28).

Outside of John 17, there are only two other brief prayers on the lips of Jesus in the Fourth Gospel. After the raising of Lazarus, Jesus prays a short prayer of thanksgiving in John 11:41–42 for the benefit of his followers. In John 12:27–28, Jesus' "heart is troubled," and this prayer is similar to his anguishing prayers in Gethsemane in the Synoptics. The "hour" of Jesus' "glorification" (John 12:26) is the hour of his death, with his subsequent resurrection and exaltation. This is the final "hour" which fulfills his mission and "glorifies" the name of the Father who sent him (John 12:28). His ultimate suffering "glory" is a triumph over the sin and darkness of "this world," which is indeed the prophetic paradox in Isaiah 52:13–15.[102]

Early high Christology

In the decades after his death and resurrection, it is truly remarkable how quickly the gospel message about Jesus Christ spread, as the believers attested to its veracity and the activity of God's Spirit in the midst opened new eyes to the reality of the Son. Following his time on earth, when did people begin to worship Jesus as the "Son of God"?

High Christology can be described as high honor and esteem given to Jesus, who is treated in a significant way as "divine." The evidence that we have within the Gospel itself does reveal a very early high Christology. Regard for Jesus as a divine figure began in the circles of Jewish followers of Jesus in Judea and blossomed rapidly across the Ancient Near East.[103] Scholars debate the Christology that is presented in the Fourth Gospel, partially because as the last Gospel to be written, they suggest that the Gospel author may reflect more of the theology of the established Christian church than the theology of the original author. On the one hand, Prof. Larry Hurtado argued that the Fourth Gospel does present a more advanced development of Christology in comparison to that which is presented in earlier texts, such as the Pauline letters.[104]

The language of the Fourth Gospel concerning Jesus is evidence that demonstrates that what is said about Jesus is quite different from all the known Greek philosophies of the first-century AD (i.e., Stoicism, Middle Platonist). Further, the presentation of Jesus as fully human and fully divine differs from all known Jewish traditions of the time. Jesus is fully divine in John 1:1, where the Logos is *Theos* (God); and like an identical "bookend," in John 20:28, one of the earliest disciples, Thomas, refers to Jesus as his *Theos* (God). In addition, Paul's letter to the Philippians includes an early poem or hymn that is evidence of high Christology (Phil. 2:6–11). The first half of the poem is about Jesus' incarnation, as he was sent by the Father to earth as a man (John 1:6). Jesus "empties himself," *voluntarily* humbling himself to be obedient to the Father even unto death (John 2:8). The second half of the poem is Jesus' exaltation as a result of his obedience (John 2:9). His lowly "human likeness" (John 2:6) is contrasted to his victory and exaltation "to the highest place" in John 2:9. The focus is on Jesus' selfless actions in coordination with the Father for the benefit of humanity. Thus, Jesus is given,

> the *name that is above every name*, that at the
>   name of Jesus,
> every knee should bow, in heaven and on earth,
>   and under the earth,
> and every tongue confess that Jesus Christ is *Lord*,
> to the glory of God the Father (Phil. 2:9–10).

What name then is the "name above every name"? The implication here is that the title of Lord (*kyrios* in Greek) is given to Jesus just as it was used for YHWH God; the title implies the sovereign ruler, authority, and power over all of creation. "Lord" was a name used for God when the Jews could not read or write the name of YHWH (see, for example, Ps. 8:9, 110:1; John 20:28). Equal to God in nature, in power, and in purpose (Phil. 2:6), Jesus received the exact same name and position as the Father. As a result, the Son is deserving of the exact same recognition, devotion, and worship as the Father (Phil. 2:10–11). When Jesus said, "For the Father is greater than I" (John 14:28), he was implying that his incarnation as a man placed him in a subordinate position to that of the "heavenly" Father.

Yet his mission on earth was temporary, and he told his followers that when his assignment on earth is completed, he would return to the glory that he had with the Father "before the creation of the world" (John 17:24). Thus, Jesus was "sent" *in the Father's name*—in the exactly the same nature, character, devotion, and intentions as the Father himself (John 5:43). Even so, Jesus' humility, honor, and glory are all done "to the glory of the Father" (Phil. 2:11). This does not imply an order of position or the subjugation of the Son; in fact, it is Jesus' *name* that assures the readers of the Son's eternal divinity, of his "one-ness" with the Father, and of his sacrificial obedience for all of humanity.[105]

Jesus devotion

Therefore, does that mean that Jesus is to be worshiped as another god? Isn't the worship of Jesus in direct opposition to the Jewish theology of *monotheism* (there is only one God to be worshiped)? Did the early believers worship God and Jesus as two different entities or gods?

Prof. Hurtado helps us out again with the concept of an observable "dyatic devotional pattern." That is, a "dyad" is a "pair" in which two individuals maintain a significant sociological relationship, such as a husband and a wife or a father and a son. In the earliest Christian tradition, the risen Jesus is placed right alongside of his Father God in a unique and distinctive manner. In the earliest worship and devotion of Jesus followers, this dyatic pattern is evident and truly remarkable. There are no parallels or predecessors, but the pattern is unmistakably derived from the earliest Christian confessional formulas and divine epithets.[106]

"Jesus Christ" appears to be a key "confessional title" for Jesus that raised him high above any other so-called god of the Roman Empire. However, there is no literary evidence from Jewish literature that the Messiah was expected to be the "Son of God" (see John 7:40–44, 12:34; Luke 3:38). Some have suggested that the recognition of Jesus as the "Divine Son" came late in time, years after Jesus lived on earth, and added to the Gospels by the early church. Yet while the Jewish written evidence is scarce, there is good reason to believe that some people did understand the role of the Messiah to be that of divine sonship. There is a great deal of authenticity given to those passages when Jesus referred to himself as the "Son"—overtly in John 17:1–3—even while Jesus rarely referred to himself as "the Christ." It appears that John fully understood Jesus to be *the* one-and-only "Divine Son" with all the rights and responsibilities that come along with that title (John 1:14).[107]

Logos

The most distinctive Johannine title used to describe Jesus is "*Logos*" (John 1:1, 14). This is a Greek word that literally means "word, speech, matter, reason." Usually translated in English as "word," *logos* is used in all four Gospels, but only in the Fourth Gospel is it used as a title for Jesus. This title is placed within the context of the entire Johannine prologue (John 1:1–18). In his prologue, the Johannine author clearly designates two "identities" of Jesus: the eternal preexistence of Jesus (John 1:1–3) and the reality of his incarnation as God's unique representative on earth (John 1:4–18). The Son has always been God (divine) and *with* God at the same time. The Son shares the eternal existence with God the Father, and as the *Logos*, he is the governing and creative force behind everything. Succinctly, John states that Jesus has existed from eternity, is cocreator with God, is fully divine, filled with divine glory, and is quite simply God (John 1:1–3, 14). The Son came from the Father to make the Father's glory visible on earth. As Father God spoke creation into existence in Genesis (Gen. 1:3, 6, 9, 11, 14, 20, 24, 26), so Jesus, the "Word," "became flesh," to reveal the "glory of God" to humanity (John 1:14). That is, Jesus was sent as a human being to earth (the "incarnation") in a distinguishable form and existence. In the Gospel of John, the author uses vivid language and imagery to help readers identify the One (and *only* One) who is fully divine and yet fully a human being.

In Greek, as in English, the word *the* appears before the title *Logos* in John 1:1; this tiny little word (the article *ó*) indicates that Jesus is not *a* son of God but *the* Son of God. The discourse or the "words" of Jesus are equated with the "words" of God—"full of grace and truth" (John 1:14, 14:24, 17:14).[108] Historically, people have tried to connect the use of *Logos* to either ancient Greek philosophy or to a Jewish wisdom background. Yet "verbal similarities do not necessarily imply conceptual similarities."[109] Reading John 1:1, we learn that the *Logos* was not created by another god; he is *uncreated*. The character and nature of the *Logos* is essentially that of God and is defined as his *Word*.

Jesus is the second Person of the Trinity through whom the world was created and who became "incarnate" as the final Revealer (the "light" in John 8:12), the final Redeemer (John 1:12; see Isa. 54:1–5), and source of life for all of humanity. He is fully human while irreversibly fully divine.[110] As the Revealer, Jesus functions as the "light" which redeems humanity from "darkness" (John 1:14–18; 12:35–36, 46). Jesus is the only One who held the power to reveal the Father to the world—"If you have seen me, you have seen the Father" (John 11:40, 12:44–46).

The Christ

The title of "Son" indicates a personal, intimate relationship with God, while "the Christ" (literally, "the Anointed One") reveals a special commissioning or an appointed task to complete. Jesus was commissioned (or "anointed") to fulfill a very unique mission on earth. The Son, as agent, was commissioned to atone for human sin, to bring "eternal life" to those who believe, and to make other sons and daughters for God (John 3:34–36, 11:52). He never sought glory for himself but said and did whatever the Father commissioned him to do to bring glory to the Father (John 2:11, 7:28–29, 8:50). Only the Son of God, the Anointed One, the One who actually shares the Father's glory, could accomplish such a task (John 4:25–26).

There is little doubt, therefore, in the mind of all the Gospel writers, that Jesus is the Christ, the fulfillment of the Old Testament–promised Messiah (John 1:33; 17:1, 3; 20:30–31). Indeed, the "Messiah" (*Messias*) and the "Christ" (*Christos*) are nearly synonymous titles for Jesus as "the Anointed One," the unique One sent from God (Matt. 16:16; Mark 8:29; Luke 9:20; John 1:41, 4:25, 20:31). In John's Gospel, there is no confession by Peter as to who is "the Christ"; instead, John defined the title "Christ" by using the distinctive epithet "Holy *One* of God" (John 6:69), a title not far removed from Isaiah's reference to God as the "Holy One of Israel."

Son of Man

Even so, Jesus preferred the title "Son of Man" to use for himself, and it is a title used thirteen times in the Fourth Gospel (see John 12:23, 34). In comparison, it is used frequently in Matthew's Gospel, along with the title "Son of David" (Matt. 1:1, 21:9, 22:42). Mark used it less frequently, but Mark's use is very important because Jesus' use of the title "Son of Man" in Mark 14:62 is a vivid image which reflects the prophetic vision in Daniel 7:13–14. In John, the authority to judge humanity is given to the Son by the Father "because he is the Son of Man" (John 5:27, 30).

In some Old Testament passages, such as the prophetic words of Ezekiel, the "son of man" was indeed just a human male figure; in fact, it implied the "frailty of *mere* humanity" (Ezek. 2:1, 3:1, 4:1, 5:1, 6:1, 7:1; Ps. 8:4, 144:3–4, 146:3).[111] However, the identity of "one *like* the son of man" reference in Daniel 7:13–14 is different and highly debated among scholars. The Daniel 7 passage was originally written in Aramaic, so it has been difficult to translate this phrase into English. It is literally translated as "one in human like-ness" (*kebar 'enas*).

This "one *like* a human being" comes "with the clouds of heaven" and "approaches" the "Ancient of Days" (God). Daniel's dream visions are from the perspective of earthly people, kings, and kingdoms. However, God sits enthroned, detached from humanity, as one who sits in judgment—from his "throne-room" (Dan. 7:9–10). The "son of man" appears *with* the "Ancient of Days" and is granted all the "authority, glory and sovereign power" that belongs to God (Dan. 7:13–14). All nations and peoples "worshiped" this individual, and his is an "everlasting kingdom" (Dan. 7:14).[112]

Goldingay points out that the individual in Daniel 7:14 is a human being in contrast to the descriptions of the four animals or "beasts" in the same chapter. If the "mythological beasts" are symbolic of evil human kingdoms (Dan. 7:17), then the "one like the son of man" could be symbolic too, representing a human authority that stands in contrast to the human empires.[113] The four earthly kingdoms are surpassed by an ideal fifth kingdom that is "forever" (Dan. 7:18).

Some scholars suggest that this authoritative figure was, in fact, an angel, perhaps the leader of the angelic host, Michael. Others have suggested that it refers to a man, "Judas Maccabee," the leader of the Jewish rebellion in the second-century BC, who was "like a king" to the Jewish people. The "son of man" could be interpreted as a symbol of a group of people, called "the saints" or "the holy ones of the Most High."[114] It would then refer collectively to godly people who are being oppressed, especially if the article *the* (signally a single individual) is not apparent. In this view, it is not a "direct reference to an individual who is a messiah or a redeemer" but may refer to an eschatological group of people redeemed by God. Hartman contends that it is not a specific title in the book of Daniel but a symbol of the people of God's kingdom.[115]

More likely, chapters 7 through 12 in Daniel emphasize the control of and the devastation perpetrated by the Seleucid ruler, Antiochus IV Epiphanes, around 165 BC (see Dan. 8:22–25). The dream visions recorded in these chapters parallel the dreams in

Daniel 1–6, but the dreams in chapters 7 through 12 are more vivid and more terrifying than those found in the first half of the book. The four "beasts" of Daniel 7 are presumably the images of four evil empires who persecuted "the saints" who worshiped the "Most High" God (Dan. 7:22). These are pictures of the Babylonian empire (Dan. 7:8; 2:36), the Median empire (Dan. 7:5, 5:28), the Persian empire (Dan. 7:6, 5:28), and the Greek empire of Alexander the Great followed closely by the reign of the Seleucid kings (Dan. 7:7, 23–24; 8:20–22). Every detail in Daniel's descriptions were images of the true nature of these corrupt human empires juxtaposed against the "forever" righteous kingdom of God (Dan. 7:27).

If the reference to "one like the son of man" in Daniel is indeed a symbol or a simile describing a single human figure, why did Jesus adopt it as a title for himself? It appears that in the New Testament, Jesus intentionally used the phrase to reveal his own true identity to those who would receive it. He did not use the title as a figurative reference to a group of people who suffered persecution. Perhaps it is because Jesus came to the earth *like* a frail human being "sent" to earth from God as a man to inaugurate the "kingdom of God" or the divine "everlasting dominion." Even so, it can be an "eschatological" title, indicating that Jesus knew himself to be the final Rescuer and Redeemer, the culminating deliverance for *all* people—the oppressed nation of Israel, as well as those people in "foreign" nations for generations and generations to follow.

In Daniel, the prosecuting *adversary* of those who followed the "Most High God" was probably a political world leader who was in direct opposition to God (like Antiochus IV Epiphanes). The opposing kings are pictured symbolically in the ancient records for fear of punishment of the author and/or the Christian community. In Revelation 12:10–12, perhaps written during the time of Roman Empire, we see that the *adversary* is the "accuser"—*Satan* is the Hebrew word for "accuser" (see Job 1:9–11—who "accused" the Christians "before God, day and night," but "has been hurled down."

This fits with the judgment scene in Daniel because the enemy had a "mouth that spoke boastfully" (Dan. 7:11, 20, 25). The fourth "beast" was the strongest and nastiest of all; this empire would "devour the whole earth" (Dan. 7:23). Yet the "Ancient of Days" judges righteously, interrupts the devastation, pronounced judgment on the enemy, and granted an eternal kingdom to those who believed (Dan. 7:11, 12, 22). Thus, Jesus Christ (the "Word" in John 1:1) is ultimately victorious over *all* "boastful," "arrogant" enemies, all *verbal* accusers and adversaries who challenge those who believe in the "One" who stands with God in the heavenly realm.

So by using the epithet "Son of Man" for himself, Jesus was declaring that he was indeed the fulfillment of Daniel's prophecy, the Messiah who came "*with* the clouds of heaven" (as a part of the heavenly realm) to redeem *all* the people of God and give them a righteous, "everlasting kingdom" (Dan. 7:27). Unlike the ancient kingdoms and the first-century Roman Empire, the Messiah's "dominion is an everlasting dominion that will not pass away" (Dan. 7:14). Of course, the ultimate, final victory of the Messiah is still in the future even today, when the Christian church will be God's completed, "everlasting kingdom" on earth (Dan. 7:27).

In the New Testament book of Revelation, the "Son of Man" is unmistakably a title for the resurrected Jesus; the glorified Jesus is "the First and the Last," and "the Living One" (Rev. 1:17–18). This is the picture we see in John 12:23 when the "Son of Man" dies on the cross and is then "glorified." Because Jesus so clearly links his own identity to the Daniel prophecy, it is certainly possible to link the Daniel prophecy to Jesus. In fact, in the Gospel of Mark, the title for Jesus and the title for God are exactly the same names as what we find in the Daniel passage:

> Again the high priest asked him, "Are you the Christ, the Son of the Blessed One?" "I am," said Jesus. "And you will see the Son of Man sitting at the right hand of the Mighty One and coming on the clouds of heaven" (Mark 14:61b–62).

Judgment and the "Son of Man"

In addition, the epithet "Son of Man" from Daniel 7:14 places emphasis on Jesus' divine authority to bring judgment on those who oppose the people of God (John 5:27, 30; 8:15; 17:2). New Testament scholars such as Andrew Lincoln and Richard Cassidy have noted a "trial narrative" theme evident in John's Gospel (see John 5:31–47, 18:19–32, 19:6–7). The first readers of John's Gospel would have been very aware of the Roman court systems and legal proceedings and of the distinct possibility that as Christians, they could be subject to arrest and trial for their belief in Christ as their only "Lord." Despite the real threat of persecution (John 15:20, 16:33), the early believers were committed to holding fast to this truth: that Jesus was the true Lord and Savior of the world and not the sitting emperor.

By referring to himself as the "Son of Man," Jesus was alluding to the promised victory of "the saints" over human oppression, tyranny, and subjugation. It must have been an encouragement to John's original readers to understand that the true Judge and "courtroom" were in the heavenly realms, and those who persevered would see the glory of Jesus (Dan. 7:14; John 17:24). They would be declared faithful in the sight of the only Judge who mattered.

John 13

As a prelude to the Farewell Discourses, John 13:1–20 is a scene that is unique in all of the New Testament, commonly called the foot-washing scene. In this scene, the disciples are attending the last Passover Supper with Jesus. They were understandably surprised and perplexed about the humble, serving actions and attitude of Jesus. The person that they thought to be the One, the promised Messiah, was acting like a common servant. So Jesus explained that it was done to demonstrate the "full extent of the Father's love" for his people (John 13:1). It was Jesus who expressed the Father's love for humanity. It was also done as an expression of selfless service, so it was a prelude to the cross. Jesus insisted that only God can truly "clean" and purify human sin, thus implying his own divinity (John 13:6–11).

Rituals of washing and cleanliness were very familiar to his Jewish listeners as an image of priestly purity before the holiness of God. So Jesus used a picture of physical cleanliness to refer to the spiritual purity of his followers (John 13:10–11). The salvation of believers by God is like an entire bath: God's gift of redemption is totally complete. As a whole bath cleanses the outside body, the one-time act of redemption of God through Jesus cleanses the whole inside of the person. As Jesus said, "You are clean" (John 13:10) if you believe in him (John 13:8b). Yet even "cleansed" believers need to repent *daily* of sins and failures, not unlike Jesus' washing of only one body part. The forgiveness of God through Christ is repeated over and over, just as a parent forgives an erring child time and again.

In addition, Jesus uses two titles for himself that were used by his followers in reference to him—"Teacher" and "Lord" (John 13:13–14). In particular, Peter seemed to like to use the latter title for Jesus (John 13:6; 21:7, 15–17, 21). These two titles succinctly demonstrate Jesus' ministry and purpose. His followers were "right" to grant him such titles because he came to preach and teach, but he also came to humbly serve and lead. This scene demonstrates something new to the listeners, which was the idea that to be a master (John 13:16) and a "Lord" meant to serve and to sacrifice for those whom he loved. Beyond his true identity, the titles in John 13 are also "examples" (John 13:15) of how his followers, especially those who were going to assume leadership in the church, were to follow in his footsteps to teach, to serve, and to love one another. These seemingly common titles were given a deeper, richer meaning, and a new face when applied to Jesus. He promised that when his followers comprehend the fuller meaning of these titles and use them as paradigms in their own lives for the work that was before them, they would be "blessed" (John 13:17). The entire foot-washing scene comes to a climax when the readers fully understand *who* it is that is doing the familiar actions in an unfamiliar way.

Self-Identity

Jesus' "self-designation" as the "Son" was used to teach his disciples and explain his mission on earth which was to "do the work of him who sent me" (John 9:3–4). In defense of his own identity and to rebuke those Jewish leaders who did not believe his words, Jesus said patiently,

> Why do you accuse me of blasphemy because I said, "I am God's Son?" Do not believe me unless I do what my Father does. But if I do it, even though you do not believe me, believe the miracles that you may know and understand that the Father is in me, and I am in the Father (John 10:36b–37).

Thus, Jesus used "the Son" as a description of himself and to focus on his unbreakable link with Father God as One with all the divine glory, power, and authority.[116] After his atoning work and ascension, the designation of "Son of Man" became a title for Jesus as a human figure but with divine purpose and attributes. It fulfilled the prophecy of Daniel as the One who triumphs over evil and who inaugurated the "everlasting" kingdom of God. The readers of the Fourth Gospel would have understood that the Old Testament "Son of Man" was indeed the divine "Son of God" with the same nature and character. By way of example, we can see that the narrative of the "blind man," the Pharisees as told in John 9, is the story of the progressive revelation of the "Son of Man" and his true identity. At the beginning of the story, the disciples called Jesus "Rabbi" (John 9:2). The "man born blind" then identified him as Jesus in John 9:11. Next, the blind man recognized him as a "prophet" in John 9:17. Jesus finally revealed himself to the one who received his sight as "the Son of Man" in John 9:35–38. The Pharisees, with physical sight but with self-seeking authority could not see that Jesus is from God (John 9:13–17, 26). The blind man received physical sight but also received "spiritual sight," or an understanding of who Jesus really is

(John 9:25, 30–33, 38). So the "Son of Man" was sent from God to judge and to give "sight" (comprehension) to the spiritually "blind." The "work of God" is demonstrated by Jesus (John 9:3–4), and those who see Jesus for who he is can *know* that he is from God.

In addition, Jesus speaks as a prophet. He uses predictive words in the Farewell Discourses and in his final prayer. He foretold of his own approaching departure (John 16:5, 17:13) and his postresurrection return (John 16:22). He proposes a new prayer life for his followers (John 16:23), and the coming Paraclete (John 14:16–20, 16:7–11). He also warns of coming persecution of those believers who are "hated" by the world (John 15:18–25, 16:1–4). Jesus' prophetic words that immediately precede the final prayer of John 17 are similar to predictive formulas found in Isaiah: "In that day" (John 16:23; see Isa. 4:2, 28:5, 52:6), "on that day," (John 14:20), and "a time is coming" (John 16:32; see Isa. 54:9–10).

"Son of God" in the Roman Empire

In later Christianity, the "Son of Man" title is virtually eliminated in reference to Jesus. "Son of God," however, has remained stable as a title over the centuries because it has been used in theology and in liturgical worship.[117] Perhaps the title "Son of God" was embraced by the Gentile congregations because of their Roman culture, and the title gained greater distinction in the early centuries over Jesus' more Hebraic self-designation as the "Son of Man."[118]

In the first-century AD, the title "Son of God" was not unfamiliar to the Roman citizens. In fact, Michael Peppard writes that "the father-son relationship was at the heart of all Roman social relationships—the crux of Roman kinship and politics."[119] The social and political focus was primarily on "the figure of the emperor—the first famous 'son of god' in the Roman Empire." The emperor Julius Caesar assumed the title of *divus Julius* (divine Julius) as a formal title of divinity. Although the title *divi filius* (son of the divine) was given to Caesar Augustus during his lifetime, it was not considered a formal title for him until after his death. But Caesar Augustus was honored with temples and public holidays and feasts because the people considered him worthy of worship. In 29 BC, Augustus' name was included in the list of the names of the Roman gods in various hymns. Cities built temples dedicated to the emperor and his family. While none of these actions and events actually deified the emperor, indeed, they are indications of the acclaim, honor, and worship given to the current emperor.[120]

Peppard revealed that it was not unusual for a reigning emperor to "adopt" a son to follow in his political footsteps. It was critical for these "fathers" of the empire to maintain their power and rule by choosing an adopted son, especially if the emperor was unable to produce a male heir naturally. Caesar Augustus, for example, was the "natural" son of the god Apollo and the divine son of Julius Caesar by "adoption."[121] Julius Caesar did not leave any natural-born sons to continue his reign in Rome, so he chose Octavius Augustus to be his "son." "The adoption of adult males helped to stabilize ruling families and formed a key part of imperial ideology."[122] In contrast, as the author of John's Gospel emphasized, Jesus was "begotten" by his Father God; he was not adopted by God as one who would inherit God's kingdom. In the face of human, imperial ideology, John declared the divine nature of "God's only begotten Son" (John 1:14, 3:16).

The writers of the Synoptic Gospels make it certain that Jesus was *not* the biological son of Joseph in their genealogy and birth narratives (Matt. 1:1–16; Luke 3:23). The ancestors in the line of Joseph were indeed in the "Davidic royal line," and this was a line of kings who were "adopted" sons of God (2 Sam. 7:13–14; Ps. 2:6–7, 89:20–27). Jesus, however, was in the line of Adam, the "'created-made' son of God" (Luke 3:38).[123] Obviously, the birth narrative is absent in John and the author preferred to emphasize the unique preexistence of Jesus with his Father (John 1:1, 14) and the "begotten" imagery in place of the "adoption" imagery (John 3:16).

It is interesting to note that the Jewish characters in the Fourth Gospel often refer to Jesus with titles that reflect their own Jewish beliefs: "the Lamb of God" (John 1:29, 36), "Rabbi" (John 6:25, 20:16), and the anticipated "Messiah" (John 1:41). But Pontius Pilate, a key Roman figure in the Gospel, attempts to exert power over the Jews by naming Jesus as their "king." Using great irony, Pilate has written on the placard over Jesus' cross—"Jesus of Nazareth, the King of the Jews" (19:19). As expected, the Jewish leaders, observing the sign, strongly objected to it. Perhaps these were the same Jews who insisted that Jesus be crucified "because he claimed to be the Son of God" (19:7). Furthermore, they may have been the same people who shouted, "If you let this man go, you are no friend of Caesar. Anyone who claims to be king opposes Caesar!" (John 19:12).

Pushed further, the chief priests cried, "We have no king but Caesar!" (John 19:15) in direct opposition to the laws of YHWH God. These insolent, brazen words from the Jewish leaders are unique to the Fourth Gospel. The "royal" scene punctuates the hypocrisy and self-interest of the Jewish leadership, who pledged loyalty to the Romans instead of to their God.

"I am He"

Readers of the Fourth Gospel cannot miss the great "*I am*" (*egō eimi*) statements made by Jesus. While such statements are an echo of the declaration of God concerning his own identity in Exodus 3:14, they more accurately reflect the words of Isaiah in 41:4 and 43:10: "I, the Lord—with the first of them and with the last—I am he," and "so that you may know and believe me and understand that I am he." Again, John alludes to the words of Isaiah where God spoke of himself as, "*I am*" or "*I am he*" in at least nine passages (i.e., John 41:4; 43:10, 13, 25). Thus, John intentionally used these words to connect the identity of Jesus with the God of Israel. John created seven self-description phrases of Jesus that are introduced by the phrase "*I am,*" spoken in the same tone as the words of God in Isaiah. These phrases are emphatic, and they are unique to John's Gospel. They are images and acclamations of Jesus' purpose and identity on earth. Using highly metaphorical language and Old Testament symbolism, Jesus said, "I am the bread of life" (John 6:35, 51), "the light of the world" (John 8:12, 9:5), "the gate for the sheep" (John 10:7), "the good shepherd" (John 10:11, 14), "the resurrection and the life" (John 11:25), "the way, the truth and the life" (John 14:6), and the "true vine" (John 15:1).

Jesus described himself as the essential elements of life: protection, provision, insight, and a full life to those who believe in his name (John 5:43). He specifically proclaimed this phrase in reference to himself before the Jewish authorities in John 8:58. During the events of his arrest, Jesus again clearly declared that "*I am he*" three times before the Roman soldiers in John 18:5–6, 8. The Jews tried to title him a "blasphemer," Pilate tried to title him a "king," but Jesus just said, "*I am HE*."

"The Way" in John 14

One of the most dramatic "*I am*" statements Jesus said to his disciples is, "I am the way, the truth and the life" in John 14:6.[124] As he prepared his earliest followers for his departure from the earth, Jesus described himself with these promises. Both New Testament scholars and Christian readers have taken a variety of approaches to the familiar verse. What did Jesus really mean when he said that he is "the way?" Perhaps it simply means that Jesus is "the way to God." If he is "the way" to the Father, is he the *only* "way?" People today may think that Jesus' words in this verse are very exclusive. They find it to be pejorative, asserting that Christianity becomes a restricted "club" and that Christians are claiming a select, privileged position before God.

In fact, Judaism is also an "exclusive" faith. The early readers of the Fourth Gospel would have recognized a distinct difference between both Judaism and Christ-followers and the plethora of ancient pagan deities. The close covenantal relationship between YHWH God and his people in the Old Testament (Israel) is redefined in the New Testament to include *all* people through the life, work, and atonement of Jesus Christ. God commanded exclusive worship of himself in the Old Testament, and that worship is expanded to include Christ in the New Testament (John 4:21–26). The only way to fully know and love the Father is to know and love the Son, the One sent from God to complete the mission of redemption of all people. This is "the way" God chose to redeem humanity. The plans and purposes of God are not a secret, and they are available to everyone who truly seeks the pathway to a holy and righteous God. Succinctly stated, "He is the way (to the Father), the truth (about the Father) and the life (from the Father)."[125]

Before Jesus' explanation in John 14:6, the word *way* is used in verses 14:4 and 14:5. The familiar expression in 14:6 is a Johannine play on words; that is, Jesus used the word *way* in a manner that was not identical to the customary use known to the disciples (represented by Thomas) in the previous verses. Jesus declared that his disciples *already* knew the "way to the place" in John 14:4. His Jewish followers may have been reminded of the "way" language used by the prophet Isaiah, but they were quite confused by his words. They did not see the connection between the "way" and the "place" of which Jesus spoke (John 14:2–4).

The disciples had just received disturbing news in John 13:33, 36. After years of being with him, Jesus was leaving them, and they could not go with him—at least right away. Jesus used the imagery of Isaiah to reassure his followers that he would not leave them or forsake them, even as he faced his own departure from this earth. The use of *way* in Isaiah 40–55 sets the scene for Jesus' use of "way" in John 14:6. In using the "way" metaphor, Jesus implied much more than the idea that he is "one path or road" to God. That is, Jesus is not saying that he is the *way to* God but that he is the *way of* God. He is the vehicle through which God's people are directed back to the path of God. Jesus used the metaphor of "the way" in the same manner as the prophet Isaiah used it; he reveals himself as the path of redemption so chosen and promised by God.

Isaiah 43:16–21 is a very vivid picture of what God, the Creator, is doing in and for his people. As their Holy One, Creator, and King, God (Isa. 43:15–21) will indeed "make a way" of redemption for the whole nation of Israel to mold them into his holy and righteous people. The "desert" is typically seen in the Old Testament as a place of difficulty and loneliness; certainly, here it is pictured as a "wasteland" with dangerous wild creatures. Human life can be like that: dangerous, threatening, dry, wasted, and empty. How does a person navigate through such a grueling life? Perhaps it would be advantageous to have someone lead the way through the trials and tribulations of this life, saving us from danger and obstacles. Thus, God promised his people that he would create "the way" and provide lifesaving "water" for the thirsty (Isa. 43:20; see John 4:13). He promised to take care of "my people, my chosen, the people I have formed for myself that they may proclaim my praise" (John 43:21).

In view of these promises, the Jewish people believed that the path or the "way" to God was through faith in Yahweh and through strict obedience to his laws (see Deut. 6:17–25). As the years passed, the people established more and more regulations, mandates, and ordinances as the basis of their relationship with God and out of fear of his authority. But the Messiah—Jesus—changed everything. A personal relationship with God did not depend on one's obedience to all the Jewish laws. We remember that the audience to whom John wrote was plausibly more Gentile than Jewish. Thus, John reveals that *Jesus* is "the way" to be in a relationship with God and not the Jewish laws.

Jesus is "*the* way" that God provided for everyone—Jews and Gentiles alike—to know God (John 14:6; Isa. 43:19b). In a manner which he could not have known, Isaiah proclaimed that Jesus is the "new thing" that provides "the way" to "the place" of redemption for everyone (Isa. 43:11–12, 45:21–22). That is, Jesus opened the door to the redemption for all people, which is just the opposite of those who imagine that belief in Jesus is too "exclusive."

The writer of the Fourth Gospel wanted to firmly plant a connection between Jesus' work on the cross and the promised redemption by the prophet Isaiah. Jesus is the redemption and reconciliation that is found in the wider contextual theme of Isaiah 40–55. In Hebrew, a common word for *way* (*derek*) is a synonym for "a path, route, road, journey, conduct," often used as a metaphor for a lifestyle or for life itself (see Isa. 30:21, 35:8, 40:3, 48:17–19, 53:6, 55:8). So Jesus is the "path" to a new, deeper relationship with Father God for the person who believes in him as the Christ. Above anyone or anything else, John presented Jesus as the *new* God-sent vehicle to place all people on the path to salvation and a new life. Redemption cannot be earned or purchased by *any* human being; it is a gift to *all* believers and not merited or deserved. This was a new concept, especially for those who assumed that obedience to God *preceded* his love.

Furthermore, salvation, redemption, and restoration is a gift from the Redeemer God and was not intended to be an exclusive action only for the individual person. In Isaiah, "salvation" is used more in a corporate sense and less for the individual. The entire nation of Israel was in need of salvation and redemption—both physically and spiritually. The community needed to get back into a right relationship with God, and the struggling nation was painfully being molded into the people of God. Jesus is the new way of redemption of individuals as well as a new way to live together—Jews and Gentiles—in a believing community, united together and made one body by a Holy God (John 17:20–21).

The "glory" that Isaiah saw in Jesus was the path of redemption as promised by God for all his people. Unbelief by the Jews in God's chosen vehicle of redemption "blinded" them to the reality of Jesus' atoning work (John 12:38–41). While God remains faithful to the "everlasting covenant" (Isa. 55:3) and brings joy and peace to his faithful people, some of his people strayed from the "path" that he established for them. Thus, God ordained that Jesus is not just a vehicle of redemption for the Jews; he is a part of God's "way-theme" to bring the entire world into "the way of the Lord," which is eternal life with him. Jesus did not come to earth to *show* the way to God; he *is* the way.

Thomas is not the only one who missed this metaphor used by Jesus (John 14:5). Many modern commentators on John 14:6 miss the connection between the Johannine "ways" and plans of God and the prophecies of Isaiah 40–55. Jesus is more than a "way" *to* the Father. He becomes a way of life of his followers *within* the prescribed "path" *of* the Father, and he "goes ahead of you on your journey" (Deut. 1:32). Metaphorically speaking, and in a positive sense, Jesus is the path to a life of obedience and love so lived by his followers. This is what the Jews in the Gospel of John were missing

(Deut. 10:24–25). They did not recognize that Jesus was the fulfillment of the plans, intentions, and promises of God—as spoken by the prophet Isaiah—and the promised redemption for *all* people through the Son and Savior (Isa. 62:11–12).

"Dwelling place"

Chapter 14 of John's Gospel opens with a rich metaphor of a "dwelling *place*" of both the Father and the Son. What does this tell us about the Son? First, Jesus tells his disciples that this "place" is not unfamiliar to them, which appears to be quite mysterious and puzzling (John 14:4). The "place" is God's provision for Jesus' followers after his earthly departure. An "eternal dwelling" designed for God's people was a familiar concept in first-century Judaism (see Luke 16:9). Like the promises of Deuteronomy 1:30–31, Jesus promised his followers that "the Lord your God, who is going before you, will fight for you…[and] you saw how the Lord carried you, as a father carries his son, all the way you went until you reached this place." As promised, "eternal life" (John 3:16) is pictured as an "eternal dwelling" with God.

The Greek word *house* in John 14:2 is fairly common (*oikia*), while the word which is translated as "rooms" in the same verse is *monai*. This latter word in a different form, *monen*, is used in John 14:23; and it can be translated as "room" or "dwelling." Thus, the "eternal dwelling" of God has "many rooms," implying that many diverse people (including the Gentile readers of this Gospel) will have eternal life with God. Furthermore, the person who loves Jesus and obeys his teachings will be loved by the Father, and both the Father and the Son will reside in the "dwelling" with the believer (John 14:23).

This is an odd "house" image for us to imagine, but even more difficult to understand is Jesus' explanation of the fact that Jesus is "in my Father, and you are in me, and I am in you" (John 14:20). Amazingly, God "dwells" inside of people and not in buildings made of stone. In fact, the Father and the Son would "dwell" in his followers forever. Jesus assured his first disciples that he was not really going anywhere; they would not be deserted by him or by the Father. As promised, it is actually the Spirit who would live in his followers after Jesus' resurrection and ascension, and who lives in believers today. In summary, we can say that Jesus is the *way of* God, the *truth of* God's promises, and the "*eternal life*" promised to those who love and obey him.[126]

Ironically, the unbelieving Jews were fearful of losing their physical stone Temple in Jerusalem—also called "my Father's house" (Matt. 21:13; Mark 11:17; Luke 2:49; John 2:16). In contrast, Jesus promised his followers a permanent eternal existence. The physical "place"—the Temple—was indeed lost to the Romans in AD 70; the spiritual place is with the Father and the Son forever. Likewise, today, people worry about frail temporary material things and false security instead of receiving the everlasting perpetual promises of God. Thomas shows that Jesus' metaphor was unclear to his original followers (John 14:5), and he reflected the original readers' uncertainty of the full meaning of Jesus' words. Like many of us, Thomas was looking for his own "road map" or an easy visual GPS to follow to assure him of eternal life.

If the reader sees Jesus as "the way" *of* God in John 14:6, as the divine guidance and divine security in this life, then it follows that the "dwelling place" (John 14:2) is the permanent eternal presence *with* God. Thus, someday, a believer can "also be where I am" (John 14:3), which is in the very presence of God. It is a metaphorical "place" of trust (John 14:1), presence, and preservation for those who understand and receive the full redemptive plan of God through his Son Jesus. In his final prayer with his followers, Jesus said, "Father, I want those you have given me to *be with me where I am* and to see my glory" (John 17:24). The glory of the Son is shared with all believers to unify them all into one church. Such words of encouragement were an assurance to early Christian believers who understood Jesus to be the gracious "way" *of* God and *to* an abundant, eternal life.

Vine-and-branches metaphor

Following the "way" imagery, Jesus immediately gave his disciples another explanation of his identity and his mission. He switches metaphors from the "way" and "place" in chapter 14 to a vineyard in chapter 15. The vine-and-branches metaphor in John 15 is a striking picture of Jesus' words in John 14:6–7. That is, Jesus used the image of the vine to illustrate *how* he is the one "true" life-giving connection between the Father and believers. Instead of struggling to earn the love and approval of God their own way, Jesus promised the growth of a close, intimate connection between believers and the Son that was planned and "tended" by Father God (the "gardener") to give people a fruitful, abundant life. The path *to* God has already been established for us as a fulfillment of Isaiah's prophecies (John 14:4); the path *of* God is his plans for redemption and direction through the promised Messiah.

Because of Jesus, people can truly "know the Father" as never before (John 14:7), they can obey God out of love for him (John 15:10), and can bear "much fruit" (John 15:8) that "will last" (John 15:16). Since God took the initiative to love his people and desires to be in relationship with them, Jesus came to earth specifically to show people how that can be accomplished. Being attached to Jesus as closely as a vine and its branches is the plan and the way of God. The "way" of Jesus in 14:6, indeed, is intended to bring a rich and "joyful" life to those who believe in the Son (John 15:11), not prejudice and discrimination. Jesus, the "true" Savior and vine, is the "way" or path provided by God so that people can "live" and thrive abundantly.

Bearing fruit

In the first-century AD, it was usual practice for young Jewish scholars to choose to follow a particular rabbi and to learn from the older authority. Yet Jesus told his first disciples that *he chose them* to follow him (John 15:16). They were chosen to come after him in his ministry and his mission to preach, to teach, to heal, and to "bear" the "fruit" of the gospel message. Ordinarily, people ask God in prayer for a "fruitful" ministry, but Jesus commissions his followers to go and "bear fruit" first and then God would "give you whatever you ask in my name" (John 15:16–17). While this is unusual, it makes sense that the joy of obedience to the Father and the Son, and "abiding" in God's love would result in successful ministry even before specific requests of God are made.

Glory

The writer of the Fourth Gospel uses the word group of "glory" and "to glorify" more than any of the other Gospel writers (forty-one times); the words are used eight times just in the prayer of John 17 (vv. 1, 4, 5, 10, 22, and twice in 24). The "glory" (*doxa*) of God is his "majesty, splendor," and is often connected to his "honor" or "to give him honor" (*kabod* in Hebrew). The glory of God was displayed in his works, in remarkable acts that only God could do (i.e., the parting of the "Sea of Reeds" in Exod. 14:21–22). His glory is emphasized among the Old Testament psalms and prophets, especially in Isaiah (i.e., Isa. 6:3, 35:2, 40:5, 42:12, 43:7, 66:18). With Isaiah, "glory" is used in the New Testament as a description of the "grandeur" of something, particularly of God or of the matters of God. The author of John's Gospel, however, emphasized the glory of Christ and the present glory Christ brought to his people.[127]

John wrote that Jesus lived in divine glory from the very beginning of time, even before his incarnation (John 12:41; 17:5, 24). His glory was revealed to people in and through his earthly life (John 1:14). Thus, the glory of the Son is his divinity, even as he took on human form. While Jesus glorified his Father (*doxazō*—to glorify, honor, praise—John 17:4), the divine glory is reciprocal, as the Father's glory also belongs to the Son (John 14:13, 16:14–15, 17:24). Since Jesus is of the nature of God, it is natural for him to reflect his Father's glory. This is especially true as shown in the "signs" of the Fourth Gospel (John 2:11, 10:37–38). The glory of the Father is revealed in the life, the actions, and the work of the Son (Isa. 40:5; John 2:11, 15:8). In fact, the crucifixion, resurrection, and exaltation of Jesus reveal his true glory because he completed the mission that he was sent to do.

In giving his life to redeem humanity, Jesus was glorified by the Father and returned to the glory he shared with his Father (John 7:39; 12:16, 23; 20:17). This was a remarkable movement of Jesus from his divine eternal glory to his earthly glory (where he deserved honor and praise) and back again to his divine glory. John repeats the idea of Jesus being "lifted up," which is prophetic of both the physical act of the raising of his cross on Golgotha and the promise of his divine exaltation back to the Father in glory (John 8:28; 12:32, 34). And as the "light of the world," shining in the world (John 9:5), Jesus was the visible, radiant glory of God on earth, just as Isaiah predicted (Isa. 60:1–3). In contrast, those people who did not see Jesus' divine glory and did not believe continued to live in "darkness" (Isa. 60:2; John 9:4, 12:41).

Jesus never sought glory and honor for himself from human beings because it was already given to him by his Father (John 7:18; 8:50, 54). His mission was to inaugurate the kingdom of God on earth and "do nothing on my own, but speak just what the Father has taught me" (John 8:28). In his departure prayer, for the benefit of his hearers, Jesus asked the Father to glorify him "in your presence with the glory I had before the world began" (John 17:5). It is a picture of a shared, reciprocal glory between the Father and the Son, equal in nature, which binds them together in the most profound manner. Glory is both given and received. Believers glorify God, and God gives glory back to his own—not because they deserve it but because the Redeemer Son deserves it.

In his departure prayer, the Son promised to leave an incredible gift for his followers. Believers will not only see the Son's glory (John 17:24), but they will also receive his glory in their own lives (John 17:22)! This is the extraordinary gift of the Holy Spirit that the Father and the Son both "send" to their own (see chapter 5 on the Holy Spirit). The glory of the Trinity is a gift not earned by the believer but is given because the Father loves those who love and obey the Son (John 17:23, 26). The redemption and salvation of Christ for his people is the renewal of the glory that he had from the beginning (John 17:19, 24). Though we cannot see Jesus physically, we can "see his glory" which is the manifestations of the Spirit who was sent by Jesus (John 16:18).

Prayer in "his Name"

Furthermore, it is worth noting that the prayers of faithful believers in the New Testament were primarily addressed to God (Matt. 6:5). But remarkably, many of the prayers of the early Christians were commonly addressed to Jesus as well. Prayers were offered to God but "in his [Jesus] name" or "through" Jesus (Rom. 1:8, 7:25; Eph. 5:20; Col. 3:17; 1 John 2:1). This was a distinctive feature of the early Christians who raised the status of Jesus to that of the Father. The exclusive place of Jesus, equal to God even in prayer, was without parallel or precedent in Jewish practice. John 17 illustrates that as *the* "Son of God," Jesus was the first "advocate" to intercede for his followers to God.[128]

In John 14 and 15, Jesus gives a brief lesson to his followers on *how* to pray. They were instructed to pray "in his name," and he would "do whatever you ask" (John 14:13, 15:16). Consistent with the Old Testament "*name*" of YHWH God, Jesus' "*name*" implies specifically that which is within his extant nature and character. Even so, we need to remember the *context* of Jesus' words. In his final discourses, Jesus addressed his immediate disciples and gave two startling promises to his followers. First, "I tell you the truth; anyone who has faith in me will do what I have been doing. He [or she] will do even greater things than these" (John 14:12). "Greater things" than what Jesus did on earth? Astonishing! Second, in the very next verse, Jesus said,

> And I will do whatever you ask in my name, so
> that the Son may bring glory to the Father. You

may ask me for anything in my name, and I will
do it (John 14:13–14).

Unfortunately, often the first of these promises (doing "greater things") is disregarded, while many Christians have grasped the idea of praying "in the name of Jesus" to get "whatever [they] ask." Because we conclude our prayers with the phrase "in the name of Jesus," it does *not* mean that God is obligated to grant all of our requests. The words of Jesus concerning prayer are often misconstrued and have been used arbitrarily by people who do not know the Father and the Son.

Most adult, thinking Christians know that God does not answer all our prayers exactly as we ask of him, and sometimes we realize that that is a good thing! Remembering the original setting of the Gospel, we understand that Jesus was speaking to his immediate disciples in preparation for his departure from the earth. A few decades later, Jesus' promises on prayer were especially meaningful to the believers to whom the author John wrote. Jesus' first promise was an assurance of the continuation of his ministry by his earliest disciples after his resurrection and ascension and then to the generations of Christians who followed after them. He promised not to leave them; in the power of his Spirit, Jesus' message would expand and grow across Asia Minor and beyond. They would faithfully continue to deliver his gospel message *without* his earthly presence. This was only possible because the followers of Jesus would work to "do greater things" in the power of the Holy Spirit and in prayer that reflected the same quality, integrity, and character of Jesus. The second promise is an assurance that God's Spirit would be with them to empower them to continue his ministry and his work in the world *to the glory of the Father and the Son* (John 14:13).

Matthew 18:19–20

Comparably, in Matthew 18:19–20, Jesus suggests that "if two of you on earth agree about anything you ask for, it will be done for you by my Father in heaven." What does the evangelist Matthew mean in this passage, and is it a different promise than what we see in John's Gospel? It is very different. In context, the entire passage of Matthew 18:15–20 focuses on sin, forgiveness, and Christian correction. Within the community of believers, people are to be treated differently. Christians, aware of what God has forgiven them, should learn to forgive one another within the directives of God. Matthew 18:18 reflects Matthew 16:19b almost word for word and thus requires readers to think about the idea of "binding and loosing."

Jesus was commissioning his immediate disciples to create a new community of believers (the "church") by granting them the authority to "prohibit" and "permit" within the sphere of church discipline.[129] Matthew 18:18 is not unlike John 20:23, where the disciples are given the authority to forgive sins within the church and by the known guidelines of God. Matthew 18:19–20 then repeats the idea presented in Matthew 18:18. Jesus is restating the limits and authority of Christian church discipline. This is *not* a verse that promises that "whenever two or three come together in my name," prayers will be answered in the manner in which we expect God to answer them.

The Greek phrase in Matthew 18:9 is *pantos pragmatos*, translated as "*any-thing*." It was used primarily in "judicial matters" and does not refer to any kind of request but to those matters specifically related to the "forgiving or retaining" of sins within the Christian church (Matt. 18:15–17).[130] However, in John's Gospel, the Greek word *ti* can be translated as "anything" or "whatever." With the verb "to ask" in the subjunctive form the word *anything* refers back to the "*works*" (*érga*) of the Father that Jesus did while on the earth (John 14:10–12). Thus, Jesus declared that "anything" that we ask for him to do *within the work of the gospel*, Jesus will help us do it "so that the Father is glorified in the Son" (John 14:13). In reality, it is the Holy Spirit that empowers the faithful believers to "do greater things" as they ask for his help in the name of the Son to continue Jesus' work on earth. The Christian community, like the original readers of the Gospel, united as the church, is to do that work which Jesus began; and they are not alone in that task.

In addition, in Matthew's Gospel, it is "the church [that] is authorized to affirm or deny acceptance into the new believing community" (Matt. 16:19).[131] This is extremely interesting since the early Christians were pushed out of the Jewish synagogues because of their messianic beliefs, which were considered "sinful" in the eyes of the Jews (see John 9:22, 34–35; 12:42–43; 16:2). The *new* "people of God" were the faithful believers in Jesus, working together to spread the good news of Jesus Christ and not the traditional Jewish gatherings.[132] To assure the advancement of the gospel message, "whatever" believers ask in prayer that continues the work of Jesus on earth and brings "glory to the Father" will be answered by Jesus to empower the body of Christians by his Spirit to spread the gospel message.

Full knowledge and obedience

The "oneness" of the Father and the Son is expressed by Jesus: "I am in the Father and the Father is in me" (John 14:10–11, 20); "all that belongs to the Father" belongs to the Son (John 16:15). Relationships do not get any closer than these expressions. The key to this divine intimacy is truly "knowing" the Father; remarkably, the same intimacy can be experienced by those who truly "know" the Father and the Son. In the prologue, John writes, "No one has ever seen God, but God the One and Only"—that is, Jesus (John 1:16)— "who is at the Father's side, has made him [the Father] known" to humanity (John 1:18). Therefore, to know the Father is to know the Son, and to know the Son is to know the Father (John 14:9–11). In his Johannine prayer, Jesus said that "the world does not know" the Father, but the Son "knows" the Father intimately and believers "know" that the Son was sent by God (John 17:25).[133]

Furthermore, as the divine Son, Jesus is perfectly obedient to the Father's will. The prophet Isaiah foretold of One who is perfectly obedient to God, particularly in his "Suffering Servant" songs. That is, the Servant has a sinless character and does the work of God without faltering. In fact, God sealed his approval on the Son when he said, "I am the Lord, that is my name! I will not give my glory to another or my praise to idols" (Isa. 42:8).

Jesus *already* shared divine glory with his Father before his earthly mission (John 17:4–5, 22). The Son is the only One who received the Father's name and his glory. Jesus did "nothing on his own" (John 5:20, 8:38) but did only that which the Father directed him to do (John 12:49, 14:31, 17:4). Jesus becomes the paradigm of obedience for those people who commit to follow the Father through the Son in the power of the Holy Spirit. Because people know and love God, they "abide" in obedience to him and "remain" in his love. That is, our love for Jesus as the "true vine" is expressed in our obedience to him and to his gospel message (John 14:21, 23). Love, like faith, cannot be separated from obedience:

> As the Father has loved me, so have I loved you. Now, remain in my love. If you obey my commands, you will remain in my love, just as I have obeyed my Father's commands and remain in his love (John 15:9).

Son and shepherd

As the "Good Shepherd," Jesus completes all the metaphors of David's Psalm 23 (John 10:11, 14). The Son "leads" and "guides" his people "for *his* name's sake" (Ps. 23:2–3). Jesus secures "rest" for his followers (Ps. 23:1–2), as well as needed provisions and protection (Ps. 23:5). The Shepherd/King accompanies his people through times of trials and turmoil (Ps. 23:4) and gives them an "overflowing" life (Ps. 23:5). John 10 is a portrait of how important names are to the author of the Gospel. This chapter about the "Good Shepherd" (as Jesus referenced himself) and his "sheep" (Christ-followers) is rooted in the Old Testament metaphors and symbolism of a virtuous caretaker of God's people (John 10:11–18). In the Old Testament, God is named and pictured as the divine "shepherd" of Israel (Ps. 23:1, 80:1; Isa. 40:10–11; Ezek. 34:11–16). As a reflection of God's reign, human leaders were given the task to care for the nation, a task which often was neglected in the nation's history. Human leaders were denounced as "false shepherds" if they did not serve God and protect the people from sin, disobedience, and idolatry (Isa. 56:9–12; Ezek. 34). The name and the image of the "Good Shepherd" reflect Old Testament prophetic traditions about a Shepherd who loves and cares for his "flock."

He is the "gate" (John 10:9) who is the one way to salvation and to the best and eternal life "to the full." The promised "green pastures" (Ps. 23:2) are the same "pastures" found in John 10:9. Because of the Shepherd/Savior, believers will "dwell in the house of the Lord forever" (Ps. 23:6), which is the same assurance from Jesus in John 14:2–4, 23. If Psalm 23 is a prayer of trust in God and a praise for his goodness, then David's words are fulfilled in the promises of the Savior/Son in John's Gospel. The beautiful metaphors of the Old Testament and the New Testament combine to reassure God's people that both the Father and the Son will always be present to protect and comfort their people.

Jesus revealed his true identity to those who would "listen" in John 10:8. He states without hesitation that "*I am* the Good Shepherd." This metaphor punctuates Jesus' own divinity and his "oneness" with the Father. The picture stands in sharp contrast to the other opposite images: hunger, darkness, false shepherds, wolves, hired hands, thieves, and eternal death. In contrast to the "hired hands"—inept, uncaring leaders—Jesus assured his followers that he is the *only* good and divine Shepherd: "I *know* my sheep and my sheep *know* me—just as the Father *knows* me and I *know* the Father—and I lay down my life for the sheep" (John 10:14–15; emphasis mine). Thus, the relationship of the Shepherd to his "flock" reveals accurate *knowledge* of the true identities of the Son and his Father.[134]

In fact, God's people are helpless without a just and righteous Shepherd. The prophet Zechariah created an image of a "shepherd" who would be "struck down" or put to death "and the sheep will be scattered," vulnerable and without a protector (Zech. 13:7; Matt. 26:31). Through this image, Jesus was passing judgment on the "false shepherds," the corrupt Roman and Jewish leadership, particularly the latter (see Jer. 23:1–2, 50:6–7).

John adapted the shepherd images from the Old Testament prophets which would have been well-known to his Jewish readers. While the Gentile readers may not have been as familiar with the "shepherd" image, they would have understood and identified the Romans leaders who did not have their people's best interest at heart. Not only the believing Jews but also "other sheep that are not of this sheep pen" (John 10:16—that is, Gentile believers) would come to believe in Jesus as the Savior and Messiah (John 10:9) and hear his voice.

The Shepherd leads his sheep out the pen *through himself* (as the "gate") until he has "brought out *all* his own" (John 10:4). He "goes ahead of them" and the sheep "follow his voice because they know his voice" and not that of a "stranger" (John 10:4–5). Again, we see that those who understand Jesus' words, *know* him, belong to him, and hear his voice. Indeed, "there shall be one flock and one Shepherd," which is a glimpse into the future Christian church. Both Jews and Gentiles follow one Shepherd (John 10:16; see Ezek. 34:23, 37:24), and all believers listen for *his* voice.

This name assures believers that he *is* the promised Messiah, who correctly loves his "flock," protects them, cares for them, and even "lays down his life" for them (John 10:11, 14). John makes it clear that Jesus used *names*; he called people by their names. People are not just blank faces for Jesus; he knows his followers by their names. He knows his people by their character and their very natures, and he loves them anyway! He demonstrated his own divinity, purpose, nature, and character by using titles or names for himself that his followers would understand. We can also see that the author of John intentionally did *not* name some people in his Gospel. We will give this more consideration later.

The Sent One becomes the Savior

Therefore, the "One sent" by God becomes the Savior of the "flock." The Good Shepherd voluntarily gave his life for his flock; no one took it from him (John 10:11, 14, 17–18). He did not leave his flock defenseless. He is the one who does only "whatever the Father does" (John 5:19–20). He is the giver of eternal life (John 3:16; 5:21; 6:27, 47), the "light of the world" to those who are blind, living in darkness (John 9:5, 39; 12:35–36), the Healer (John 9:36–37), the "Good Shepherd" to the flock of Israel and beyond (John 10:11–18). He is the Servant who washed the feet of those he loved (John 13:13:1–5), the Prophet (John 13:19–20, 16:1–4), the only "true vine" to which believers can cling. He is the "King" who stood unmoved before his enemies (John 18:37–39). He is the "Resurrection and the Life," with authority over death itself, to demonstrate "the glory of God" (John 11:25–26, 40; 20:8–9). Ultimately, he is the Judge, and he is the co-sender of the Holy Spirit (John 16:7) who continues to guide believers and "convict the world" in regard to "sin and judgment" (John 16:8–11).

In summary, the "sending" words of Jesus in the Johannine Gospel reveal who he is: One with the Father, the agent and messenger of God, the One deserving the same honor as the Father, and deeply loved by his Father. He was sent from the Father to do the Father's work of redemption on earth and to form a "people" for himself. He did the Father's will—to teach, judge, and bring peace.

The response then by people is "to believe in the one he sent" (John 6:29), to hear and follow his voice (John 10:3–5), to fully accept him, to give him honor, to obey him, to love him, and *to know God through his Son* (John 10:30). Finally, just as he was sent from God, Jesus has the right and the honor of sending human beings into the world as *his* agents, messengers, and peacemakers so that everyone will "believe in his name" (John 20:21, 31). The "One sent" fulfills his mission and becomes the "Savior."

The Johannine Jesus is presented as a paradox:

> He is the King who chose to wear a crown of thorns.
> He is the Priest who chose to sacrifice himself.
> He is the Prophet who fulfilled the other prophets' dreams.
> He is the Judge who was misjudged by human leaders.
> He was "raised up" even as others "brought him down."
> He is the Suffering Servant who died so that all humanity can live.

Conclusions and responses

Thus, the prayer of John 17 is a *benediction* of his life and mission, spoken by the Son. It was the Son's prayer to the Father but for "the ears" of his human followers—including believers today!—to prepare them for the imminent future and for "eternal life." It is a prayer that reveals the identities, natures, and the characters of both the Father and the Son to people who chose to "abide" in obedience and follow the ways of Christ today.

In the prayer, Jesus asked the Father to bless and protect his faithful followers, *united* together as his church—one "flock"—that they might *return* glory to the Father and the Son. How do we return his glory? We reveal the divine glory by the way we treat other people. First, Christian leaders who truly care for their people must teach and preach *Christ*—not just trendy philosophies on life, selfish financial gain, events in the news, or feel-good ideology. People need to *know* Christ, first as revealed in the biblical texts and then as applied to modern-day contexts. This will have a positive effect on everyone's prayer life. Second, it is imperative that Christ-centered leaders live Christ-centered lives. We must believe and live what we teach without judgment and be examples of the truths we propagate. We share our very lives with people with genuine humility and love. The Apostle Paul wrote to the church at Thessalonica:

> Just as a nursing mother cares for her children, so
> we cared for you. Because we loved you so much,
> we were delighted to share with you not only the
> gospel of God but our lives as well (1 Thess. 2:8).

Most of my adult life, I had a fear of praying in public. I was terrified that someone would ask me to pray out loud at the close of a Bible study or before a family meal and my words would not be eloquent enough. One of my seminary professors set my mind straight when he said that, indeed, public prayer was a simple reflection of private prayers with God. So I learned to walk and talk to Jesus, just like I would a constant companion. I learned to trust his presence, be honest with him, and believe that he really did hear me. Later, when I was called on to pray in a group of people, it was far less scary. I learned by doing; I am less formal, more transparent, and I just reveal my heart. I don't worry so much about using the "correct" words; I try to make the focus on God and not on what I say. My prayers emphasize who *they* are, not who *I* am. With Jesus in John 17, and in humility, we ask only to be a part of the Father's plan and to bring glory to the Father and the Son. Our prayers are *to* the Father *through* the Son and *by* the Holy Spirit (John 14:20, 25).[135]

After the resurrection and the return of Jesus to his initial divine glory, it is the "Paraclete," the Holy Spirit, who is sent by the Father and the Son to indwell believers—to live "within" them. The Spirit helps us to pray and to point us in the "way." After the Son physically left the earth, his Spirit empowers every true believer permanently and eternally, just as Jesus said he would (John 14:17–18). It is to this third Person of the Trinity that we now turn.

Notes

[88] Michael Horton, *Rediscovering the Holy Spirit* (Grand Rapids: Zondervan, 2017), 16.

[89] Ayman S. Ibrahim, *A Concise Guide to the Quran; Answering Thirty Critical Questions* (Grand Rapids: Baker Academic, 2020), 109–110.

[90] Ibrahim, 111.

[91] Ibrahim, 112–115.

[92] Larry H. Hurtado, "Even Higher Christology in the Gospel of John: Frey's Edinburgh Essay," *Word Press*, 2019, https://wp.me/YZXr-2hA, accessed February 19, 2019.

[93] David R. Bauer, "Son of God," in *Dictionary of Jesus and the Gospels*, ed. Joel; Green, Scot; McKnight, and I. Howard Marshall (Downers Grove: InterVarsity Press, 1992), 769–75, 772.

[94] Bauer, 775.

[95] Andreas J. Köstenberger, *John; Baker Exegetical Commentary on the New Testament*, ed. Robert; Yarbrough and Robert H. Stein (Grand Rapids: Baker Academic, 2004), 188.

[96] Bruce Henning, "Jesus as the Rejected Prophet and Exalted Lord: The Rhetorical Effect of Type Shifting in John 12:38–41," *J. Evang. Theol. Soc.* 62.No 2 (2019), 329.

[97] Henning, 329.

[98] Henning, 330.

[99] Henning, 332.

[100] Henning, 333.

[101] Henning, 338.

[102] Henning, 339.

[103] Hurtado, "Even Higher Christology in the Gospel of John: Frey's Edinburgh Essay," accessed May 24, 2019.

[104] Hurtado, "Even Higher Christology in the Gospel of John: Frey's Edinburgh Essay."

[105] Lynn Cohick, *The Story of God Bible Commentary; Philippians*, ed. Tremper Longman and Scot McKnight (Grand Rapids: Zondervan, 2013), 120–124.

[106] Hurtado, "Even Higher Christology in the Gospel of John: Frey's Edinburgh Essay."

[107] Bauer, "Son of God," 772–773.

[108] D. H. Johnson, "Logos," in *Dictionary of Jesus and the Gospels* (Downers Grove: InterVarsity Press, 1992), 481–84, 481.

[109] Johnson, 483.

[110] Johnson, 483.

[111] John Goldingay, *Daniel; Word Biblical Commentary*, ed. David Hubbard et al., Vol. 30. (Dallas, Texas: Word Books, 1989), 168, author's emphasis.

[112] Goldingay, 168.

[113] Goldingay, 168–169.

[114] Louis F. Hartman and Alexander A. Di Lella, *The Book of Daniel; the Anchor Bible*, Vol. 23. (Garden City, New York: Doubleday & Co., 1977), 5.

[115] Hartman, 89–90, 94–95.

[116] I. Howard Marshall, "Son of Man," in *Dictionary of Jesus and the Gospels*, ed. Joel Green, Scot McKnight, and I. Howard Marshall (Downers Grove: InterVarsity Press, 1992), 775–81.

[117] Michael Peppard, *The Son of God in the Roman World; Divine Sonship in Its Social and Political Context* (New York: Oxford University Press, 2011), 10.

[118] Peppard, 15.

[119] Peppard, *The Son of God in the Roman World; Divine Sonship in Its Social and Political Context*, 4.

[120] Peppard, 4.

[121] Peppard, 135.

[122] Peppard, 4.

[123] Peppard, 135.

[124] Köstenberger, *John; Baker Exegetical Commentary on the New Testament*, 428.

[125] Matt Searles, "'These Things I Have Said to You': An Investigation of How Purpose Clauses Govern the Interpretion of John 14–16," *JETS* 60.3 (2017): 511–32., 516.

[126] Kostenberger, *John; Baker Exegetical Commentary on the New Testament*, 426–427.

[127] G. M. Burge, "Glory," in *Dictionary of Jesus and the Gospels* (Downers Grove: InterVarsity Press, 1992), 268–70.

[128] Larry Hurtado, "Jesus in Early Christian Prayer," *Word Press*, 2013, http://wp.me/pYZXr-r6, accessed April 14, 2018.

[129] Craig L. Blomberg, *The New American Commentary; Matthew*, ed. gen. ed. Dockery, David, vol. 22. (Nashville, Tennessee: Broadman Press, 1992), 254, 281.

[130] Blomberg, 280.

[131] Köstenberger, *John; Baker Exegetical Commentary on the New Testament*, 576.

[132] Köstenberger, 576.

[133] Bauer, "Son of God," 772–775.

[134] Köstenberger, *John; Baker Exegetical Commentary on the New Testament*, 306.

[135] Horton, *Rediscovering the Holy Spirit*, 224.

Chapter 5

The Johannine "Paraclete"

Imagine what it would be like to have a task given to you by your boss, but no one gave you anything to help you complete the task. You were told to write a list of e-mails, for example, but no one gave you a computer or told you how to tap into the internet. How frustrating! Imagine then a god who tormented his people with a long list of rules and regulations and expected them to follow all of them without any guidance or help.

Our God, however, has granted us endless help in living the kind of life that he requires of us. This "Helper" is the Holy Spirit. Only a gracious, loving God would set boundaries for his people (for their own good) and then give them the means by which they can live within them. The fourth unique and distinctive epithet used by the author of the Fourth Gospel in the Farewell Discourses is the "*Paraclete*." Father and Son are understood as "Persons," but who is this mystical Spirit? What is his role and function in our everyday lives?[136]

Michael Horton contends that Christians today tend to "depersonalize" and "marginalize" the Spirit in our teaching, preaching, and even in our prayers. Indeed, the Spirit may be the least understood and the most ignored Person of the Trinity. Often, church songs and liturgy refer to him as the "Holy Ghost," so there is little wonder why people (especially children) avoid interaction with this mysterious "apparition." Craig Keener suggests that there are some churches that ignore a "vast number" of passages that speak about the Spirit, while other churches "experiment" with spiritual experiences and "neglect the biblical foundations and safeguards for such experiences."[137]

Thus, Horton writes,

> Like the cry of a child at birth, the first springs of prayer are that of dependence, lament, need and trial. Prayer is the filial cry of the child. But one day there will be no more prayer, any more than there will be preaching and sacraments. We will no longer lament, invoke, weep, confess, or long in an inchoate way for the "new song" that God has written for his symphony. It will be the everlasting song in the immediate presence of the Father, in the Son, by the Spirit.[138]

What is a paraclete?

The Greek word *paraklētos* literally means "one who is called alongside." In particular, it refers to someone who assists alongside someone else in a judicial situation. In the courtroom, it is an advocate or defense attorney who sits next to the accused. Thus, *advocate* seems to be the best English translation of the word. Other English versions use the translation of "Counselor," "Helper," "Exhorter," (from the word *paraklēsis*) or "Comforter" (taken from *parakalein*—"to encourage"). However, these translations lose the important functions of the One called the "Paraclete," who is the Holy Spirit, the third person of the Trinity. Indeed, "comfort" and "encouragement" are included in the roles of the Holy Spirit, but to understand the Holy Spirit as *only* a "Comforter" is misleading and limits his role and functions. The Paraclete is so much more than one who grants people comfort, ease, and contentment in this life.[139]

The gift of the Paraclete is a promise made by Jesus; he makes it a point to say that the Holy Spirit is "*another*" Advocate, "of the same kind" as himself. Both Jesus and the Spirit are "sent" into the world by the Father (John 3:16–17, 5:43, 16:27–28). Both are involved in the process of "rebirth" or regeneration (John 3:5–6, 8). Both are characterized by "truth" (John 1:14; 14:6, 17; 15:26; 16:13). Just as Jesus reveals his Father and bears witness to him (John 1:18, 4:25–26), so the Spirit witnesses to and reveals the glorified Son (John 15:26–27, 16:13–14). The role of Spirit could be considered "legal" (John 14:16, 16:7–8) because the Advocate sustains believers no matter what so that they can be assured of his guiding presence. As a picture, the "legal" redemption secured by Jesus is implemented *for* us and outside of us while the Spirit's transformative restoration part is carried out *within* us.[140] The close interrelating between Jesus and the Spirit can be called *perichoresis* or the mutual indwelling of the persons. It is the inseparable, "incomprehensible," "eternal and immutable" relationship between the Father, Son, and Spirit.[141]

The Spirit, moreover, is a unique Person and not just an "energy force" or a mystical apparition. He is fully God, and he is fully "Lord." The Spirit is neither inferior nor subordinate to the Father and the Son. While Andreas Köstenberger names the Paraclete the "Other Helping Presence," Michael Horton writes that there is "distinction without division":[142]

> The Father sent the Son, and the Spirit clothed
> the Son *in our nature*; the Father and the Son
> sent the Spirit *into our hearts*, regenerating and
> uniting us to Christ, the living vine.[143]

The Spirit is described by various biblical names, such as: "Spirit of God" (Gen. 1:1; 1 Sam. 10:10), "Spirit of grace and supplication" (Zech. 12:10), "Spirit of the Lord" (Judg. 6:34, 11:29, 13:25), "Spirit of Life" (John 6:63; Rom. 8:2), and the "Spirit of Truth" (John 14:17, 16:13). Note the English word *of* in the proper titles, implying a description of the Spirit. Perhaps the most familiar name, simply the "Holy Spirit," has become a title as well as a description (Matt. 28:19; Acts 2:38, 4:31, 6:3, 8:15; Rom. 15:13). In fact, the Spirit is titled and described so many times in the Bible that modern readers have become unaware that the titles all relate to one Person who has existed since eternity past (Gen. 1:2), who has many functions and duties and who executes and completes the plans and purposes of God. The presence of the Holy Spirit is quiet and calming, not loud and boisterous in individuals and in the corporate church. Sometimes, we forget that he is even there—until we need him. Jesus attempted to convince his closest followers that his departure was for their benefit (John 16:7). In exchange for his physical presence *beside* them, he would send the Holy Spirit to live *in* them (John 14:20).

It is the task of the Spirit to make known and to decipher the words and the work of the exalted Jesus because they are of the same nature, character, and kind. Jesus came to earth to give life to humanity (as we see in John 1:4, 3:15, 5:21, 6:40, 10:10, 14:6, 17:2–3, 20:31), and so does the Spirit (John 6:63). The coming of the Holy Spirit at Pentecost (see Acts 2:1–4) is parallel to Jesus' incarnation; both are the piercing entrance of God into the earthly human world. Both the Son and the Spirit are deserving of human worship (John 4:23–24). The Spirit reveals the knowledge of and the truth about the Father and the Son. The unity of the Paraclete and the Son is so strong that Jesus can speak *as if* he himself will continue to be with his people in his human form (John 14:16–20). The Spirit is the "permanent replacement" for the Son on earth. The Spirit takes over where the incarnated Jesus left off, so to speak.

The words of a person in his/her last will and testament do not go into effect until after that person's death. So the Farewell Discourses in the Fourth Gospel are Jesus' last testament, his last promises, and his plans and purposes for his followers that would be completed by the Holy Spirit after Jesus returned to the Father:

> The Holy Spirit glorified Christ himself, in his person decisively and publicly, by raising him from the dead. The Spirit who had been responsible for uniting the eternal Son to our humanity now raised him from the dead and clothed him in immortal glory as the first specimen of the new creation. The Spirit ensured that the incarnate Son who abased himself for us would recover the

glory that he had with the Father before all the ages (John 17:22–24).[144]

John 7:37–39—Living Water

By way of historical background, we realize that the Jews knew from their Scriptures that the Spirit of God filled special people for a short time to fulfill a special task. Yet "on the last and greatest day" of the Feast of Tabernacles, Jesus promised his followers "streams of living water will flow from *within* [them]" (John 7:38). What does this "living water" symbolize? The Johannine author explained to his readers that "by this he meant the Spirit, whom those who believed in him were later to receive. Up to that time the Spirit had not been given, since Jesus had not yet been glorified" (John 7:39).

The "Feast of the Tabernacles" (or the "Feast of Booths") was an important week of celebration that reminded the Jewish people of God's abundant provision to the nation during the time that they wandered in the wilderness (Lev. 23:33–43). Streams and moving water (often a rare sight in the Israelite desert) symbolized God's flow of care and rich legacy for his people physically and spiritually. But the nation rejected him as their Lord, and he was forsaken for the idols of other nations (Ps. 46:4, 65:9; Jer. 2:13–19; Ezek. 47:1–12; Joel 3:18–21). In view of the past sins of the nation, water was poured out at the Temple during this feast, symbolic of life-giving rain (Zech. 14:16–19) and of God's flowing abundance. In a spiritual sense then, water became a symbol of the future age to come and a hope for the Lord's salvation of his people from "drought" and oppression from pagan nations. Once again, God would inhabit the Temple and reign over all his people:

> On that day, living water will flow out from Jerusalem, half to the eastern seas and half to the western sea, in summer and in winter. The Lord will be King over the whole earth. On that day,

there will be one Lord and *his name the only name* (Zech. 14:8–9).

The "*only name*" for God was given to Jesus, who was sent *in the name* of his Father to give life to humanity (John 1:14; 10:30, 34–38). The Spirit gave physical life to Jesus and resurrected him from death to life. In the same sense, the Spirit gives *spiritual* life to those people who believe in the Son (John 7:38–39). "Eternal life" for believers is both present and future, initiated by Jesus and empowered by the Spirit. After Jesus was glorified and he returned to the Father, the Holy Spirit of God came to rule and reign *within* his people (John 7:38–39). In the Gospel narrative, Jesus' earliest followers had not yet experienced the work of the Holy Spirit, but later, we can assume that most of John's readers had received the Holy Spirit as believers. They had experienced his work in their lives, and so the "living water" symbolism would strike a chord of refreshing recognition.

New Testament scholar Prof. Jörg Frey comments that the Johannine author placed strong emphasis on the "Spirit-Paraclete" and observed that the author gave a "noticeably personalized role and status" to the Spirit. In Frey's judgment, the Fourth Gospel presents the Father, Son, and Spirit "in a more vividly personal union" compared to the other Gospels. In addition, the Gospel of John shows the "post-resurrection revelatory work of the Spirit" to a greater extent than what is presented in the Synoptics, which makes sense if the Fourth Gospel was written years later. The development then of the Spirit in John's Gospel reflects a Christology and a belief in the Paraclete that has "no precedent or parallel" in either Jewish or Hellenistic religions. The risen Jesus is placed next to God the Father in a characteristic manner, and the Spirit is presented as a part of the triad, uniquely different from any presentation of God's spirit in the Hebrew Bible.[145]

The Paraclete Discourses

The promises concerning the Spirit spoken by Jesus in his Farewell Discourses, in his departure lessons, assure and prepare his followers for their own missions and ministries to come.[146] Three passages within John's Farewell Discourses are unique in all of the New Testament, and they introduce both the identity and the purpose of the *Paraclete*/Holy Spirit: John 14:15–28, 15:26–27, 16:6–11. We will look at these specific passages within their contexts.

John 14:15–28

This is the first lesson that introduces the Paraclete. Chapter 14 is a very tightly woven passage, permeated with literary metaphors and images. The hasty departure of Judas (John 13:30) opens the door for Jesus to discuss his own departure. It is understandable that the remaining disciples would be confused. Jesus' departure was not literally a geographical "exit," so Jesus had to explain his "going" (John 14:4, 28). The chapter is bracketed by Jesus' repeated words of reassurance: "Do not let your hearts be troubled" (John 14:1, 27). The disciples did not need to be "troubled" for two reasons: first, they would be intimately connected to the Father and the Son, even as Jesus went away from their presence (14:20). Second, because Jesus had to go away, the Holy Spirit would be with them on a permanent basis. In fact, the Father and the Son would "come and dwell" *in* the believers, and "make their home" with them (John 14:2, 23). The disciples were instructed to "trust" and "believe" in Jesus because the startling events regarding his departure were certain and inevitable, if not inconceivable (14:1, 11, 29). Jesus reassured his followers by the linked themes of love and obedience. Belief in the Father and the Son means loving and obeying them (John 14:15, 21, 23–24). Jesus promised that this love is reciprocated, as the Father loves those people who love and obey the Son (John 14:21).

Yet the primary focus of chapter 14 is on the Paraclete, the so-named "Counselor" and the "Spirit of truth" in the NIV (John

14:16–17). The Spirit is a pledge to those who already know Jesus that they will continue to "see" and "know" him because he will live "*in*" them *in the form of the Spirit* (John 14:17–21). Furthermore, "the Spirit of *truth*" shines his light on Jesus so that, *with veracity*, believers will be assured of his continuing presence, even if he is not physically with them (John 14:17–19, 28).

This section on the Spirit is also bracketed by Jesus' words: "If you love me" (John 14:15, 28b). If his followers would receive his words with truth and belief, they would then obey his words *in love*. Within this passage, three roles of the Holy Spirit emerge which encourage those who believe: first, the Spirit is a "teacher of all things," not unlike Jesus himself. The Spirit does not, in fact, uncover startling new or private revelation apart from Jesus' words, but he gives understanding to the true meanings of Jesus' words. The Jewish rabbis, of course, highly valued the role of a teacher who could explain and apply the biblical texts. It was not unusual that Jesus was addressed as a "Teacher" (John 13:14) and recognized as a "Rabbi" (John 3:2) during his earthly ministry, and the Spirit continues this teaching role.

Second, the Spirit "reminds" Jesus' followers of "everything" Jesus taught them (John 14:26). Some scholars observe that teaching and recollection are the one and the same, and that may be true. Again, in the Jewish culture, "remembering" was an important part of their tradition.[147] Certainly, these two roles do complement one another; if only we could remember everything we are taught!

Believers can "*know*" that the Spirit of truth lives within them, bringing Jesus' words to their remembrance and giving needed guidance on how to interpret those words and obey them. Because the Spirit lives within his followers, Jesus promised that they will never be alone in the navigation of this world (John 14:18–19a). This is both conviction and assurance that the very presence of the Spirit helps believers to continue to know the truth, to love Jesus, to obey his "commands," and to remember his words. Even today, the Spirit has an impact on how one "sees"—and "knows"—biblical truth. It is the task of the Holy Spirit to teach and to remind writers, readers, and teachers of the words of the Father and the Son now available in our written texts.

Third, the Holy Spirit is the one who brings "peace" and the absence of fear even during troubled times (John 14:27). John 14:27 expands on John 14:1 because Jesus was leaving a kind of peace that overcomes human "troubles." This is not the kind of peace that was promised by the Roman Empire in the first-century AD ("*Pax Romana*"). Roman "peace" was actually an illusion imposed on ordinary people by the elitist few, who engaged in greed, violence, and military strength. The peace brought by the Spirit does not depend on outward circumstances; it is composure, confidence, and grace even in times of conflict (see John 15:18–25). The Father "gives" the Spirit to the believers in John 14:16, but the Spirit is also sent "*in the name* of Jesus," whose name brings peace to his people (John 14:26; 20:19, 21–22). The horrific events of Jesus' passion would terrorize his first followers. For the earliest disciples, his impending departure would mean great sadness, grief, confusion, and fear.

The "prince of this world" would invade their lives in ways they could not imagine (John 14:30; see John 17:12). Indeed, for the later readers of the Gospel, those in John's congregation, opposition from the Jews (John 14:29; 16:2–4) and from the surrounding Roman culture cast uncertainty, fear, and doubt over the young church. But the presence of the Holy Spirit in their midst brought a "peace" that was unknown to the "world"—the peace of the Spirit (John 14:27). In summation, Jesus concluded this discourse by saying that he revealed "all this" to his followers so that they would *know* the Father, "believe" in the Son, and anticipate the Holy Spirit (John 14:25, 29).[148]

John 14: Imagery

To his earliest followers, Jesus made paradoxical promises: Before long, the world will not see me anymore, but you will see me. Because I live, you also will live. On that day, you will realize that I am in my Father, and you are in me, and I am in you (John 14:19–20).

John, then, created two visual images in an effort to make known the purpose of the coming Spirit. First, Jesus spoke of a remarkable "triangle": the Son is *in* the Father, and the believer is *in* the Son, and the Son is *in* the believer, in the form of the Spirit (John 14:19b–20). In John 14:10–11, we grasp the unity of the Father and the Son, while in John 14:19–20, the believer is part of that unity through the gift of the Spirit. Jesus provided a picture of *how* he would remain with his followers—that is, as the Spirit (John 14:12, 28–29). This is a "triangle" image of the Father, Son, and Spirit-filled people who all "live" in the Spirit instead of in the "world" (John 14:17). Furthermore, the image shows that it is possible for people to return the love of the Father back to him in obedience to the Son (John 14:2, 23–24). Being a part of this triad, the believer is secure in the teaching and reminding of the Spirit and can rest in his peace.

John employed a second image by using a "house" (*monē*) or a "dwelling." This is a picture of Jesus "dwelling" in the Father and the Father "dwelling" in the Son (John 14:10–11). In his full humanity, Jesus "made his dwelling among us" (John 1:14); the Greek word used here for "to dwell" (*skēnoō*) means "to pitch one's tent." It has its roots in the Old Testament word that is translated "to tabernacle." In Leviticus 26:11, God pledges to "put my *dwelling place* [my tabernacle] among you…I will walk among you and be your God, and you will be my people." This is the essence of "covenant" that the God of the universe agreed to take up residence among his people. If the people upheld their end of the covenant, then the nearby presence of Yʜwʜ was their reward for obedience (Lev. 26:1–13). In a similar manner, Jesus promised that his followers would know the presence of God in their midst. They would be "dwelling" all together in a "house" with both the Father and the Son (John 14:2, 20, 23b). Eugene Peterson, author of *The Message*, pictures it this way: "The Word moved into the neighborhood."[149] A "dwelling place" in the ancient world implied a permanent fixture, filled with good things, as opposed to a transportable tent with sparce furnishings (see Deut. 6:10–12). Thus, the indwelling Holy Spirit in the life of a believer grants him/her a share (or a "room") in this loving, permanent, triangular relationship with the Father and the Son.

John 14:23 may be the only place in the New Testament where both the Father and the Son are said to "indwell" the believer.[130] Again, the "dwelling place" is not a geographical location or a physical building; it is not a "condo" in heaven that is "prepared" for us based on our human merit. It is a metaphor that explains the gift of the indwelling Holy Spirit who resides in believers on a permanent basis and is a key source of blessings.

John 15:26–27

To clarify, an illustration of the "triangle" relationship with believers is seen in chapter 15. Jesus instructed his followers to "remain in me"—but how is that possible if he is leaving? How do believers "remain" in Jesus? In the first section of chapter 15, the readers can see the mutual loving relationship in the picture of the "vine and the branches." It is possible for Jesus to remain *in* the believer in the form of the Holy Spirit (John 14:17, 20) so that believers can "remain" (or "abide") in him (John 15:4). Together, the believer and the Holy Spirit will "bear much fruit," yet without the guidance of the Spirit, people "can do nothing" (John 15:5). The "vine and branches" imagery was a positive assurance to his disciples who were about to embark on their own ministries after the death and resurrection of Christ.

They were reassured not only of Jesus' continual presence (in the form of the Holy Spirit) but also of his great love for them. Jesus gave two commands to his followers to "remain" in this relationship: they were to love him and obey his "words"—his teachings and commands (John 15:7, 9). By following his commands, his followers became his "friends," and serving Jesus would become a voluntary privilege, not a duty (John 15:14–15). Love and obedience go hand in hand, such that the person who loves and obeys Jesus experiences "much fruit" in a godly, productive life and ministry, as well as complete "joy" (John 15:11).

In fact, the disciples did not choose to follow Jesus; he chose them (John 15:16). He chose them for a distinct purpose—that purpose was to demonstrate the loving, "abiding," empowering relationship that existed between the members of the divine Trinity before the world began. Thus, those people who love and obey Christ are to exhibit this deep, mutual trinitarian love by loving one another (John 15:12, 17):

> The eternal love of the Trinity is to be manifested to the world by the disciples who have been brought into this Trinitarian love. Given the relational nature of the whole of the Farewell Discourse, it is entirely appropriate that the central section focuses on the love of the Father for the Son, the love of the Son for his people, and that the purpose of this section is that the disciples—who have been brought into this Trinitarian relationship—should love one another.[151]

In addition, Jesus spoke twice about *prayer,* which is an important aspect of this remarkable relationship. If it were not so, Jesus would not have engaged in the practice of prayer with his Father (see Matt. 14:23; Luke 3:21, 6:12, 9:29). Initially, those people who "remain in Christ" *pray* appropriately, knowing and believing the "words" of Jesus (John 15:7). Being filled with the Holy Spirit, believers can ask "whatever they wish" with respect to holy living and ministry, and their prayers will be answered "to the Father's glory" (John 15:7–8). In the context of his passage, answered prayer is linked to the idea of "bearing much fruit." That is, God is glorified by answering the prayers of those people who "remain" in Jesus, guided and directed by his Spirit to do the work and the will of God. This excludes the self-centered, self-glorifying prayers of people who demand from God anything outside of what is appropriate for Jesus' disciples (John 15:8).

Next, Jesus chose his followers for the purpose of living lives that would bear "eternal fruit"—"fruit" that would "last" (John

15:16). The immediate disciples were chosen to continue the mission and the ministry of Jesus after his departure from this earth. They were "appointed" to spread the gospel in the world which would not receive them well (John 16:16,18). Prayer would be a very critical aspect of their ministries as they preached and taught in a hostile worldly environment. Jesus chose to encourage them by saying that their prayers would be answered, guidance would be given, and the "abiding" Spirit would empower them in their ministry tasks. The author of the Fourth Gospel was actually doing exactly what is expressed in this verse (John 15:16). He was chosen and appointed to write an account of Jesus' life and ministry so that many people would come to *know* Jesus would "believe" and experience "eternal life" (John 22:31).

Finally, Jesus promised that "when the Spirit comes [that is, after Jesus' exaltation]…he will testify about me" (John 15:26). Certainly, a major role of the "Spirit of truth" is to reveal and testify concerning Jesus Christ—who he is and what he did for humanity. In chapter 15, the role of the Spirit is to bear witness to the true nature of the Son and to the veracity of his words and works. The Spirit emanates from the Father to believers to verify everything about the Son (John 15:26; see also John 16:13). In spite of the witness of the Spirit, there are those people who refuse to receive the truth about the Son. The result is "hatred" from "the world" toward those who do *know* the truth of Christ (John 15:18–19). Sadly, the hatred toward believers was due to the *lack of knowledge* of God (John 15:21–25, 16:3). Even though Jesus clearly revealed the Father to the Jews, who already knew the Old Testament, their rejection of Jesus was without "excuse." Hatred flared up into the "persecution" of the believers (John 15:20–21).

This must have spoken directly to John's congregation as well; the readers experienced stressful opposition in the Roman Empire, as well as rejection from the Jews, for their faith in Christ (John 16:1–3; see John 9:22). Thus, the Holy Spirit brought to their remembrance the pain and sorrow Jesus went through at the hands of his enemies *for* them (John 15:18), as well as his warnings *to* them (John 15:20). Jesus' immediate followers could endure the hatred of their enemies because the Spirit would be present in their lives. There would be a direct connection in prayer so that they would be empowered to accept the responsibility of testifying about Christ. Positively, the Spirit would help all the early believers to boldly testify to the truth about Christ (John 15:27) within their respective antagonistic cultures.

John 16:6–16

The third significant discourse in John concerning the Paraclete is in chapter 16. Knowing the persecution that was ahead of them, Jesus continued to prepare his disciples by saying, "*All this I have told you* [chapter 15] so that you will not go astray…I have told you this so that when the time comes, you will remember that I warned you. I did not tell you this at first because I was with you" (John 16:1, 4; emphasis mine). Then, Jesus opened a new discourse (John 16:1) with warnings for his followers after reassuring them of the coming promised *Paraclete* (John 15:26). The Holy Spirit would be with them to keep them from doubt and apostasy—going "astray"—in the midst of hatred, persecution, and uncertainty.

Regardless, they were "filled with grief" at the thought of his departure (John 16:6). He warned them about future events so that "when it happens," they would not turn back in their faith but continue in belief (John 14:29) and "remember" everything that Jesus had taught them (John 16:4). Jesus told his disciples that it was for their benefit that he had to leave this earth (John 16:6–7), which was even more confusing to them. Jesus unfolded the reality of the Spirit and declared that the Spirit would "convict the world." Although the Spirit indwells *believers*, this is a passage about the work of the Spirit on *unbelievers*. For those people, the Spirit is not a "Comforter"; he is a "Convicter." After Jesus' departure, it is the Spirit's job to:

> Convict the world of guilt in regard to sin, because men do not believe in me. Convict the world in regard to righteousness, because I am going to the Father. Convict the world in regard

to judgment, because the prince of this world
now stands condemned (John 16:8–11).

As such, the Spirit is not a picture of a "harmless dove" but of
the sovereign God who brings about stern judgment.[152] While most
of the words in the New Testament concerning the Spirit are for
believers, this passage is a promise to "the world," which is John's
shorthand name for "those who do not believe in me" (John 16:9).
Certainly, conviction and condemnation are not comfortable; but
the promise is that, ultimately, righteousness wins and evil in the
world *already* "stands condemned" (John 16:11).

Once more, we see that the verb "to convict" has judicial over-
tones. In Greek, *elegchō* means "to expose, to convict, to cross-exam-
ine for the purpose of convincing or refuting an opponent, especially
in legal proceedings."[153] Behind every believer stands an "accuser"
(Satan) or a "prosecutor" ("the prince of this world" John 16:11) who
is trying to defeat the righteousness of God everywhere. It is "the
accuser" that deceives believers, convicts wrongly, and showers guilt
without cause.

Thankfully, it is the Spirit who stands with us against such
evils, supporting and helping God's people to "rebuke" known sin
and malice. The Spirit is the "conscience" of the faithful, showing
us where we have misjudged, transgressed, and fallen short of what
we know to be acceptable to God. This passage warns that the Spirit
will be less forgiving for unbelievers because he cannot help those
who refuse to believe. At times, he may be a "defender"; but at other
times, it is the Spirit who prosecutes the sin, unrighteousness, and
injustice in the world. Indeed, the unbeliever's life of temptation
and struggle is similar to the experiences of the Israelite nation, wandering without God's Spirit. Those who do not know Jesus do not
know the Spirit, nor do they see themselves as sinners (John 14:9, 17;
15:21; 16:3; 17:7, 25).

It is the Spirit who acts on unbelievers to bring them to the
point of repentance, acceptance, reconciliation, and belief. Yet the
Apostle Paul wrote that even believers can "grieve" the Spirit, refus-
ing his help and advocacy to their own detriment (Eph. 4:30; see Isa.

63:10). The Spirit can be ignored; and believers can find themselves involved in "every form of malice" including "unwholesome talk, bitterness, rage and anger, brawling and slander" (Eph. 4:29–31). Sin, especially in the lives of his people, brings "grief" to God and to his Spirit.

In John 16:12–15, Jesus again addressed the role of the Holy Spirit for those who believe. The promises in this section were first given to the disciples who were left to carry on the gospel message after Jesus' return to the Father. For Jesus' earliest followers, the coming Spirit was the anticipation of the extraordinary events of Pentecost which were "yet to come" (John 16:13). The "Spirit of truth" does not disclose any "new *gnosis*" or "secret" words of wisdom to Jesus' followers.

The Spirit speaks only "what he hears" (John 16:13) in the same pattern as Jesus, who spoke only what he received from the Father (John 8:26–28, 15:15, 17:7–8). In fact, the Spirit does not put himself into the spotlight; he shines his light on Jesus, revealing all of Jesus' glory to humanity, which was given to the Son by the Father. All the Father's wisdom, knowledge, character, nature, love, and *glory* belongs to the Son (John 16:15, 17:4). Then, the Spirit takes all of that which "belongs to Jesus" and makes it "known" to the believers (John 16:14–15, 17:25–26). Those people who "accepted" the teachings of Jesus and "knew with certainty" the divine origin of Jesus, believed by faith through the revelation of the Spirit (John 17:8).

> The "new creation" inaugurated by the Son is carried out by the Holy Spirit: Creation exists from the Father, in the Son, by the power of the Spirit; in the new creation Christ is the head while the Spirit is the one who unites the members to him and renews them according to Christ's image to the glory of the Father. The Father works *for* us, the Son works *among* us, and the Spirit works *within* us.[154]

The gracious presence of the Holy Spirit in the lives of human beings gives people dignity. We are all God's creation, and he highly values humanity. Remarkably, he has chosen to indwell us by his Spirit. If that were not so, he would never have sent his Son to die for us, nor would he have sent the Spirit to constantly guide and direct us. He does this because of his unfailing love for us (John 14:21, 17:26).

The Spirit's mission and ministry

The *Paraclete* is a title of *function*; it tells us what the Spirit *does*. The visual signs of the Spirit are always life-giving, healing, edifying, and restoring. It seems that John picked this title intentionally to reassure his readers that the Spirit is *doing* something special for them. The Spirit should not be known *only* by his distinctive work (like the giving of spiritual gifts) because he does have various important roles to play in the shared work of the Godhead both now and in the future. The Spirit is the faithful, powerful defending *presence* standing with Christians in the face of evil and/or opposition. The Spirit restrains *evil* in the world while preserving the goodness of God in spite of human corruption. By using the title of *Paraclete*, perhaps John was telling his readers that they could rest assured that one of the Spirit's most important jobs is to be "another" Advocate (just like the Son) for the people of God.

Furthermore, the Spirit is engaged in *life*—as the only power that can truly overcome human death. The Spirit is involved in all of creation, as well as the renewal and redemption of human *life* (Job 33:4; Ps. 104:30; John 1:4, 4:14, 6:63, 10:10, 17:2; 2 Cor. 3:6). In the Old Testament, the "pouring out" of the Spirit was a picture of abundance, overflowing grace and prosperity (Isa. 32:15; Joel 2:23–32). It was the Spirit, then, "the giver of life," who put himself into the womb of Mary and gave Jesus "flesh" to live among humanity (Luke 1:35; John 1:14). The Spirit raised Jesus from the dead; he is the "first-fruits" of all who believe and who will one day disable the terror of physical death. Death has no power over those who have the Spirit, and he will be the One who will ultimately renew and resurrect believers' frail human bodies to grant believers "eternal life" in the future.

If we think about the theme of legal proceedings, we can see that the author of John's Gospel presented the ministry and mission of Jesus as "the extended metaphor of a cosmic trial."[155] In a world of both good and evil, Jesus came to renew and redeem. Like all human beings, he faced "prosecution" from his enemies. He was his own "advocate" in the face of unrelenting antagonism (John 18:19–24, 28–39). Jesus raised other "witnesses" concerning his own identity, including Moses and John the Baptist (John 5:31–47).

His mission was to reveal his Father throughout his earthly ministry (John 5:19–30). Upon completion of his mission on earth, Jesus sent the *Paraclete*, who "prosecutes" the case against human unbelief, guilt, disobedience, sin, unrighteousness, and false judgment (John 16:8–11) but who "advocates" for faithful belief, righteousness, truth, obedience, and love.[156] In spite of opposition (sometimes very strong), the third mission of the Spirit is to make it possible for people to follow a holy God in obedience. "To be holy is to obey the commands of God for love's sake. And this is what the Holy Spirit has come to enable us to do."[157]

Next, the Spirit is particularly involved in divine redemption. The saving work of Christ on the cross was necessary before the sending of the Spirit to redeem believers. Some people say that the primary reason Jesus came to the earth was to suffer and die so that humanity could be saved. However, the primary reason Jesus had to die and be resurrected was to cleanse humanity so that God could indwell his fallible, sinful creatures. This is not to take away anything from the tremendous sacrifice of Christ but to recognize that a holy, righteous God cannot fill corrupt containers.

We tend to separate the Spirit's ministry from that of Jesus, but the saving work of Christ is groundwork for human redemption, and the mission (or the function) of the Spirit is to continue and complete the redemption process. Once people are forgiven and cleansed of their sins, then the Holy Spirit can live within them, just as the God of the Old Testament could fill the Temple with his presence only after the cleansing sacrifices of his people. The renovation work of the Spirit releases power and judgment into those people who willingly allow the sanctification process to transform their lives. That is, the infusion of holiness and righteousness from God through the Spirit allows people to judge correctly, act fairly, and to have the power to do what is right. The Spirit forgives sin, removes guilt, and empowers people to live righteously.

Evidence of the Spirit residing in a believer is expressed by the Apostle Paul as the "fruit of the Spirit" (Gal. 5:22–25). We can note that the "*fruit*" in this passage is a singular noun, meaning that we cannot choose to engage in one or two select virtues—"love *or* patience *or* goodness"; it is a total package. In reality, it is virtually impossible in our human nature alone to "love one another" and find true "joy" and "peace" without all the other virtues: "patience, kindness, goodness, faithfulness, gentleness, and self-control." Thus, the character of Christians is produced by the indwelling Spirit and not by a person's own attempts at moral discipline. Testimony of the presence of the Spirit in one's life is more than merely "following the rules" created by culture; it is a transformation by the Spirit to create a new way of thinking and behaving that is glorifying to God (John 15:1–6; 2 Cor. 3:17–18). The righteousness that justifies remains external to the believer because it is accomplished by Christ, who became one of us but is now in heaven. Yet,

> we receive this verdict because the Spirit convicts us inwardly of our guilt and gives us faith to embrace Christ in the most intimate union. Again, this is precisely why we need *both* advocates—the one outside and above us and the other within us.[158]

In addition, the age of the Spirit, which began at Pentecost, established a new access for believers to God (John 16:25). The Spirit opened the "door" for believers to ask the Father directly *in Jesus' name* (John 16:26), so it was not necessary for Jesus to intercede for the disciples and speak to the Father on their behalf. The Jewish priests often prayed for the people at the Temple, but with the assurance that God loves Jesus' followers, a new path of communication is open for them to go straight to the Father in prayer (John 16:27). As Jesus prayed directly to God and addressed him as his Father (John 17:1), those who love and obey Jesus can speak honest, straightforward prayers to the Father through the Son by the Holy Spirit.

In the end, the Spirit brings a person into a loving, obedient relationship with both the Father and the Son, and that is like finally "returning home" to the place where we all truly belong. After his resurrection, Jesus returned to his "home" with his Father, but he promised to send the Spirit to his followers to grant them the permanence and security that he left behind on earth. Another mission of the Spirit, then, is to guide believers from their earthly "home" to a more permanent, "peaceful dwelling place" (Isa. 32:14–18). Someday, yet in the future, Jesus promised to "come back" and take his followers "home" to "the place where I am going" (John 14:3–4), which is their "eternal home"—the *future* part of "eternal life"—to be with him and the Father. There, in our final "home," believers will see and experience Christ's full glory! This, he promised to all believers in his final prayer with his earliest disciples in John 17:24.

Baptism by the Holy Spirit

The picture of the Holy Spirit descending upon Jesus is mentioned in all four Gospels (Matt. 3:13–17; Mark 1:9–11; Luke 3:21–22; John 1:31–34). In the Fourth Gospel, John the Baptist connects the unique epithet of "the Lamb of God" with the baptism of Jesus; in doing so, John the Baptist realized (and was a witness to) Jesus' divine nature and purpose (John 1:29).

John the Baptist gave testimony about Jesus and spoke of the difference between himself and the promised Messiah: John baptized people with *symbolic* water. Jesus the Messiah baptized people with the *Holy Spirit* (John 1:33). In Jewish tradition, John the Baptist baptized with water to cleanse and purify "for repentance" and to prepare the nation for the coming of the Messiah (John 1:23–26, 31;

Matt. 3:11). However, he testified that he saw Jesus baptized *by* the Holy Spirit visible "as a dove" (John 1:32; Matt. 3:16–17). Baptism had nothing to do with Jesus' sinless nature but was a visual sign to people that the Spirit of God did indeed rest and *remain* on him to empower Jesus to do his ministry on earth (see Isa. 61:1–3).[159] The baptism of Jesus was his inauguration into the very same mission and ministry that had already been started by the Holy Spirit: to give life and redemption to humanity.

The descent of a "dove" (John 1:32) may be a reference to the Jewish concept of the Spirit who temporarily came to rest on specific persons for specific reasons. But the Spirit "remained" on Jesus, confirming his true identity (John 1:33) and as a sign that the Spirit would never leave him throughout his entire ministry.[160] We might imagine that, knowing what he was sent to earth to do, at times the assignment may have been overwhelming to Jesus. If he needed the assurance of the constant presence of the Spirit in his life, how much more so do we need that pledge and privilege of the Spirit?

The baptism event reported by John is a parallel to Jesus' words in his prayer in John 17:19—"For them I sanctify myself that they too may be truly sanctified." Of course, why would Jesus need to "sanctify" or purify himself if, indeed, he is sinless? The Old Testament background of the word "sanctify" is the consecration of the priests for their holy callings/work in the Temple (Exod. 28:41; Lev. 20:7–8). Jesus separated himself from the world to obediently do the Father's will and work on earth. As the Son, Jesus was anointed as "the Christ" and ordained *by the Spirit* to complete God's plans and purposes on earth so that humanity—"them/they"—can know the Father, be holy, and experience "eternal life" (John 17:3).

Following his example, human beings experience "baptism" as an outward sign of inward transformation that comes only from God. That is, the Spirit comes to true believers and "remains" in them. The human being is completed and given eternal life by the "one and only Son" (John 3:16–18a). The indwelling Spirit is a new experience, a "new covenant" with God, and a part of the "new creation." The individual person, therefore, can experience a "new birth" *because* of Christ and *by* the Holy Spirit (John 3:3). Now water baptism is a public *sign* of one's "new birth" in and through the Son and the Spirit. Baptism is a public sign of a personal inward renovation that unites all believers into one "body" of Christ (the church) (see 1 Cor. 12:12–13).

Some people debate as to whether or not there is a separate act of the filling of the believer by the Holy Spirit after the person has committed to belief in Christ, called the "second filling." There is little debate over the fact that the Spirit does fill believers, but it is the timing that is disputed. The most cited scriptural passage from the New Testament concerning the filling of the Spirit is Acts 2:1–21, recalling the Old Testament passage from Joel 2:28–32. The point of Peter's sermon in Acts 2:17–21 was to verify that *all* believers receive the Spirit, regardless of gender, age, ethnicity, or position. Peter connected the filling of the Spirit with the act of repentance, but *he does not call for another act or event* (see Acts 2:38–41). Upon their expression of faith, "everyone who calls on *the name* of the Lord will be saved" (Joel 2:32). This Old Testament passage, with Peter's sermon in Acts 2, indicates that the indwelling Spirit and the salvation (or regeneration) of individuals—"all people"—through the Messiah are simultaneous.

To have Christ is to have the Spirit and vice-versa—"we are baptized *into Christ by the Spirit*." All persons who are united with Christ through faith are forgiven ("saved") and receive the "new birth" of *life in* Christ (John 14:19–20; see Eph. 4:5).[161] Over the centuries, the Christian church has attempted to establish an event which deepens the person's faith in Christ and is manifested in unique "gifts" given by the Spirit as empirical evidence of a richer, more profound faith. However, there is nothing in the Gospels nor in the letters of Paul that require *another* baptism by the Spirit in the lives of believers.[162] To say that some Christ followers have more or less of the Spirit than others, or perhaps no Spirit at all, is to force God into a position of creating a hierarchy system of belief, which is not biblical.

Craig Keener concludes that,

> we are complete in Christ and dead to sin, but in
> practice that means neither that all of us always

138

live accordingly nor that we always appropriate the power of the Spirit that enables us to do so. Conversion gives us access to all we need, but neither conversion nor a single experience after conversion frees us from the need to seek God's empowerment in practice... The Spirit transforms us when we come to Christ; from that point forward, we must continue to depend on his power to carry out the mission Jesus gave us.[163]

Eucharist and the Holy Spirit

Another point of disagreement among scholars is the meaning and essence of what is called the "Eucharist" or "Holy Communion" or the "Last Supper." We recall that the teachings of Jesus concerning the Holy Spirit (John 14–16) took place at his last Passover supper with his immediate followers (John 13:1). At their final meal together, Jesus prepared his followers for his departure from this earth by expressing "the full extent of his love" (John 13:1). He did this by instituting the Eucharist ritual with his immediate disciples for their "cleansing" and their remembrance. The bread and the wine are visual and vivid reminders of "Christ's body and blood"—or the atoning work which he did on the cross. As we continue this "remembrance" today, we are reminded of three things: (1) Jesus really did die a sacrificial death physically; (2) but he is still alive among us by his Holy Spirit, and the bread and wine represent his very presence; (3) the Holy Spirit brings to remembrance all that Christ did for us and indwells us as a "pledge" of *our* "final redemption."[164]

The Eucharist without the Holy Spirit would be just another "snack," even if the elements are "blessed" by another human being. It is the Spirit who places the substance and significance into Christian rituals, and without the Spirit, ritual practices become routine and useless to touch human hearts. Sacraments or rituals such as the Eucharist and baptism are "points of grace" for an individual, but they are also vital for the unity of the community of believers, the corporate church. Through "word [Scripture] and sacrament," then, the Holy Spirit acts inwardly to increase a person's faith; and it is he who unites the members of the body of Christ into "one body, one faith, one baptism; one God and Father of all, who is over all and through all and *in all*" (Eph. 4:4–6; emphasis mine).[165]

"The Spirit of glory"

In the Old Testament, God's "glory" was his unique qualities of "power, mystery, and separateness."[166] His holiness, righteousness, and justice are revealed in his glory; he is "high and lofty" (Isa. 57:15). Glory is not an attribute of God but "the luminous manifestation of his person, his revelation of himself."[167] It is not something that he has; it is something that he *is*. The Old Testament pictures the glory of God as a "light" (Gen. 1:3; Isa. 60:1–3, 19–20), and the "light" that filled the earth at creation is the Spirit. The Spirit guided the nation of Israel by his presence in the "fire and a cloud" (Exod. 13:21; Deut. 5:23–24). Creation was God's first light-filled, glorious "temple," and his glory filled the whole earth (Ps. 72:19; Isa. 6:3). Then, God's glory filled the Tabernacle and the Temple of the Israelites where it appeared as a "cloud" (Exod. 40:34; 1 Kgs. 8:10–11). His light has broken into human existence since the beginning, guiding, renewing, and giving knowledge and insight to those who truly seek God (i.e., Ps. 4:6, 18:28, 19:8, 27:1, 36:9, 89:15, 119:105). The glory of the Lord was revealed in his acts of deliverance and the salvation of his people (see Exod. 40:34–38; Ps. 19:1, 29:1, 57:5).

Nevertheless, the nation rebelled in disobedience and turned away from God, who had to remove his glory from their midst. In a very intense scene, the glory and presence of the Lord departed from the Temple, leaving the whole nation vulnerable to hostility and destruction: "Then the glory of the Lord departed from over the threshold of the temple and stopped above the cherubim...and the glory of the God of Israel was above them" (Ezek. 9:3, 10:18–19).

The "Spirit of the Lord" revealed to Ezekiel that the glory of the Lord had to depart from the Temple because of the sins of the people—"the land is full of bloodshed and the city is full of injustice" (Ezek. 9:9). Only later did the glory of the Lord return to the Temple. "I saw the glory of the God of Israel coming from the east. His voice was like the roaring of rushing waters, and the land was radiant with his glory" (Ezek. 43:2, 4). It was the Spirit who "lifted" the prophet and brought him into the "inner court," and "the glory of the Lord filled the temple" (Ezek. 43:4–5).

Moving into the New Testament, we find that there are overlapping meanings for the concept of glory. The idea of *doxa* (radiance, honor, fame, repute) is something that was always given *to* God, but it is also that which radiates *from* him.[168] Again, the glory of God is pictured as light: at the time of Jesus' birth, the angelic host appeared to the shepherds at night, and "the glory of the Lord *shone* around them, and they were terrified" (Luke 2:8–9; emphasis mine). Matthew wrote that the Gentiles (even so, the Gentiles!) "have seen a great light…a new light has dawned" (Matt. 4:16). It is the Spirit who fills believers and makes *them* "the light of the world" (Matt. 5:14–16). On earth, Jesus is seen as "light" in John's prologue (John 1:4–5, 7, 9) and in Jesus' great "I am the light of the world" statements (John 8:12; 9:5; 12:35, 46). In the Fourth Gospel, it appears that Jesus shared glory with this Father before his incarnation—"before the creation of the world" (John 17:24). Upon his return to the Father, his eternal glory returned, not unlike the glory of God which departed from the Old Testament Temple and then was eventually restored (John 17:5, 24).

On the other hand, we also see that the "glory of God" was revealed on earth in the illness and death of Lazarus so that the "glory of the Son" was demonstrated in the giving life by the Spirit to his friend (John 11:4, 40). Glory was given to Jesus on earth, and the Son glorified the Father through his sacrificial death and the glorious redemption as a result. It was the cross itself that was Jesus' ultimate glorification because he totally, obediently fulfilled his Father's plans and purposes (John 13:31–32). Thus, the "Spirit of glory" of the Father and the Son was actually seen by believers in the words and acts of Jesus on earth. After his work on earth was completed, the risen Christ once again resumed his position of divine glory in heaven with the Father (John 17:1–5).

It must have been quite difficult for Jesus' earliest followers to understand Jesus' words and grasp the concept of "glory" prior to his death and resurrection. So after his departure, the Holy Spirit was given to believers to give them insight, to testify about Jesus, to disclose "truth" about him, and to continue the very presence of God on earth. Looking back at Christ's passion events, the Holy Spirit helped the readers of John's Gospel to understand that the glory of God was revealed in Jesus on earth (Isa. 40:3–5; John 1:14) and that the Father's eternal glory is shared with the (risen) Son (John 17:1, 4, 22). Someday, still to come, Christ will finally return to earth "in all his glory" (i.e., Rev. 1:6, 4:11, 5:9, 21:22–26). In the meantime, it was and is the Spirit who makes the disclosure of Jesus' glory to his people.

Jesus indwells each believer in the form of the Spirit, just as the Father is "*in*" the Son. This is the remarkable reciprocal "triad" that Jesus pictured in John 14:11, 20 (also John 17:22–23). The Son brings glory *to* the Father (John 14:13), and the Son is glorified *by* the Father (John 1:14; 17:1, 5). After the coming of the promised Paraclete—"On that day" (John 14:20)—the Spirit fills believers so that the glory of the Father and of the Son is displayed. The Spirit teaches and reminds believers so that they will truly *know* the glory of the Father and the Son (John 17:26). Christ is glorified by those people who accept his words and his salvation (John 17:10b), and believers are glorified by Christ through the Holy Spirit (John 17:22, 24). The church is protected and glorified by Christ, and the church glorifies her Savior in word, ritual, and actions. Furthermore, it is the Spirit who unites all believers as "one" (John 17:21, 23). Indeed, both this "circle" of glory and the unity of believers are amazing gifts of the Spirit and not achievements of human power and position (John 17:20–23).

Divine glory is made known as believers "love one another" (John 15:17). It is made known through the unity of faith in the revealing of truth (John 16:12), in joining God in his work on earth

(John 15:8), in facing opposition with confidence (John 16:20), in living life to the fullest and showing his peace (John 14:27). His glory is apparent when people turn from sin, "remain" in Christ, and self-lessly love one another, just as Christ loves his people (John 15:12). It was the design of God to send the Holy Spirit who would fill Jews and non-Jews alike (Col. 1:27). It is remarkable in our day too that we have "Christ in me—the hope of glory." This is not earned by human merit; "Christ in me" is the Spirit, helping us to practice in this life the position ("in Christ") that he has already granted to us. And with great anticipation, someday we will "see" his full glory (John 17:24).

Future glory/eternal life

In the visions recorded in the Book of Revelation, God confirmed the fact that one day, Christ will return to "a new heavens and a new earth" (Rev. 21:1). Through an abundance of symbols and metaphors, we can "see" the future of the world and we can hope for God's newer and better "cosmos," the "dwelling place" of God. Jesus has returned to the Father, but he is also very present with us in the form of the Spirit—now and always. It is the Spirit who sustains the "now and later" redemption in every believer. We are "already" saved and justified through Christ, but we are "not yet" fully sanctified. One day, in the future, we will be with him and share his glory (John 17:22).

Each person truly "born of God" will reflect the glory of God in the present life and in the life to come *by the Holy Spirit* (John 1:12–13). All true believers will one day experience the fullness of the glory of the Father and of the Son without pain, without suffering, and without sin. The continuing presence of the Spirit now assures believers of their *own* complete glorification in the future. Jesus promised, "I am the resurrection and the life. [The one] who believes in me will live, even though he/she dies; and whoever lives and believes in me will never die" (John 11:25). Further, Jesus said, "Did I not tell you that if you believed, you will see the glory of

God?" (John 11:40). As Jesus was raised from the dead, so believers will be resurrected from the dead by the Spirit:

> The Spirit who brooded over the waters of chaos, the Spirit who indwelt Jesus so richly that it became known as the Spirit of Jesus: this Spirit, already present within Jesus' followers as the first fruits, the down payment, the guarantee of what is to come, is not only the beginning of the future life, even in present time, but also the energizing power through which the final transformation will take place. The early creed spoke of "the Holy Spirit, the Lord and giver of life." That is exactly true in the New Testament (John 1:4; 14:6).[169]

Essentially, the story of the Holy Spirit is found from the beginning to the end in the biblical narrative. His story begins at creation, long before Jesus, and it spans far into eternity in the lives of Christians. If Jesus is "God-in-the-flesh," then the Spirit is "God-in-reality." As we fully recognize and remember what the Spirit *does*—that is, defends, protects, gives life, seeks truth, transforms lives, grants new access to the Father, and promises a glorious "home"—we realize that we cannot truly live without him.

It is he who allows us to speak and act authentically as Christ followers and to bring life, not death, to the world around us. We can live "paradoxical" lives—peace in a time of turmoil, joy in a time of sorrow, abundance in a time of loss, and love in a time of hate. He grants a ministry of power and blessing for those who believe. On the other hand, our Advocate condemns evil, convicts the sinner, and argues with the human mind and heart to combat sin and iniquity. The indwelling Spirit makes it possible for believers to live and look forward to the day when we are all gathered together in the presence of the holy Trinity (see Eph. 1:3–14). "Day by day Christ grows more and more into one body with us, until he becomes completely one of us."[170]

Prayer and the Holy Spirit

The resurrection and ascension of Jesus radically changed the prayer relationship between the Father and the believer. Because of the completed work of the Son, and our faith in his name, a bridge is established between people and the Father. That bridge is the indwelling Holy Spirit. The Spirit is a gift to believers so that the holiness and the righteousness of the Father and the Son can reside in us and empower us. That means that the same intimacy between the Father and the Son is available to the person who prays to the Father, believing in Jesus as the Son, with the Holy Spirit. The gracious gift of the Holy Spirit is proof that God does not desert his children after their initial acceptance of faith in Christ; he wants to see all of his children fully sanctified and in unity with one another (John 17:23).

In the introduction to this book, we said that the prayer of John 17 is an illustration of the *development of prayer* in a biblical sense. After Jesus' departure from the earth, the Father and the Son sent the Holy Spirit to fill the believers to set up "residence" in them, making prayer an intimate conversation between the believer and the Triune God whose presence is as near as one's own shadow. Prayer moved from temple ritual to an intimate relationship because of the *indwelling* Holy Spirit. Thus, prayer is a gift of the Holy Spirit. His presence in us alters the communication experience with God. It is he who teaches us what to say, what to pray for, and what to expect in terms of answered prayers (Rom. 8:26). It is a gift to be able to pray to God in the name of Jesus through the Holy Spirit.[171] Prayer is communion with all three, but it is most affected by the Spirit living within us.

God has not changed, but people have and our perception of him has. The continuing revelation of who God is has modified how people have known him and related to him. It happened to people over time and history, and it happens to each individual person. As we seek him, we find him, and we know him better. What the author of John's Gospel is *doing* in the Farewell Discourses is putting followers of Christ into a brand-new living prayer relationship with God through Christ and by the Holy Spirit. The transformation of people into children of God is "sealed" and accomplished by the Spirit, which transforms prayer from an obligatory duty to a cherished conversation.

Conclusions and responses

Never before in the history of the world had the Spirit of God filled an ordinary person on a permanent basis. Thus, the words of Jesus in John 14–17 are an explanation of a new, exciting intervention of God into the world. Even so, for believers today, the Farewell Discourses are a clarification of the significance of Jesus' death and resurrection; but they are also a *preparation* for the filling of the Spirit who came after Jesus. The "cross is one step toward Pentecost," and this places more emphasis on the continuing work of the Holy Spirit in the lives of believers. We would do well to remember that, in his love, the Father sent the Son to atone for human sin and the Spirit is sent by the Father and the Son to allow humanity to love them back. The Spirit is the "perfecting agent" and his presence in believers "changes everything."[172]

But it doesn't end there. The function of the Spirit is to *prepare and equip* Jesus' followers to continue his mission and his ministry on earth. As he was sent by the Father, so the Son "sends" his followers to perpetuate his words and his work (John 17:17–18, 20:21). If the church seeks the Father's will concerning Christian ministry and mission, he will answer. It is the Spirit who responds to our requests as he prepares and equips us for our labors in the world and in the continuation of the gospel message. Since we are included in the "household" of God and in the intimate "triangle" picture with the Trinity, we should desire more than anything to allow the Spirit to act in us to advance what Jesus Christ began. The Spirit's enablement of believers is hollow if no one knows anything about him.

Remarkably, the power of the Spirit molds and energizes ordinary believers to do extraordinary things for the gospel. One does not have to be specifically ordained to serve Christ; the Holy Spirit equips all of us to do exactly what we are called to do. He uses our past—warts and all—to help us navigate and serve other people in the present and the future. Nevertheless, this is where we must consider "yieldedness." The Spirit cannot use us if we are not fully yielded to God's plans, purposes, and power. Western culture tends to worship "self-control" and even those people who assent to the existence of God depend heavily on "doing things their own way." But in the Old Testament, we see patriarchs and prophets who yielded to God to preach his words and warnings to a rebellious nation. In the New Testament, John the Baptist yielded to God to prepare the nation and be a "witness to testify concerning the light [Jesus] so that through him all might believe" (John 1:6–7).

Young Mary surrendered to the Holy Spirit and did an incredible thing in her culture, bearing the Son of God in her womb (Luke 1:35–38). There are countless examples then and now of people who yielded to God with a real willingness to allow his Spirit to totally prescribe and determine every part of their lives. The practice of yielding to someone else is not always easy for human beings; but the Spirit "comes along side" of us to guide, direct, and help people to follow God in obedience. Ultimately, it is too painful *not* to yield to the One who loves us and wants the best for us.

Every believer is called to be a part of Jesus' mission, empowered and impassioned by the Spirit. We can find the Holy Spirit alive and well in the ordinary, simple work of God on earth, from shoveling snow for a neighbor to knitting nursery items for babies in Africa. It is amazing what God can do through people who are committed to his agenda! God prepares and equips his people to be surrendered to his will, and then he empowers us with his own Spirit. As Horton said, "We should not be looking for the works that are done uniquely by the Holy Spirit, but the unique role of the Holy Spirit in every work."[173]

Notes

[136] Michael Horton, *Rediscovering the Holy Spirit* (Grand Rapids: Zondervan, 2017), 25–26.

[137] Craig S Keener, *Gift and Giver; the Holy Spirit for Today* (Grand Rapids: Baker Academic, 2001; 2020), 210.

[138] Horton, *Rediscovering the Holy Spirit*, 224.

[139] Horton, 125–26.

[140] Horton, 126.

[141] Horton, 32, 34.

[142] Andreas J. Köstenberger, *John; Baker Exegetical Commentary on the New Testament*, ed. Robert; Yarbrough and Robert H. Stein (Grand Rapids: Baker Academic, 2004), 434; Horton, *Rediscovering the Holy Spirit.*, 325.

[143] Horton, *Rediscovering the Holy Spirit,* 301, author's emphasis.

[144] Horton, 284.

[145] Larry H. Hurtado, "Even Higher Christology in the Gospel of John: Frey's Edinburgh Essay," *Word Press*, 2019, https://wp.me/YZXr-2hA, accessed May 24, 2019.

[146] M. M. B. Turner, "Holy Spirit," in *Dictionary of Jesus and the Gospels*, ed. Joel; Green, Scot; McKnight, and I Howard Marshall (Downers Grove: InterVarsity Press, 1992), 341–51; Köstenberger, John; Baker Exegetical Commentary on the New Testament, 434–35.

[147] Köstenberger, 442–43.

[148] Matt Searles, "'These Things I Have Said to You': An Investigation of How Purpose Clauses Govern the Interpretation of John 14–16," *JETS* 60.3 (2017): 511–32., 515–16.

[149] Eugene Peterson, *The Message: The New Testament* (Colorado Springs, Colorado: NavPress Publishing, 1993), 185.

[150] Köstenberger, *John; Baker Exegetical Commentary on the New Testament*, 441.

[151] Searles, "'These Things I Have Said to You': An Investigation of How Purpose Clauses Govern the Interpretation of John 14–16," 519.

[152] Horton, *Rediscovering the Holy Spirit*, 177.

[153] Cleon L. Jr. and Cleon L. III Rogers, *The New Linguistic and Exegetical Key to the Greek New Testament* (Grand Rapids: Zondervan Publishing, 1998), 219.

[154] Horton, *Rediscovering the Holy Spirit*, 35–36.

[155] Turner, "Holy Spirit," 350.

[156] Turner, 350.

[157] John N. Oswalt, *Called to Be Holy; A Biblical Perspective* (Anderson, Indiana: Warner Press, 1999), 129.

[158] Horton, *Rediscovering the Holy Spirit*, 208.

[159] Oswalt, *Called to Be Holy; A Biblical Perspective*, 91.

[160] Köstenberger, *John; Baker Exegetical Commentary on the New Testament*, 69–71.

[161] Horton, *Rediscovering the Holy Spirit*, 189–90.

[162] Mary Rose D'Angelo, "Baptism in the Holy Spirit," *St. Lukes. J. Theol.* 22.3 (1979): 229–32: James D. G. Dunn, Baptism in the Holy Spirit: A Re-Examination of the New Testament Teaching on the Gift of the Spirit in Relation to Pentecostalism Today (Philadelphia: Westminster Press, 1977).

[163] Craig S Keener, *Gift and Giver; the Holy Spirit for Today* (Grand Rapids: Baker Academic, 2002; 2020), 168–169.

[164] Horton, *Rediscovering the Holy Spirit*, 263.

[165] Ibid, 260–61.

[166] John N. Oswalt, *Holy One of Israel: Studies in the Book of Isaiah* (Eugene, Oregon: Cascade Books, 2014), 43.

[167] S. Aalen, "Glory," in *Dictionary of NT Theology, vol. 2*, ed. Colin Brown (Grand Rapids: Zondervan Publishing, 1971), 44–49, 45.

[168] Aalen, 44.

[169] Aalen, 163.

[170] Aalen, 210–12; Searles, "'These Things I Have Said to You': An Investigation of How Purpose Clauses Govern the Interpretion of John 14—16.," 522—523.

[171] Horton, *Rediscovering the Holy Spirit*.

[172] Horton, 40–41.

[173] Horton, 41.

Chapter 6

The Trinity and the Church

It is not the intent of this book to present a treatise on Trinitarian theology, but our theology of prayer is inexorably linked to our theology of the Trinity. In fact, God planned for a community of believing people who express the same love and unity to one another as the Trinity itself. How we minister to others and how we pray are a reflection of our knowledge of and our sincere belief in the nature and character of a trinitarian God. Furthermore, our "ecclesiology," or the concept of the universal Christian church, is founded on our understanding of the Trinity and on our theology of prayer.

"Trinitarian" theology

The Gloria Patri
Glory be to the Father and to the Son and to the Holy Ghost.
As it was in the beginning, is now and every shall be,
World without end. Amen.

The "*Gloria Patri*" (Latin) or the "*Lesser Doxology*" has been a part of Christian ritual, worship, and prayer for as long as anyone can remember. An ancient prayer, it may date to the second-century AD as a confessional prayer response by believing Christians. The very early believers used this doxology at the beginning or at the end of every prayer to recognize and remember to whom they were praying. Still today, it is sung or recited at the end of many church worship services. The prayer succinctly names the three Persons of the Trinity and acknowledges the existence of the Trinity from eternity past, to the present, to eternity future. It is a summation of God's revelation of himself to humanity.

The doxology is based on the risen Jesus' words to his followers in Matthew 28:19–20, which is the most lucid reference to the Trinity in the Synoptic Gospels:

> All authority in heaven and on earth has been given to me. Therefore, go and make disciples of all nations, baptizing them in the name of the Father, and of the Son, and of the Holy Spirit, and teaching them to obey everything I have commanded you. And surely, I am with you always, to the very end of the age.

Here, we see *one name* for three distinct Persons: *the* (singular) name of the Father, the Son, and the Holy Spirit. The "going," "making," "baptizing," and "teaching" by the early church, as instructed by Jesus in these verses, was made possible because of the faithful Holy Spirit. Likewise, all ministries of the church even today should be centered around these directives—missions, evangelism, discipleship, ordinances or sacraments, prayer, teaching, and instruction—under the guidance of the Holy Spirit. Whatever the church "does," therefore, must be bathed in prayer to secure the Spirit's guidance.

Like the "Lord's Prayer" in Matthew 6, the *Gloria Patri* declaration can become so familiar to practicing Christians that the depth and meaning of it can be lost or ignored. Yet this short liturgy reveals *the heart of all prayer*: prayer is the human response to the glorious revelation of the eternal trinitarian God. With this ancient prayer in mind, it seems only right that all Christian prayer should be trinitarian in nature: to the Father, through the Son, and by the Holy Spirit.[174]

The Trinity

The very nature of the trinitarian God can be incredibly difficult for human beings to understand. John does not use the word "Trinity" in his Gospel. In fact, the term is not explained anywhere in the New Testament; the Bible does not promote nor refute the Trinity. It is a doctrine that developed in the early centuries of the church as a clarification and a confession of faith.

Certainly, in the first-century AD, at the time of John's writings, the very idea of a "one-in-three" deity was unheard of and was regarded as unlikely, if not absurd, especially by unbelievers. Even so, the Trinity remains a challenge to fully describe in our present culture. The Father, Son, and Spirit are "of equal essence and therefore in an equal sense, God himself." The New Testament does cite a "fixed, three-part formula" in which all three are mentioned together (see Matt. 28:19; 1 John 5:8). God is One in three, as he is Three-in-One (see Eph. 4:4; Gal. 4:4). "God first sends the Son and then the Spirit of his Son to continue the work of Jesus on earth."[175] However, the Trinity is three Persons, not just three mystical ideas fused into one concept. Each Person is unique, but all are united. There is "distinction without separation."[176]

In the early centuries of Christianity, the doctrine of the Trinity was hardly a settled matter among the budding Christian congregations. It is evident, however, that John "saw" the character and nature of the trinitarian God; and he concurred with the foundational beliefs concerning the Trinity. This is shown by his use of the various distinctive names for all three Persons: Father, Son, and *Paraclete*. No doubt the believers to whom John wrote had already *experienced* the Trinity. They knew the Father God of the Jews. They had heard direct witness accounts of his incarnate Son, Jesus, and they had personally witnessed the redemptive power of the Holy Spirit in their individual lives and in their believing community.

So by naming God the "Holy," and "Righteous" and caring "Father," John is denoting the identical features of the other members of the "Holy Trinity." That is, the Holy and Righteous Son is "one" with the Father" (John 10:30), and the Holy and Righteous Spirit is "another advocate," just like the Father and Son (John 14:16). The Johannine discourses in chapters 14–17 confirm the completion of the three Persons into the "oneness" of the Trinity. The agency and the position of Jesus Christ as the promised Messiah is inexorably linked to the Father in John 17:1–3, and the *Paraclete* (the Holy Spirit) is sent forth by the Father and the Son as a gift of life to believers (John 14:16–20; 16:7, 12–15).

Yet how is it that people can *know* the trinitarian God? In Johannine theology, God is known by "seeing," "hearing," and "believing" (for example, see John 20:27–29). How can people have faith in a God they cannot see? It is a question of faith, and this is a key theme in the Old Testament. It is a challenge for frail humanity to perceive of a holy, righteous, invisible God. The cultures around the Israelites had visible gods, made of stone and wood, but Yhwh is a living God, even if he is hidden from human eyes. Thus, the Lord revealed himself in his creation (see Rom. 1:20) and in his divine acts and promises. He showed his power and his judgment through his prophets, who spoke in images and metaphors to reveal God's nature and to reveal his plans and purposes for his people. The faithful "see" God in his acts, his love, his grace, and in his glory (Isa. 64:1–4). Thus, "seeing is believing."

Furthermore, God told people about himself through his Word. His Word came through patriarchs, prophets, and spokesmen with the common expression, "Speak to the Israelites and say to them" (i.e., Lev. 15:2, 23:2). God spoke creation into being (i.e., Gen. 1:3, 6, 9, 11, 14, 24). He speaks and then he acts (Num. 23:18–20). His people were to hear God's words (or "his voice") and were never to doubt the veracity of the message (Isa. 45:19; Ezek. 10:5). God called his people to "hear" and to obey his "decrees and laws." The "Great *Shema*" is the word of God that became a Jewish affirmation of faith. In Hebrew, the word *Shema* is a command to "hear!" (Deut. 6:4–9), but to truly hear the Lord meant to love and obey the Lord. "Hearing and obeying" is believing.

Thus, characters in John's Gospel know the Father and the Son by "seeing," "hearing," and "believing." In John 9, for example, there is a blind man who cannot "see" but gains "spiritual sight" (knowledge of Jesus) in contrast to those Jewish leaders who were "spiritually blind." Physical "sight," the ability or the inability to "see," is used to convict those who could not "see" the true identity of Jesus (John 9:39). In the Johannine version of the resurrection story, the author highlights the theme of "seeing." Mary Magdalene ran to the other disciples from the empty tomb of Jesus and declared, "I have *seen* the Lord!" (John 20:18). Soon after, the risen Jesus appeared to his followers. Amazed, they said, "We have *seen* the Lord!" (John 20:25). The sceptic Thomas, however, stated that he could not *believe* until he had *seen* the physical marks of the crucifixion on Jesus' body (John 20:25). When Jesus does reveal his hands and his side, he told Thomas to "stop doubting and *believe*" (John 20:27). "Because you have seen me, you have believed; blessed are those who have *not seen* and yet have believed" (John 20:29). In fact, this included the readers of John's Gospel in the first century who had personally not seen Jesus in the flesh and all believers who know Jesus from his time until today.

Jesus said, "Very truly I tell you, whoever hears my word and believes him who sent me has eternal life and will not be judged, but has crossed over from death to life" (John 5:24). That is, of any generation, all those who *hear* and truly *believe* the words of the unseen Father God and who *see* the only exalted Son, *hear* his message, and *believe* are filled with the Holy Spirit. It is the "Spirit of Truth" who shines his light on the other two members of the Trinity, and it is he who "testifies" about them *within* the believers (John 14:17, 15:26). We can *see* Jesus through his Spirit and *hear* the voice of God all around us, if we truly *believe*. We have a visible Trinity that lives within those *people* who speak and act according to God's will, who love and obey and "remain" in Jesus. John's Gospel assures us that true "hearing" and "seeing" results in "believing" and *knowing*, which prepares all believers, then and now, to "testify" and share the truth about the Three-in-One God (John 15:26–27).

On the other hand, the unbelieving "world" cannot *know* the Trinity because, primarily, they do not know the Father, the "first Person" of the Trinity. Quite bluntly, Jesus told the Jewish leaders that "whoever is from God hears the words of God. The reason you do not hear them is that you are not from God" (John 8:47). If they knew and loved the Father, they would also love the Son and they would know the One they sent, the Spirit (i.e., John 5:37–40, 16:13–16).

In the Farewell Discourses, *knowing and obedience* go hand in hand: "If anyone loves me, he/she will obey my teaching. My Father will love him/her and make our home with him/her" (John 14:21, 23–24; 15:10). In addition, Jesus made it clear that *knowing and loving* are so linked together (14:21, 25–26). Perhaps the most familiar verse in the entire New Testament, John 3:16, is a priceless promise: we can know with certainty that those who are faithful to the Father and the Son will have the gift of eternal life from the Spirit. Yet sometimes we neglect to read the next few verses, which say that those who refuse to know, obey, and love each member of the Trinity "stand condemned" (John 3:16–18).

Knowing God

We know the Trinity because the Father sent the "Light," his "Word," and Jesus is the "Light" and "Word" (illumination). And the Spirit casts light on them both (John 1:4–9; 3:19–21; 8:12; 9:5; 12:35, 46; 16:13, 16). Key to knowledge is revelation. John used the words of Jesus to reveal the remarkable truth about the nature of the "Three-in-One": the "One True God" (John 17:3) is actually the "Holy" and "Righteous Father" who is *one* with his "Son" (John 10:30, 14:10–11, 17:11). Both the interrelated Father and Son are revealed to the world through the indwelling Holy Spirit, who is a gift sent from both the Father and the Son (John 14:16–17, 16:7). Before his physical departure from the earth, Jesus made it "*known*"—with "certainty" (John 17:8)—to his followers that they are protected, "sanctified," and commissioned by all three Persons of the Trinity (John 14:16–21, 15:26–27, 17:17–18).

Jesus promised that those people who "*know*" all three Persons will be "in" Jesus, just as he will also be "in" them (in the form of the Spirit, (John 14:20–21, 16:14–15). The Trinity "sets up residence" within God's people (John 1:14; 14:2, 23). Finally, being filled with his Spirit, those who believe are "sent" into the unbelieving world to reveal the Holy Trinity that is truly known to them (John 17:15–16, 18). By Jesus' directives, and through the power of the Holy Spirit, those who know the Trinity can complete Jesus' commission in Matthew 28:19. The most important disclosure of the Trinity to the world is the love and obedience of Christ-followers empowered by the Spirit (John 15:9–17).

More than revealing merely some of the attributes of God, the chosen epithets in the Farewell Discourses disclose the essence of the divine: who the Father is, who Jesus is, and who the Spirit is, as well as the role of believers within the unchangeable plans of God. From our investigation of the backgrounds of the prayer of John 17, we can deduce that Father God is unique, holy, pure, loving, righteous, and just. All his plans, actions, and even his silence are true and trustworthy. In the discourses, the Johannine author also pronounced who God is *not*. He is *not* unjust, unfair, self-serving, and capricious. He is not an "absentee father" who does not care about his creation. In his behavior and in his nature, God is completely different from other gods and known human rulers; he is Spirit and he has chosen to indwell his people by his Spirit. The Father, through the Son, has "cleansed" every believer so that he can indwell his people by his Spirit in a trusting, loving relationship:

> I believe that the immense cynicism and overwhelming fear that we see in the postmodern West could rightly be called a non-knowing of the Father—[that is,] an experiential knowing… God-knowledge is not abstract knowing, which Western people prefer. *True knowing is deeply loving*. God refuses to be known except through trustful, loving relationship. You cannot know God with your mind alone.[177]

Knowing the Son

The biblical events of two thousand years ago are real and not fiction. We can know that the Son "became flesh" (John 1:1–2, 14) and was sent to reconcile imperfect humanity to a holy God. Eyewitnesses saw Jesus in human form, watched him, touched him, ate with him, and spoke with him. They shared their experiences with us in writing in what we call the New Testament Gospels (the "good news of Jesus Christ"). Following Jewish tradition, they wrote down what they could recall from their time with him, aided by the Holy Spirit for truth and precision. We are now called to "remember," in word and in rituals, the life, death, resurrection, and exaltation of the second Person of the Trinity. The Prologue of John's Gospel is a succinct summary of who Jesus is. In the Fourth Gospel, Father and the Son are pictured as being so close to each other and to the believers that they are "in" one another (John 14:20, 17:21).

Jesus was with the Father from eternity past to eternity future (John 1:1, 17:5). In obedience to the Father, Jesus was sent to restore humanity, to forgive, and to release people from the bondage of sin so that the holy God can fill his creation with himself. The "Son," the "Servant," was appointed to bring justice and salvation to the earth (Isa. 42:1–4, 49:6). While the Old Testament nation of Israel had sacrifices and offerings, belief in the work of Jesus Christ is the "new" way provided by God to irradiate iniquity and cleanse persons to be his children (John 14:6–7). People are holy only because God is holy; Christ followers are righteous only because he is righteous. True holiness, justice, and selfless love in human beings was modeled by the Son who made it possible for the world to *see* God on earth.

Knowing the Spirit

The *Paraclete*, the Holy Spirit, will continue to make known the redemption, the righteousness, and the love of God to a needy world (John 17:25–26). God infuses humanity with his Spirit so that he can work through such a person to witness to the world about who he is and who he is not. By sending the Holy Spirit to fill his followers, Jesus completed the trinitarian Godhead. That person who believes in the Son is empowered to do so by the Holy Spirit, honoring both the Father and the Son. If the intent of the Gospel writer was to demonstrate the true identity of Jesus beyond human doubt (John 1:1–5, 20:31), it is the Spirit who authenticates the truth of John's discourse (John 14:16–17).

While their natures may be different, we know that the three Persons of the Trinity are united in terms of aims and resolve. Truly, the complete unity of the Trinity radically changed all human relationships with God and with each other:

> God's power is not domination, threat, or coercion, but instead is of a totally different nature, one that even Jesus' followers have not yet adjusted to. If the Father does not dominate the Son, and the Son does not dominate the Holy Spirit, and the Spirit does not dominate the Father or the Son, then there is *no domination in God. All divine power is shared power, which should have entirely changed Christian politics and relationships.*[178]

Everlasting covenant

Reconciliation is the "new covenant," an "everlasting covenant," sealed by the blood of Jesus and made actual in human beings by the Holy Spirit. This is an internal covenant, not external one, like the Old Testament law; and it is accomplished by the Spirit's guidance, protection, conviction, and encouragement. The Spirit is the vehicle by which believers have reciprocal love with God. The complete restoration of the world and the total realization of all of God's purposes on earth is yet future, but divine redemption has begun in our present. At some point in time, *all* the nations will gather together to seek the Lord and the gathering will be the culmination of the "everlasting covenant." This is God's promise from the days of the Old Testament prophets (Isa. 55:3–5).[179] Perhaps Jesus was referring to this glorious gathering when he addressed the unity of God's people in John 17:11, 21–23. One day, the whole world will know the "Holy and Righteous Father"; the whole world will be united because of the completed mission of the Son, and everyone will experience the advocacy of the Holy Spirit.

In effect, this is the picture of redeemed humanity in God through Christ and by the Holy Spirit. God is still faithful in his promises so that when people turn from disobedience and seek to know God through Jesus, they receive the promised Johannine "eternal life" (John 17:3). Someday, in God's "new age," all those who "turn to the Lord" will receive God's "mercy, pardon," glory, and "splendor" (Isa. 55:3–7, 12–13; 43:18–21; 44:22–23). The future hope of the glorification of the people of God and a complete renovation of this world is what keeps the church going forward, with the certainty of a "full" life (John 1:4, 10:10) in Christ and in the Spirit, beyond suffering, beyond sin, and beyond death (Rom. 8:18–21).

Family of God

Jesus came to fulfill the promises of God spoken to the prophet Isaiah (Isa. 61:1–9; see John 12:37–41; Matt. 11:5; Luke 4:16–21), and then the Holy Spirit inaugurated the time of the redeemed Christian church, the "fellowship of believers" (Joel 2:28–32; Acts 2:1–47). The church is a symphony of believers, all witnessing to the world as to the "music" of the Trinity. The Word makes known to believers the essence of God, and then we experience his love, his promises, his acts and purposes through the Son and by the Spirit. This happens in our own individual lives and in the lives of other believers around us, which unites us in "one Spirit," one divine work of art. Each note and each chord is important to the whole structure of a symphony to express complete harmony.

We can imagine another metaphor: the Johannine community of believers was assured that they were truly "children of God," firmly an integral part of the "family" of God because of their common belief in the Son. The family was very important in the Jewish world, and children (especially sons) were always given their family name to carry on the traditions and legacies of their ancestors. The trinitarian nature of God is a picture of the *unity* of his people—with common goals, purposes, and love for one another, committed to and shared with each another (John 17:21–23). Even so, today, just as the members of the Trinity have reciprocal love for one another; so the church must show reciprocal love for one another. The church "abides" "in Christ," just as Christ "remains" in the church. The Spirit fills the church, just as the church is to be filled with the Spirit. Christ followers are indeed brothers and sisters in Christ—"children of God" dedicated to the Lord and to each other (see 1 John 2–3). We can picture little children kneeling, praying to God with innocent faith, and parents praying ardently for wayward or sick children. In prayers, in words and actions, and in harmony, the church can replicate the familial "oneness" of the Trinity, demonstrating to the world the love, obedience, devotion, faithfulness, goodness, and godly living which are characteristic of the children of God who are known by his "*name*" (John 15:16–17, 17:10–12).

The Trinity and the kingdom

In the first century, John's readers knew very well what it was like to be ruled by a despot emperor; the idea of a kingdom is far less familiar to Americans living in the present age. Yet the Christian church exists today because of the power of the Father and the authority of the Son, who is head of the church (Eph. 1:19b–23). Not to be forgotten, it is the Spirit who energizes, equips, protects, and edifies the church, which is the kingdom of God in the present (Eph. 1:17).

The New Testament "treats the church as the kingdom [of God] in this present age." All three parts of the Trinity are involved in the creation and the support of the church while it is God's kingdom on earth. His kingdom is not limited to the boundaries and bricks of the organized institution because it is the *people* who gather as a unit to carry out the plans and purposes of God. The Holy Spirit equips, leads, and empowers the church to do so, even within a hostile human social culture. Individual and communal prayer is a crucial part of the connection and communication between the gathering of believers and its Head. As we assemble as "one body" to encourage one another, we learn to worship, to pray, and to share the acts of the Spirit collectively (Eph. 1:23; Acts 2:42). All believing communities—past, present, and future—are in the hands of a holy and righteous God, to be his witnesses in the world of his great glory and love.[180] Moreover, in spite of rumors to this effect, God *will not* allow his church to fail!

"The Messiah will establish the kingdom of God not only on earth but in their hearts."[181] As the kingdom of God on earth, metaphorically and in reality, the church is ruled by God (not a board of people). It is judged by the Son (John 5:22, 30) and energized by his Spirit. It is a place where a person can both give and receive, loving and serving others while being loved and served by God.

There are those people who, while professing belief in Christ, reject the idea of attending a church. They dislike the Sunday morning commitment and like the idea of "worshiping" God at a football stadium or at their children's soccer game. It is not unusual to hear folks complain that "I got nothing out of that sermon." In fact, perhaps the concept of "church" as a body of believers has more to do with *giving* to others than *receiving* for the self. True *worship* may be more about serving others and listening to the Spirit than it is about criticizing the choir director (John 4:23–24). In accordance with the divine "sending," believers are "sent" by the Trinity into the world to witness to the valid existence of the kingdom now and to the authority of the divine King (John 17:23, 25). This is also succinctly expressed in Jesus' prayer in the Gospel of Matthew: "Your kingdom come, your will be done, on earth as it is in heaven" (John 6:10). Thus, God's kingdom did come to earth in the incarnation of his Son, and his will continues to be done in the church through the direction and guidance of his Spirit.

Godly unity

As Horton said, within the Trinity, there is "distinction without separation."[182] Each Person is a unique strand, but they are knitted into *one* God. The very same concept, in fact, can be applied to the church. The church is composed of many unique and distinctive people, each with his or her own gifts, talents, personalities and "bents"; but we are all united together into one "body of Christ" (Eph. 4:4). Moreover, each believer in the church has the freedom to be whatever God created him/her to be (Gal. 5:1, 13). If, indeed, every person fulfilled God's calling, uniquely designed for that person, the strength and the power of church could be truly unleashed. Not everyone is called to be a kindergarten Sunday school teacher, but what an impact that one teacher can have on numerous little lives! Some people are called to preach; some are called to watch over the congregation financially (see 1 Cor. 12:4–11, 27–31).

Talented church leaders, hearing the voice of the Spirit, should encourage staff members, volunteers, and laypeople to do whatever fits each person most appropriately. We just need to know what God created us to be, to know how we can use who we are to best serve him, and what the Spirit empowers us to do. Experience has taught many people that trying to serve God outside of one's passions and giftedness is very difficult, if not damaging. In the same vein as the Trinity, there should be no selfish competition, envy, or superiority, "gender hierarchy," or jealousy in the church because every piece of the puzzle is important. The Apostle Paul's metaphor is very clear:

> God has arranged the parts in the body, every one of them, just as *he* wanted them to be…God has combined the members of the body and has given greater honor to the parts that lacked it, so that there should be no division in the body, but that its parts should have *equal concern* for each other. If one part suffers, every part suffers with it; if one part is honored, every part rejoices with it (1 Cor. 12:18, 24b–26; emphasis mine).

A church body without "an eye or an ear" or "a head or a foot" is truly "inactivated" (1 Cor. 12:14–21). The idea is that there is an interdependency of all the parts to make a whole and that no one "of less importance" is expendable. Christians can contribute something somewhere in this world, even as they exercise their distinctive gifts and talents. Truly humble church leaders know this to be true; their focus should be on releasing and empowering other people to engage in God's plans and operations. Again, Paul wrote:

> Be completely humble and gentle; be patient, bearing with one another in love. Make every effort to keep the unity of the Spirit through the bond of peace. There is one body and one Spirit—just as you were called to one hope when you were called—one Lord, one faith, one baptism; one God and Father of all, who is over and through all and in all (Eph. 4:2–6).

Jesus' prayer of John 17 reveals that the unity of believers is, in fact, *already achieved* (John 17:20–23). Jesus is "in" the Father, and the Father is "in" Jesus (John 17:21). Then, by extension, the Spirit is "in" believers (John 17:23), who is the unifying force of the Trinity. This means, of course, that Christian churches do not achieve unity on their own by their own human-driven power and programs.

Christian unity is a gift that has already been given by God; Jesus has already completed the restoration and reconciliation of his people and the Spirit is permanently engaged. We are unified by faith in Christ as Lord, and the infilling of the Spirit makes all Christians "one" (John 17:20). Human plans cannot guarantee a unified people of God. For example, the elimination of church denominations would not make people and doctrines any more unified than they were before. It is the common Spirit that unifies believers.

Church unity does not necessarily mean *uniformity*. There is diversity and variety, and that is good! The world does not need cookie-cutter Christians. But Paul told his Corinthian church that all the "spiritual gifts" given to believers "are the work of the same

Spirit, and *he* gives them to each one *as he determines*" (1 Cor. 12:11; emphasis mine). In fulfilment of his promises, each and every believer is equipped to fulfill his/her God-given assignments. We are redeemed, purified, and empowered by the Spirit for God's purposes, not our own desires of fame, power, and position. God is happy to reveal his plans for us. The nudging of the Spirit is not forceful and rude, but if we truly listen, we can hear his leadings. Someday, every Christ follower will see the glory of the Son who will rejoice with us in our completed tasks on earth (John 17:24–26). As a result, the total, complete, glorious unity of the church (on this earth and in the life to come) is not human compromise or organization but a gift from the Father to the people that he loves (John 17:23).

Indeed, the "church" is not a building; it is not worship services that we "go to" or educational curriculum. This, I learned from serving as an associate pastor. The church is not new, exciting, different programs or productions. The church is a flock of sheep, trying to follow the "Good Shepherd." It is a collection of diverse people, all sinners, but redeemed by a gracious God. It is a wonderful conglomeration of voices and hands and feet, of loud babies and aging saints who are hard-of-hearing. It is like taking all the leftovers out of the refrigerator and throwing them together into a warm and hearty soup that tastes very good. The purpose of the church is to bring more people into the glorious kingdom of God, to make more Christ followers, and to grow them up in the Spirit. As the church "mirrors" the Trinity in so many spiritual and practical ways, it is our job to transform this world with the love of God that is inside of each one of us. C. S. Lewis was correct:

> For the church is not a human society of people united by their natural affinities, but the Body of Christ, in which all members, however different (and He rejoices in their differences and by no means wishes to iron them out), must share the common life, complementing and helping one another precisely by their differences.[183]

Responses: God's kingdom and prayer

God's kingdom on earth is both attained and released through prayer. Prayer is the glue that "sticks it all together." Prayer softens our hearts toward others. Someone said that you cannot hate someone for whom you are praying. It is critical for believers to maintain a private prayer life that connects the individual to God and to other people. It is also crucial that the "body of Christ"—all believers, all over the world—be united under the Head of the church (Christ), and pray in unison for his will to be done on earth. Even without the internet, the prayers of faithful believers can spread across the globe—helping, encouraging, supporting one another, and building God's kingdom together. No doubt the church today is in a spiritual battle, and our enemy attacks the church with great force. But our mighty King, present in us as the Holy Spirit, is stronger than any other opposition. Collectively, prayer is our best defense to stay together, play together as a global symphony, and to realize that the Conductor is always standing by to lead and direct us. We keep going with joy, thanksgiving, grace, peace, strengthened by the Spirit of God.

Notes

[174] Michael Horton, *Rediscovering the Holy Spirit* (Grand Rapids: Zondervan, 2017), 224.

[175] J. Schneider, "God," in *NIDNTT, vol. 2*, ed. Colin Brown (Grand Rapids: Zondervan Publishing, 1986), 66–86, 84.

[176] Horton, *Rediscovering the Holy Spirit*, 131.

[177] Richard Rohr and Mike Morrell, *The Divine Dance; the Trinity and Your Transformation* (London: SPCK, 2016), 149, emphasis mine.

[178] Rohr, 95, author's emphasis.

[179] John N. Oswalt, *Holy One of Israel: Studies in the Book of Isaiah* (Eugene, Oregon: Cascade Books, 2014), 12.

[180] Horton, *Rediscovering the Holy Spirit.*, 317. See also, Scot McKnight, *Kingdom Conspiracy: Returning to the Radical Mission of the Local Church* (Grand Rapids: Brazos, 2014).

[181] Oswalt, *Holy One of Israel: Studies in the Book of Isaiah*, 120.

[182] Horton, *Rediscovering the Holy Spirit*, 131.

[183] C. S. Lewis, *Letters of C. S. Lewis*, ed. W. H. Lewis (New York: Harcourt Brace Jovanovich, 1966), 224.

Chapter 7

How Do We Respond?

> Prayer, then, is listening to that voice—to the
> One who calls you the Beloved.[184]

We have been thinking about the power of prayer and how our knowledge, understanding, and love of God affects our prayer life. The intent of this study is to add to our understanding of prayer based on our knowledge and familiarity of the One who listens to our prayers. Furthermore, our practice of prayer speaks of our *anthropology*—how we view ourselves in relation to God. Who are we, imperfect human beings, in relation to a holy, righteous God? Too often, what we think about ourselves is based on current social media (like television and Facebook) and not on the word of God. First and foremost, and in truth, human beings are frail and fallible. Our physical bodies break under the stresses of life, demands, disease, and exhaustion. We are recognizing more mental illnesses in our society than ever before. And spiritually? People crave some spiritual connection with something or someone outside of themselves—sometimes with great peril. How do people survive if this world is "all that there is?"

Mike Glenn observed,

> The joke among my Baptist friends is when
> another Baptist says, "I'm going to pray for you,"
> it simply means they're leaving. It doesn't mean

anything else. They're probably not going to pray. They're not going to do anything. They're just leaving. These speakers are like most of us. When we hear someone say they are praying for us, we don't expect anything to happen. We aren't looking for them to do anything that will really help. That's sad.[185]

What is prayer indeed?

For some people, including professing Christians, the whole concept of prayer is confusing and even daunting. Even when we seek to understand it, we tend to evaluate our "prayer-life" based on the answers we receive (or not). Doubt and suspicion arise about God when it seems that he is completely deaf to our prayers. Truly, our prayer practices reveal what we know and believe about the Triune God to whom the prayer is addressed. Likewise, a lack of prayer practices also reveals one's basic beliefs and knowledge of a remote and inaccessible God.

First, it can be said that prayer is beyond *human definition*. Every time we try to define it, we put limits and boundaries around it. Second, prayer is beyond *human methodology*. That is, every time we try to fit prayer into one pattern, one method, or one technique, we find failure. To limit prayer into one or several human structures is to limit the One to whom we are praying. *Prayer is like a bird.* Sometimes prayers "fly away," to be ignored and forgotten. Sometimes, they come to rest, protected and secured. But if we try to find one set definition of prayer, or if we limit it to one methodology, it is like putting a bird into a cage. The disciples asked Jesus "how to pray" in Matthew 6 because they did not know how to do it either. The prayer that Jesus gave them is a *model prayer*, certainly, and it is a beautiful example of how we can approach Father God. But it is just that—one example. It is a beginning point, a starting line, like the beautiful little prayers we teach our children to say.

Faith is the bird that feels the light and sings
while the dawn is still dark.
(Anonymous)

Prayer is a gift, perhaps one of the best gifts that we can both give and receive:

> The man whispered, "God, speak to me," and a
> meadowlark sang.
> But the man did not hear.
> So, the man yelled, "God, speak to me," and the
> thunder rolled across the sky.
> But the man did not listen.
> The man looked around and said, "God, let me
> see you," and a star shined brightly.
> But the man did not notice.
> So the man shouted, "God show me a miracle!"
> and a baby was born.
> But the man did not know.
> The man cried out in despair, "Touch me, God,
> and let me know that you are here!"
> Whereupon, God reached down and touched the
> man,
> But the man brushed the butterfly away and
> walked on.
> Don't miss a blessing because it is not packaged
> the way you might expect.
> (Anonymous)

Prayer is a bit like the internet. God wants us to stay attached; he wants us to keep the lines of communication open. During the horrible Coronavirus/Covid-19 pandemic, people used technology to stay attached to one another; with the need for "social distancing," it was all that we could do. During this time, we often thanked God for the internet—can you believe that?—so we could communicate with and "see" our friends and family, albeit not perfectly. It is not hard to "get online" and "share" with God, and we can disclose anything we want to with him, while he totally respects our privacy. Unlike the internet, however, God never "goes down" and he never "malfunctions." He is available any time, any place, and in any weather. And I think he receives our happy emojis!

Years ago, I had a dear friend who said that she awoke about four o'clock every morning and spend three hours in prayer. I also heard that the great reformer Martin Luther practiced hours and hours of prayer on a daily basis. My gut reaction was, what can you possibly have to say to the Father for all that time? Since then, I have come to realize that prayer is more than me talking to God. More often than not, it is about God talking to me.

Prayer is reading, studying, thinking about his Word, and listening for his voice in Scripture. It is "hearing" him in the quietness of a sunset or in a meandering stream—and in music—he is so alive in music! Prayer is all my theological books and blogs that draw me closer to him. He knows what I need before I say it, but I don't think he ever gets tired of hearing my prayers of gratitude and praise. So prayer is necessarily *spontaneous and honest*. We cannot limit ourselves to one "right" or "wrong" way to pray to our Father and our God. He hears every little, humble, meek, and heartfelt prayer, even if it is not "the way we were taught to pray." In the end, Christian prayer is characteristically trinitarian. Horton writes that we should pray *"to the Father, in the name of the Son, and through the Holy Spirit,"* remembering each vital part of the Trinity.[186] While this is indeed quite biblical, it is not a "secret formula" to use when we want something from God. Without a doubt, it is a genuine recognition and a reminder of *who it is we are talking to.*

Another friend once told me that she was afraid to pray "boldly" because she was afraid of God's answers—or the lack thereof. There is also a fear of praying specifically because that is like telling God what to do. Many of us can identify with these fears! Thus, our prayers become repetitive and habitual or just mumbled general requests that are not new news to God. Our fears are rooted in a lack of faith, and our lack of faith is rooted in an emaciated knowledge of God. With humility and honesty, we can tell God about our fears, and he can renew our faith in him and in his perfect will. That is our response to the awesomeness of the Triune God.

> God's commands are designed to guide you to life's very best. You will not obey him if you do not believe him and trust him. You cannot believe him if you do not love him. You cannot love him unless you know him.[187]

Prayer is a weapon

In addition, prayer has been pictured as a "battlefield." If we acknowledge that God is holy and righteous and that the earth is filled with wickedness and unrighteousness, we can imagine an intense conflict happening between "the enemy" and the good God. Some people see prayer as our way of entering into this good/evil "battle."

On the one hand, we know the familiar image of the "armor of God," pictured by the Apostle Paul, where believers were urged to "be strong" and "take a stand against the devil's schemes" (Eph. 6:10–11). This image is a reminder of the military armor worn by the Roman army in the first-century AD, and each part of the armor is protection from the enemy except the "sword of the Spirit, which is the word of God," which is an offensive weapon (Eph. 6:17). This "battle" image is followed by specific instructions on prayer, as Paul told the Ephesians to first "pray in the Spirit, on all occasions, with all kinds of prayers and requests." Second, they were told to pray "for all the saints, and pray for me also…pray that I may declare it [the gospel] fearlessly, as I should" (Eph. 6:18–20). Thus, prayer is a weapon on the battlefield of life, and there is a whole army of other believers to stand with us so that we do not have to do the battle alone.

Jesus was in the midst of conflict when he was on the earth; in the heated battle, if Jesus needed to pray to stay in contact with his Father, how much more so do we need to pray for his strength and shield? Paul faced accusations and conflicts throughout his ministry, as did so many other saints of God who carried the gospel truth across the known world. In his final prayer of John 17, Jesus prayed for "protection" for his people against the "evil one" (John 17:15) and acted as an intercessor for them in the spiritual clash on earth, knowing, of course, that ultimately, the battle has already been won. Certainly, we face battles every day most of our lives. We can read his Word and pray to be sure we are with God in the daily "battle plan": "Jesus prayed in Gethsemane, and as he humbled himself under the call of the cross, he still had to endure the cross. Gethsemane was not a substitute for Calvary."[188]

Trial scene

In previous chapters, we have also expressed prayer in of terms of legal and judicial imagery. As we saw in an earlier chapter (chapter 4), this imagery comes out of the Old Testament prophecies. In Daniel 7, the earthly conflict is pictured as a legal one, where God—the "Ancient of Days" (Dan. 7:9) and the "Most High" (Dan. 7:18)—is on his throne in heaven. He is the final and ultimate Judge. In this courtroom scene, "the court was seated and the books were opened" (Dan. 7:10), and the evil human empires are judged. The "prosecuting attorney" is the "enemy," the "fourth, unnamed beast"—perhaps Satan and/or a picture of the Roman Empire. The enemy *speaks* with condemning *words*: he boasts, blames, and accuses people of a variety of faults, failures, and weaknesses. This is one who desires to "crush and devour" the Christian church—the "saints" (Dan. 7:7).

No wonder the Son had to come as the "Word" of God (John 1:1) to argue against the words of the enemy. In the courtroom, there is also a "defense attorney," "another Advocate," the Spirit of God, who "comes alongside" of each and every Christian who is enticed by the enemy's lies and accusations. The Righteous Judge "pronounced judgment in favor of the saints" (Dan. 7:22). Ultimately, the enemy does not win the case against God's people. Thus, with the Son and through his Holy Spirit (Dan. 7:13–14), believers are ultimately vindicated:

> Then the sovereignty, power and greatness of the kingdoms under the whole heaven will be handed over to the saints, the people of the Most High. His kingdom will be an everlasting kingdom, and all rulers will worship and obey him (Dan. 7:27–28).

In addition, in the prophecies of Micah, the Lord brings a legal case against Israel, culminating in the familiar verse:

> He has showed you, [people], what is good. And what does the Lord require of you? To act justly and to love mercy and to walk humbly with your God (Mic. 6:8).

And Isaiah said,

> So [humanity] will be brought low and [humankind] humbled, the eyes of the arrogant humbled. But the Lord Almighty will be exalted by his justice, and the holy God will show himself holy by this righteousness (Isa. 5:15–16).

The trial scenes in the Old Testament reinforce the idea that God alone is perfectly righteous and just and not the arrogant human rulers who seek personal power and self-gratification. Therefore, moving into the New Testament, it is the "Lord Almighty" who judges humanity with righteousness and justifies and redeems his own. In the prayer of John 17, Jesus' followers (the "saints") are given the assurance that they are indeed vindicated and justified by the holy and righteous God.

Most often, we bring our prayers before the Judge (the Father) when we encounter disagreements, struggles, and overpowering enemies (such as disease). When we pray, there is a "prosecutor"—the "enemy," Satan—who resists our prayers, accusing us and finding fault. Even when we pray righteous prayers within the will of God, often they are not answered in our timing and we can sense a real struggle going on. In other words, in this world, it is difficult to overcome the wickedness and evil, and sometimes, we really need someone in the courtroom who is on our side. The accuser is just the accuser; but our Advocate, the *Paraclete*, is the just, righteous Spirit of God who will defend us against false accusations. And God's verdict will be in our favor. Indeed, Dietrich Bonhoeffer said, "God does not give us everything we want, but He does fulfill His promises, leading us along the best and straightest path to himself."[189]

This is illustrated by a story. A judge was sitting at his bench, hearing cases of misdemeanors and traffic violations. A young man came in with an attorney by his side. The young man was accused of a traffic violation and was ticketed by the police. The attorney said that it was his first offense, and he was sorry for the mistakes. The judge looked at the young man and gave him a severe lecture on responsibility and safety. He ordered the young man to pay a hundred-dollar fine to the court, a fine that was impossible for him to pay. Then unexpectedly, the judge stood up, removed his robes, walked down to where the boy was standing, and paid the fine for his son.

John 15—"remaining" and "bearing"

Jesus taught, quite simply, that prayer is *"remaining."* The image John included in his Gospel is the image of a vineyard. In John 15, various forms of the word "to remain" appear at least ten times (John 15:4). To "remain" with Jesus implies that people have the power and/or the inclination to move away; it is not Jesus that moves. Prayer is remaining connected to the nurturing Source; it is "bearing much fruit" (John 15:5) and "remaining" in the love of Jesus (John 15:10). It is to feel the "joy" of Jesus (John 15:11) and to work alongside of him. The Spirit who lives within us never leaves us and teaches us what to say and do. This means that we cannot hide but that he is only a whisper away when we need him. So to "remain" in Jesus is to love him, to obey his commands, to feel his joy, and then share it with others (John 15:4, 10–12, 16). To fully know God is to love and obey him and to love those people whom God loves (John 15:12). Then, we can be his "hands and feet" on the earth with actions that reveal who he is. To stay connected to him is to be prepared by God to do the "master's business" (John 15:15). "Remaining" in him, directed by his Spirit, we are ready to do "battle" and to do whatever we are asked to do.

To be sure, prayer does *not* take the place of *action*.[190] The Bible illustrates this over and over again. If someone is disconnected and does not remain in Jesus, actions can become self-serving and done to seek human control and/or attention. Such a person (apart from Jesus) is like a dried-up branch that is "thrown into the fire and burned" (John 15:5–6). To actively take part in God's kingdom, "to bear much fruit," is to remain "in Christ" as his disciple and to bring glory to the Father (John 15:8). Christianity is a "participatory" faith, and participating in his holiness and righteousness is a dynamic movement. There is no demand for those who want to "sit on the sidelines" or just relax in their "position" of being "saved." Sometimes, even if we think we are "remaining" in Jesus and doing his work, the struggle can become intense. Then we start questioning God—and ourselves. Although times of doubt and uncertainty are common, we cannot lose faith in who God is and who we are in him. The Holy Spirit knows this, and he is faithful to comfort and encourage. If we promise to pray for people, we are also called to minister to them—with action. At any point in time, we must be ready to be an instrument in God's hands, as he may use us to be the answer our own prayers by our words and actions. We talk to God sincerely about what *he* can do and then ask him to make us aware of what *we* can do: a visitation, a phone call, or at least an e-mail, a warm meal, a cup of coffee, or a card to encourage and support one another in times of need. "We should weep with those who weep and then, we need to get up and do something."[191]

Places and positions

Some teachers have suggested that a "successful" prayer life—which, in reality, is difficult to define or demarcate—necessarily involves the proper *place* for prayer; and the proper *position* of the one praying. Both of these stipulations have their foundations in the biblical literature. In ancient Jewish tradition, the proper *place* of prayer was indeed the Temple. With sacrifice and worship, prayer took place in the Temple, often with the assistance of the priests. A good example of this is the story of Hannah in 1 Samuel. At the altar of the Lord, Hannah "poured out her soul to the Lord" in prayer (1 Sam. 1:15–16). God answered her prayer by giving her the son Samuel (1 Sam. 2:26). In the New Testament, we hear the prayer of two faithful ("righteous and devoted") people, Simeon and Anna, who prayed and waited in anticipation for the promised Messiah. Luke tells us that Anna "never left the temple but worshiped night and day, fasting and praying" (Luke 2:25–38).

Before the construction of the Jerusalem Temple, it was a mountain that was the holy place of God. In the ancient days, the divine forces were often worshiped on a mountaintop, assuming the one praying was closer to the deity. Abraham called his place of sacrifice and worship the "mountain of the Lord" (Gen. 22:14), and the psalmist recognized the "city of our God, his holy mountain...Mt. Zion is the city of the Great King" (Ps. 48:1–2).

Other sacred events took place on mountaintops, where God felt close (Deut. 5:4; Mic. 4:2; Isa. 42:11; Ezek. 28:14). The Temple was the central place of prayer and worship. After the Temple was destroyed in AD 70, the rabbis considered prayer to be the temporary replacement for the Temple until the third Temple is built.

In the OT, the position of a person submitted to God in prayer and worship was indicative of the beliefs held concerning the One being worshipped. It was common in the ancient days to bow before the stone images of gods or even to prostrate (face on the ground) before an image in prayer and petition. This was a position of humility and supplication before gods and before emperors. The Israelites knew that they were never to "bow down" to "an idol in any form" or to "worship" them (Deut. 5:8–9). The psalmist's songs echo the position of reverence: "Come, let us bow down in worship, let us kneel before the Lord our Maker" (Ps. 95:6), and "I will bow down toward your holy temple, and will praise your name" (Ps. 138:2). In fact, through the prophet Isaiah, God said that someday he will receive all the veneration he deserves:

> Before me every knee will bow; by me every tongue will swear. They will say of me, "In the Lord alone are righteousness and strength" (Isa. 45:23b–24a).

In the New Testament, it was Jesus' habit to use a private place for prayer. He prayed in the "desert" alone and fasted for "forty days" (Matt. 4:1); he prayed in a "solitary place" (Mark 1:35). Jesus went to his "usual place" on the Mount of Olives. This practice was a contrast to the showy practices of some Jewish religious leaders—"those hypocrites"—who prayed in a public place "to be seen by men" (Matt. 6:5–8). Jesus' teachings on prayer in the Sermon on the Mount point to a personal, intimate relationship with the "unseen" God who hears all sincere prayers.[192] The Isaiah 45 passage above, describing a person's low position before an exalted God, is repeated in both Romans 14:11 and in Philippians 2:10 in reference to the divine position of Jesus Christ. In addition, anticipating the great sacrifice before him, Jesus "knelt" in prayer in the Garden of Gethsemane (Luke 22:41), where his prayer was so intense that "his sweat was like drops of blood falling to the ground" (Luke 22:44).

Thus, while Jesus did not limit people to a required place or position of prayer, he did set an example of an *attitude of humility* before a holy and righteous God. Many prayers in the Bible show the freedom of people to choose a posture and a place but to be *humble, honest, and sincere* in their hearts before God. Outward positions for prayer and sacred places may be very helpful and very personal. The point is that every authentic prayer is different, and every humble prayer is important no matter where or when the pray-er joins his/her heart with God.

Meeting God in the physical world can also be a matter of *practice*. Where do you go to feel God's presence on a consistent basis? Where can you go to limit distractions and still energize your prayers? Eyes open, do you see him in nature? Hands unfolded, maybe arms spread wide, do you feel his sun on your face? Pray with a friend, pray out loud, sing the familiar hymns/songs in the car, and praise him "continually." Read his Word and pray a response to what you find there. In the end, God doesn't really care how and where you pray, as much as he cares *that* you pray honestly and frequently! As we practice our prayers, we can pray with more confidence but with genuine humility because we *know* an awesome God (John 15:9, 17:23).

Each of us has a personal, unique relationship with the triune God, and no prayer pattern or technique is going to fit every person in every situation. We must not be intimidated by people who pray in a way different from the way we were "taught" to pray, or those people who tell you that your prayers are ineffective because you are not doing it "right."

At one point in my life, I was very sad that I did not manifest the visible gifts of the Holy Spirit like "speaking in tongues." I had friends who prayed "in tongues," and I felt less than a "spiritual" Christian. I prayed and prayed, asking God to grant me this ability—but to no avail. I finally realized that, while a person may have this gift of "special tongues," it did not *necessarily* indicate in a closer walk with God. Truly, what did I want? To be like my friends or to be closer to God? I chose the latter; even without a special "prayer language," I think he hears me just fine.

> It is my hope, therefore, that those who recognize in these prayers the cries of their own hearts, will also recognize the quiet prayer of God's Spirit in the midst of their own halting and stuttering words.[193]

Prayer is subversive

Eugene Peterson notes that "Jesus was a master at subversion."[194] In the first half of John's Gospel, Jesus intentionally kept his true identity a secret from his opponents and kept his miracles "under cover" from select groups (i.e., John 2:18–22, 7:4–10, 10:24–25). He spoke to the "crowd" in riddles, in metaphors, and parables (John 2:19, 4:34, 6:53–58). Even his most immediate followers did not always understand his figurative language (John 16:16–18, 25, 29):

> Parables aren't illustrations that make things eas-
> ier; they make things harder by requiring the
> exercise of our imagination, which if we aren't
> careful, becomes the exercise of our faith.[195]

If, indeed, Jesus was subversive in his speech, we can also say that the author of the Fourth Gospel was subversive in his writings to a gathering of Christians in the first-century Roman Empire. Peterson explains that there are three assumptions that are "implicit in subversion": first, "the status quo is wrong and must be overthrown if the world is going to be livable." Second, there is another world that is much more "livable," and third, ordinary means (like tyranny or military force) by which a new world becomes a reality are "unacceptable."

The purpose of subversion is to bring about change.[196] Sadly, we see a great deal of injustice, greed, and arrogance in our culture. Thus, human prayer, in unison with the Holy Spirit, is an attempt to alter the world and make it more "livable." Prayer can bring about transformation in human behavior, in worldly circumstances, and in ourselves. We are bombarded with self-centered feelings and emotions and the promise of happiness and success as a result of material items that we "need." Indeed, millions of hamburgers are made just to "guarantee" our happiness.[197] This is the image of the culture in America that prayer must expose and deflate:

> Prayer is a subversive activity. It involves a more
> or less open act of defiance against any claim

by the current regime…As we pray, slowly but surely, not culture, not family, not government, not job, not even the tyrannous self can stand against the quiet power and creative influence of God's sovereignty. Every natural tie of family and race, every willed commitment to person and nation is finally subordinated to the rule of God.[198]

Quietly, intentionally, nonviolently, believers can subversively create a culture of true justice, moral righteousness, and sacrificial love for one another with God and through prayer and acts that reflect God's righteousness. During the cataclysmic COVID-19 pandemic, ordinary people did extraordinary things for each other, in every town and in every neighborhood—even for complete strangers—without seeking any praise for themselves. It was a glimpse into a real Christlike society. Again, Peterson writes,

Our task is that we develop a self-identity as Christians and do these things not incidentally to our lives but centrally. By encouraging one another, by praying together, by studying Scripture together, we develop a sense that these things are in fact the very center of our lives.[199]

Jesus was subversive because he was not "flashy," flamboyant, or self-gratifying. He unobtrusively did the work of his Father, preaching and teaching, and ultimately completed his assignment (John 5:19, 30; 7:16; 19:30). He did not pray for more updated, electronic things for his followers to make their lives more comfortable. He prayed for more love, more joy, more unity, and more of himself "*in*" them (John 17:23).

Prayer is submission

Prayer is a relationship with a living God, and all relationships need work. A good relationship is a product of true commitment and an investment of time. Parents invest in their children with their own time; teachers invest in their students; and pastors invest in their congregation with their time, care, concern and knowledge. In the same way, prayer is an investment. It is the careful tending of a relationship, like watering a beautiful blooming plant. It takes time, commitment, and patience. Prayer is a way to love God in return, to bow before him in recognition of who he is, and allow him to change and transform us at *his* discretion into what *he* wants us to be.

In a successful relationship, each party is quick to own up to mistakes and ask for forgiveness. He is perfect, but God graciously forgives and forgives and forgives us if we truly repent. To humbly confess our sins before him is to recognize who is God (he is) and who is not God (me). We submit to *him* and to *his* plans and purposes, not the other way around. He does not submit to *us* and our human demands. Confession is making things right before our Father God and then with the appropriate human beings. Only then can God cleanse us, strengthen us, renew us, and put the relationship back where it belongs. We first humble ourselves and then we ask for his forgiveness and direction so that faults are not repeated and compounded. Part of confession is praise!

Praise is an emotional reaction to his God-ness and to our humanness. We praise him for who he is! He answers our prayers in his way and in his timing, and we gladly listen carefully. Surrendering to God is to see ourselves as we really are and to place our trust in him. Because we rarely have full knowledge of any situation and we are limited in our view of reality, we do not always have the correct answers. God knows so much more than we do. Thus, we are *invited* to submit our wills to God's will and to voluntarily place our total trust in him (Matt. 26:39; Luke 22:42). It seems that most often, we eventually submit to God anyway—happily, or kicking and screaming.

The same is true for the body of believers who meet together to join in Christ's work on earth. The church is the "bride" of Christ and shares an intimate relationship with him. In fact, the entire gathering of Christ followers is *invited* to "the wedding supper of the Lamb" (Rev. 19:7–9), which is a picture of a voluntary, joyous, cherished relationship with the Messiah who is the head of the church. Christian congregation or organization, then, should be in submission to the Holy Spirit, well before any human leader or board. Without prayer, the actions of a person and/or the programs of a church can become random, thoughtless, self-seeking, and reactionary. Prayer and humble submission to his leadership gives us time to think through a matter and to consult with God to be sure our decisions truly reflect the mission and intentions of God.

Presence and absence of God

The absence of God can be very overpowering and suffocating. It has been called the "dark night of the soul." Sometimes, we may feel that God does not care or is totally unaware of our situation. How can a loving God allow something bad to happen to his children? Paradoxically, his absence may be God's way of leading us to a new sense of his presence. The dreadful cross and the darkness of the earth were only a preface to the new light that shone on Easter morning.

Perhaps we experience something like what the earliest of Jesus' followers experienced—they did not fully understand what was happening and what Jesus was saying. They must have been terrified to think that he would leave them, and they would have to go on without his physical presence. How could he do this to them? The crucifixion was the end of all their hopes and dreams—and maybe even their own lives. Was all of this for nothing? Everything they learned, was it all a myth? Was Jesus really who he said he was? Only after he left this earth did they fully realize how close they had been to him, how much he had meant to them, and how much they needed him.

But shortly after, they experienced Jesus' resurrection. God, who loves his children so much that he allowed his Son to die for them, does not leave his people waiting in the dark for long. Gently, profoundly, with love and hope, the Spirit moves softly, almost hidden from our perception. The Spirit brought an unexpected light and life from the Father and the Son who are really never far away. His Spirit testifies to this truth: Jesus may have left the earth, but he really isn't gone. God is never really gone. In his "omnipresence," he is always with us:

> Prayer is the moment the pilot checks the flight plan before taking off. Prayer is the meeting of the generals to go over the battle plans before the battle is engaged. Mechanics check over the race car one last time before the race, and coaches talk about the game plan just before the game starts—that's prayer.[200]

Answered prayer

Learning to ride a bicycle is a challenge for a young person. Each time a child struggles to keep his/her balance, teetering back and forth, learning to steer, and keep pedaling, the task becomes easier. Suddenly, they "get it" and off they go with stability, newfound freedom, and confidence. Prayer is the same in many respects. We teeter and struggle with unanswered prayers and become confused by the advice given to us by more mature, experienced "pray-ers." Each answered prayer, each connection to God's Spirit, brings hope and joy that maybe, just maybe, we "get it!" It renews our commitment, our faith, and our sheer freedom to connect with the Almighty God.

When prayers are not answered in the way that pleases us, we should ask if our main desire is to bring glory to the Father. Answered prayer always brings glory to the Father through the Son by the Spirit. The Bible is filled with examples of how events and miracles are God's answers to human prayers, which ultimately brings glory to

God (i.e., 1 Sam. 1:10–20; 2 Chron. 32:20–23). Forgive the alliteration, but praise and glory are the preface of petitionary prayers (Ps. 63:1–3, 69:30, 86:12; Isa. 12:5, 63:12; John 12:27–30, 13:32; Rev. 16:4–9).

A prayer that is answered in the way we would like it to be answered should be a lesson to us about the love of the Father, and he should receive the glory, not we ourselves. It is noteworthy that often, God answers our prayers in ways that are surprising and unexpected. Who are we to tell God how he should go about answering our prayers? In his infinite wisdom and unbounding love, God answers our prayers in exactly the right way, in the right timing, and in ways that we cannot even imagine; and this brings him glory. The Lord is very gracious to answer *any* of our prayers, so perhaps we should think more about *answered prayers* and less about *unanswered prayers*.

C.S. Lewis admits, "I ended my first book with the words *no answer*. I know now, Lord, why you utter no answer. You are yourself the answer. Before your face, questions die away. What other answer would suffice?"[201]

Learning to pray

Why do well-meaning speakers and writers tell us that prayer is "mysterious" and baffling, challenging us to keep working on it as if it were some lofty goal? We must understand that a worthy and "successful" prayer life is neither an achievement nor a reward. Hopefully, this is not just another book on "how to have a successful prayer life." Countless books and sermons have endless tips on "how to pray," so readers do not need any more methods to consider here. We have been told that we need the right time, the right place, the right position, keep a journal, have patience, pray with someone else, pray alone, meditate, play music, and my favorite, pray with a decaf mocha.

Seriously, prayer is not as enigmatic as some would have us to believe. Perhaps we succumb to the common human "fear of failure." We do not speak boldly to God because we fear that our communications are too trivial, too weak, too inconsequential to bother the Almighty God. We fear no response from God or a response that we do not want to hear. And yet, there is no reason for fear or disappointment in prayer. Richard Rohr says that the most *personal* thing we do as believers is to pray: "Christian prayer thus becomes much more a merging than a manipulating, much more dancing than dominating, much more participation than partisanship. You rest in God, not in outcomes."[202]

Indeed, for Henri Nouwen, prayer can be very *simple*. It is, as he said, "Opening your hands before God." To him, prayer meant total surrender. It is turning off the news of the world and relaxing the tension, releasing the grasp of the world. It is finding a place of stillness *in our heads* where we move beyond words into a state of *shalom* (well-being) *in our hearts*.[203] Thus, we can feel loved by a gracious Father and get beyond the human guilt and the chaos to reach the hope. When we open our hands to God, we can see that he opens his hands to us and gives us whatever gifts he has in store for us. It is a new melody and a new path; it is not simply a duty but a breath of life:

> Praying is living. It is eating and drinking, acting and resting, teaching and learning, playing and working. It is the unceasing recognition that God is wherever we are, always inviting us to come closer and to celebrate the divine gift of being alive.[204]

Transformation

Generally, the role of parents does not end at the birth of a child or when the adoption papers are signed. It is the natural desire of mothers and fathers to nurture and guide their children as they grow up; they naturally want to see their children reach their full potential as human beings. Likewise, God does not forget about those who are his children by faith (John 3:5–7; 1 Pet. 1:3–5) but grants believers an "inheritance" of eternal life.

God wants to purify those who he has redeemed and see them grow "in the Spirit" (John 3:5). It is the love and grace of God that truly transforms us. We often pray for God to transform our circumstances, to change our situation, or even alter another person. But we forget that maybe what really needs to be done is to transform us. Transformation is evident in changed human behavior or in new attitudes or perspectives. It is God who determines how one should change; we are not responsible for telling God how to do it.[205] By faith, we turn the controls of our lives over to God and allow him to mold and shape us for his use. Through the Old Testament and into the New Testament, it is the will and purpose of God,

> to transform human behavior in this world with the consequent possibility of living with God through all eternity…[U]nless Christians are truly transformed into the character of God, the whole purpose of the Church's existence becomes blurred and confused.[206]

Furthermore, through prayer we learn to trust in and depend on God to protect us as he transforms us (John 17:15–17). We are transformed so that our whole lives are a testimony to both the love and the grace of God (John 15:27, 17:18). Like the first readers of John's Gospel, we cannot trust self-promoting human political leaders to really help us live better lives; we can only trust God (John 14:1). While we are grateful for the material blessings in our lives, they do not bring eternal happiness or eternal life. We can trust that through times of suffering and affliction, in circumstances beyond our control, it is God who hears our pleas and who loves us, redeems, and transforms. We can ask God to take away the heartaches, or we can ask him to be very present *in* them and show us how to get through the suffering in ways that bring glory to him. Trust is knowing God and believing (beyond a shadow of a doubt) that he does care and is very near to us during our times of peaks and valleys.

While we may still want to be in total control of our own lives, in fact, "dependence [is] the most characteristic attitude for the radical disciple."[207] John Stott said that "to attempt to live without him [God] is precisely what is meant by sin."[208] We are dependent upon one another as human beings, and we are all dependent upon God. Think of Peter, the Christ-follower, who was rash, excitable, and impetuous but who became such a worthy disciple of Jesus. Peter had to become completely dependent upon God to become the person God wanted him to be (John 13:36, 38).

The same is true for all of us; our pride and our sense of self-control can stop God's intended transformation process and silence the prayerful communication between us and God. While a person may be terrified of disease and/or death, it might be better to ponder *what does God want me to do with my life of health*? Those who are strong in this life—physically, mentally, and spiritually—must contemplate how they can help those people who are not as strong, even if the only thing that we can do is to pray. The goal of prayer should be to interrupt the physical world with the spiritual strength, love, and grace of God. Even so, how many other lives would be transformed by God and by our prayers if we could get beyond ourselves and truly believed in the power of our prayers for other people?

At one time, I knew a relatively young woman who was plagued with cancer. She put up a good fight against such an enemy. While she was in the hospital for treatments, she took up knitting. For hours—lonely, painful hours—she just talked to God and knitted. She created numerous blankets and tiny garments for the newborn babies who started their lives in that hospital. She did not revel in self-pity but affected so many lives in a positive way in spite of her pain, weakness, and distress. She gave all the glory to God until she could do it no more.

Community transformation

Moreover, what can we do about the painful injustices that cripple our society? Is it outdated to ardently desire and pray for true righteousness and justice in our world? Or is it just "pie-in-the-sky-by-and-by" to imagine a just and righteous kingdom on earth? Isn't it all about me? To truly desire the same things that God desires for his creation is to submit to his wisdom and authority and to catch a glimpse of a bigger life beyond ourselves. It is God's intention to transform and remold humanity individually and collectively into devoted Christ followers in what we call "the church." The glory of Christ is given to the church not based on human merit or achievements. Believers are empowered and united by God "to let the world know that you [God] sent me [Jesus] and have loved them even as you have loved me" (John 17:23). The point of individual redemption is to be unified with all those people who are being transformed to "testify" about Christ to the unbelieving world (John 15:27, 17:15–18).

Each one of us is not an island in the middle of the tumultuous sea of life. We are transformed by God *so that* we can love and "come alongside" other people to build and sustain others. We are not alone in our struggles, and we are not alone in the joy of being together "in Christ." Prayer allows God to be the guide for those *unified* in a confusing world; we look to him as the Source when human beings run out of their own resources. God is the Respirator when we cannot breathe anymore.

He is compassion in a world of hate and injustice; he is forgiveness in the depths of sin and peace in every turmoil (John 21:21–22). As we all need God, we also need each other to bring about his "kingdom on earth." In fact, unity in the church is not an achievement but a gift from the Father and the Son because each person is "in Christ" and all persons have Christ "in" them (John 17:20–23). To be sure, it takes a while to fully comprehend that sinful humanity is loved by God no matter what. He is bigger than all our sins. Love is his identity (see 1 John 7–8). In spite of the human battles, in spite of the prosecution of the world, we are indeed his "beloved"; and that being so, *we must respond by loving others well.*

Knowing God, loving Jesus, and praying in the Spirit

In this study, we have shown that the epithet "Holy Father" in John 17 is a title that the first Jewish disciples would have recognized in the same vein as the "Holy One of Israel" highlighted by the prophet Isaiah. "Righteous Father," in the prayer of John 17, is an epithet that would have been received by the Greek and Roman readers of the Gospel, especially as they experienced the *unrighteous* Roman Emperor. We pray "in faith" *to* the holy and righteous *Father* because we truly believe that he is who he says he is and that he cares for us.

We *know* him. He is always right and just, and we can trust that he wants what is best for his own. In his great holiness, he has graciously promised to hear our most feeble human prayers. When we fully understand the love and graciousness of the Almighty God of the universe (if indeed we can ever *fully* understand), it is only natural that we must "bend the knees of our hearts" before him in love and in awe. And *we can stop questioning his motives.*

Second, we pray "in the name" of the faithful and wonderful Son with love and obedience. The Trinity is "made known" to the unbelieving world by the followers of Jesus through the love of God and of his Son (John 17:23, 26). As the "Sent One," Jesus became like one of us, who then suffered and died so that we might be in a relationship with him and with his Father. Equal to God in nature, united with him in purpose, the Son is the Savior who sacrificed his life so that humanity can have an "abundant" life. To pray and ask "in Jesus' name" is not a blanket magic "formula" which, attached to any prayer, guarantees that Jesus will do whatever we ask him to do (see Matt. 18:19–20). They are the recognition of a holy and righteous God whose true character, nature, glory and will are shared with his Son. To pray in his name is to express an ardent desire to be a part of the work in God's kingdom with Christ.

Third, it is by the Spirit that we can talk to God at all. The Advocate *lives inside of us*; and it is his desire to guide us, to empower us, and to counsel us in all circumstances. Sometimes prayer is waiting for his "way" and his timing, both of which are always perfect. Those who believe will see the glorified Jesus (John 17:24) through the "eyes" of the Holy Spirit, who will be "in them" (John 17:23, 26). Thus, John Bunyon said that prayer is "a sincere, sensible, affectionate pouring out of the soul to God, through Christ, in the strength and assistance of the Spirit, for such things as God has promised."[209]

Self-identity and God identity

While attending seminary, I did a study on the word *humility*. It was not for a class or for a grade; I just needed to do it for myself. For many years, I struggled with my own self-worth and value, which I discovered was not particularly unusual for a woman. There was always a tension between my esteem and significance among my peers and my humility before the Lord. I fought to balance who I am and who others perceived me to be. To be a woman in a man's world of theology was not an easy road. I felt like I had to "run faster and jump higher" than my male counterparts. Notice the word *felt*. What I was *feeling* was affecting what I was thinking. Was I trying to excel for me or for God?

Funny how God works, but my thought process changed when I studied John 17. The jigsaw pieces of the puzzle of my life and work rarely fit together until I fully understood the title "Holy Father." Yes, I stand before an awesome, holy, powerful, perfect God, striped of my pretenses, with all my imperfections, and with the ludicrous idea that he needed me to do something for his kingdom. And yet, filled with emotion, I finally understood that he first loved me just as I am and would ever hope to be. He is so holy, but he is my gracious Father who *knows* me and still loves me. There is a wholeness, a *shalom* in the heart when we stand before God *with Christ* and *with* the *Advocate*. It was time to really get to *know* him because who I am to God surpasses and overcomes who I am to other people.

I have been given many titles in my life: Mrs., Dr., mom, professor, pastor. Names describe what I *do*; they are descriptions of me but not who I am. The same is true of the trinitarian God. While we try to describe him and his nature and give him honor through titles and names, he remains holy, separate, and indescribable. Humility, then, is a balance that is both functional and positional: with Paul, "I can do all this through him who gives me strength" (Philippians 4:13). I am in a position of training and willingness to do whatever God asks me to do—but I cannot do it without him.

Conclusions

To be received by God as a *loving* Father who always receives his wayward child is the basis for great gratitude. We can become so focused on our own desires that we forget to recognize who we are talking to and what he has done for us already. By nature, human beings tend to see only what they lack instead of what they have been given by God. In Exodus 16, God graciously provided manna and quail for the Israelite community as they wandered in the desert. But they "grumbled" against the Lord (Exod. 16:2, 7–8) because they lacked the rich, familiar foods they had in Egypt *in slavery* (Exod. 16:3). God graciously gave them freedom and food, but all they could see was what they did *not* have.

Prayer can be like that; if all we do is demand from God and never recognize the love and grace and compassion which he has already given to us, his presence can be an oversight. God can teach us a great deal through *his* provision when we think we need something more or something else. We discover that the more we humble ourselves before him with gratitude, the more we see his presence in his gifts. "Thankfulness is a soil in which pride does not easily grow."[210] Gratitude can heal wounds and change our perspective. Nouwen said,

> The discipline of gratitude is the explicit effort to acknowledge that all I am and have is given to me as a gift of love, a gift to be celebrated with joy. There is always the choice between resentment and gratitude...Indeed, I can choose to lament about the many misfortunes which have plagued me in the past, and thereby wrap myself up in my resentment. But I don't have to do this.[211]

Further, we can miss God's presence looking for something else. Years ago, I was able to go to a prayer-retreat center in the mountains. There, I participated in a "silent retreat" over a weekend, focusing on God and what he wanted me to do with my life. I wanted so much to "see" God during this time of refreshment. I began by sitting on a rock, all by myself, and opened the Bible to the middle to the lengthy Psalm 119. A long time was spent in that psalm (it's a long psalm), and the message of obedience was loud and clear. But I did not feel him near me. Later in the day, I sat down by a tumbling stream. The sound of the water, surrounded by silence, was cathartic. In my mind, I could not connect my direction to read Psalm 119 and the soothing sounds of the stream. I finally stopped thinking and gave in to the stillness, thirsting for him. I realized that, like the water, God is always moving. His Spirit is alive in his Word. He flows like the water *in* and *through* me. It moves me to *want* to be obedient. I heard his Spirit in the silence, and I drank deeply from the water of life (John 3:5, 4:10, 7:37–39).

In view of all of this, I have learned that prayer is less about me and all about *knowing* God. We should do less of the talking and more of the listening. If we *know* and love God, prayer is not a duty or a tiresome ritual; it is a privilege to be in his presence. Guilt about prayer methodology is not from God. Jesus made the Father *known* to us and his Spirit lives within us individually and collectively (John 14:9–11, 16–17). The world does not *know* the Father, so they do not *know* the Son and the Spirit. So the world wants to put prayer in a box and control it, like a caged bird. There is freedom in understanding that the only way *to* God is *through* God.

I share one of my favorite poems, the "Franciscan Benediction," from Philip Yancey's excellent book on *Prayer*:

> May God bless you with discomfort
> At easy answers, half-truths, and superficial
> relationships
> So that you may live deep within your heart.

May God bless you with anger
At injustice, oppression, and exploitation of
    people,
So that you may work for justice freedom and
    peace.

May God bless you with tears
To shed for those who suffer pain, rejection, hun-
    ger and war,
So that you may reach out your hand to comfort
    them and
To turn their pain into joy.

And may God bless you with enough foolishness
To believe that you can make a difference in the
    world,
So that you can do what others claim cannot be
    done
To bring justice and kindness to all our children
    and the poor.

Amen.[212]

Notes

[184] Henri J. M. Nouwen, *The Only Necessary Thing; Living a Prayerful Life*, ed. Wendy Wilson Greer (New York: Crossroad Publishing, 1999), 66.

[185] Mike Glenn, "Prayer Isn't the Opposie of Action," Patheos Jesus Creed, 2019, https://www.patheos.com/blogs/jesuscreed/2019/08/16/prayer-isnt-the-opposite-of-action/?utm medium=webpush&utm source=evangelical&utm campaign=JesusCreed.

[186] Michael Horton, *Rediscovering the Holy Spirit* (Grand Rapids: Zondervan, 2017), 224.

[187] Blackaby, "http:// www.Christianquotes.info," accessed July 30, 2020.

[188] Glenn, "Prayer Isn't the Opposie of Action."

[189] Dietrich Bonhoeffer, http://www.Christianquotes.info, accessed September 15, 2021.

[190] Glenn, "Prayer Isn't the Opposie of Action."

[191] Glenn, "Prayer Isn't the Opposie of Action."

[192] Scot McKnight, *The Sermon on the Mount*, ed. Tremper Longman III and Scot McKnight (Grand Rapids: Zondervan, 2013).

[193] Nouwen, *The Only Necessary Thing; Living a Prayerful Life*, 197.

[194] Eugene Peterson, *The Contemplative Pastor* (Carol Stream, Illinois: Word Publishing, 1989), 41.

[195] Peterson, 42.

[196] Peterson, 43.

[197] Peterson, 17.

[198] Peterson, 17.

[199] Peterson, 18.

[200] Glenn, "Prayer Isn't the Opposie of Action."

[201] C. S. Lewis, *Till We Have Faces* (Grand Rapids: Eerdmans Publishing, 1966), 308.

[202] Richard Rohr and Mike Morrell, *The Divine Dance; the Trinity and Your Transformation* (London: SPCK, 2016), 154.

[203] Rohr, 154.

[204] Nouwen, *The Only Necessary Thing; Living a Prayerful Life*, 40.

[205] John N. Oswalt, *Called to Be Holy; A Biblical Perspective* (Anderson, IN: Warner Press, 1999), 2.

[206] Oswalt, 3.

[207] John Stott, *The Radical Disciple: Some Neglected Aspects of Our Calling* (Downers Grove: InterVarsity Press, 2010), 109.

[208] Stott, 100.

[209] John Bunyon, http://www.Christianquotes.info, accessed September 15, 2021.

[210] Stott, 106.

[211] Beth Porter, Susan Brown, and Philip Coulter, eds., *Befriending Life; Encounters with Henri Nouwen* (New York: Doubleday, 2001), 238.

[212] Philip Yancey, *Prayer; Does It Make Any Difference?* (Grand Rapids: Zondervan, 2006), 105.

About the Author

Dr. Judith A. Diehl did her PhD work at the University of Edinburgh in the New Testament. Her dissertation was on the prayer of John 17, and the "Gospel of John" remains an area of strong interest. This book reflects her ardor for the Fourth Gospel. At Denver Seminary, she taught New Testament and Hermeneutics. She authored three journal articles for Scot McKnight in the *Currents in Biblical Scholarship* which addressed the "Roman Empire in the New Testament," followed by the Introduction to the book *Jesus Is Lord, Caesar Is Not* edited by Scot McKnight and Joseph Modica.

In 2020, she wrote the commentary on 2 Corinthians for the Zondervan series, the "Story of God Bible Commentary Series" edited by Tremper Longman III and Scot McKnight. This series of commentaries is unique and especially useful for church leaders and people interested in teaching the Bible and serving in God's kingdom.

Dr. Diehl served as an adult education pastor in Colorado for over four years, and her ministry has been focused on teaching the Word of God to adults. She is, by nature, a teacher and has worked in churches all of her life. After retiring from Denver Seminary, she currently enjoys writing, blogging, teaching, and preaching occasionally at her church. She lives in the Rocky Mountains and enjoys skiing in the winter and hiking in the summer. A wife and mother, she and her husband have two grown sons and a grown daughter.

Milton Keynes UK
Ingram Content Group UK Ltd.
UKHW010929231123
433129UK00001B/177